MW00966588

Tomorrow is a Lovely Day

Tomorrow
is a
Lovely Day

Garfield Thomas Ogilvie

To Father Bill,

A loyal & true priest to God and his friends.

Gary O.

Thank you.

PENUMBRA PRESS
www.penumbrapress.ca

Copyright © 2005 Garfield Thomas Ogilvie and Penumbra Press
Designed by Mag Carson
Cover designed by Mag Carson after a painting by Marjorie Orange
Printed and bound in Canada

No part of this publication may be reproduced, stored in a retrieval system, or
transmitted, in any form or by any means, without the prior written consent of the
publisher or a licence from The Canadian Copyright Licensing Agency (Access Copyright).
For an Access Copyright licence, call toll-free to 1-800-893-5777
or visit www.accesscopyright.ca

LIBRARY AND ARCHIVES CANADA CATALOGUING IN PUBLICATION

Ogilvie, Garfield Thomas, 1931-
    Tomorrow is a lovely day / Garfield Ogilvie.
ISBN 1-894131-86-X
    I. Title.
PS8629.G54T6 2005   C818'.6   C2005-906026-3

Canadä

Penumbra Press gratefully acknowledges the financial support of the Government of
Canada through the Book Publishing Industry Development Program (BPIDP) for our
publishing activities. We also acknowledge the Government of Ontario through the
Ontario Media Development Corporation's Ontario Book Initiative.

DEDICATION

My parents
Tom and Eva Ogilvie
My children
Catherine, Mary, Tom and John
My grandchildren
Laura, Colin, Kathleen, Sarah,
Heather, Rebecca and Shawn
Who with my wife, Marilyn,
Were kisses from God.

Acknowledgements

The assistance of my wife, Marilyn, in the formation of this book deserves my deepest appreciation. Without her personal and professional competence, its satisfactory completion would have been impossible.

Ditto for publisher, John Flood. The expertise of John and his staff have made the preparation and distribution of *Tomorrow is a Lovely Day* extraordinarily pleasant.

Not to be overlooked is the kindness and support of Jack Kinsella, my dear friend since my adolescence.

I would also like to acknowledge certain friends who over the years have helped me shape a philosophy of life that formed a basis for my writing:

Father Leo Cormican, English Professor Emeritus, St Patrick's College
Genevieve O'Keefe, my grandmother, who taught me faith
Basil and Angus O'Keefe, cousin and uncle, my boyhood idols, who
    taught me kindness
Marjorie O'Grady Orange, my sister-in-law, who taught me empathy
Sister Margaret Power, who taught me obedience
Rodney Andrews, a teaching compatriot, who taught me humility
Dr. Brian Brett, who taught me grace
Albert O'Grady, my father-in-law, who taught me patience
Earl Hogan, a cousin, who taught me courage

Foreword

Authors who write about people and places they have personally known have best impressed me. Their firsthand observations of real-life experiences give their literary works freshness and truth.

Greene knew the intrigue of the spy world and it showed in his masterful categorizing of the human heart at war and play. Wordsworth wrote of nature's Spirit as he stood knee-high in wild flowers beneath wandering clouds.

Johnson and Boswell stage-coached their way through the dales and caps of the British Isles. London mirrored the wilds of the North, O. Henry, the bowery, and Maugham, the West Indies and Virgin Islands. Thackeray, Yeats and Keats travelled the byroads.

And what of Burns's poetry about the heart of Scotland, Mark Twain's childhood on the Mississippi, and Joyce and O'Casey's sketches of the hidden Ireland as found in its laneways, pubs, docks and ghettoes?

Two authors directly responsible for my writing anything were Robert Gibbings and H.V. Morton. Gibbings literally walked across parts of Ireland in the 1930s and 1940s. Once in Gougane Barra, Cork, I met a lady who as a child listened to her parents and Gibbings chatting about Irish ways. Gibbings would stay a few days with certain families and later jot down his observations. As a botanist and lithographer, as well as a writer, he did some amazing work, preserving folklore and botanic findings in print and wood. Morton applied the same principles of hands-on reporting across the British Isles and parts of Europe. His travel books on Scotland, Wales, South Africa, Middle East, England and Rome are collectors' items.

These two men sat by the roadside fires and peat-moss lums of ordinary folk; they drank in the dens and snugs of taverns and hotels; they stopped by gates, streams, barns, fairs, markets, fords and linns. They met tinkers, gypsies, labourers, minstrels, fishmongers, vagabonds, farmers, masons, and milkmaids. They saw and wrote of a vintage world on the verge of change. They were kings of the road.

I have tried to imitate them. I have tried to meet people on their own turf and talk with them about life. I never pried, prodded, or snooped and during our dialogues I never wrote anything down. I merely steered the conversations in accordance to the rhythms of the moment and the wishes of my hosts. A person's memories of anything are his own and not to be shared readily with anyone. For many, I was a stranger in their midst. And I respected that.

My primary intention in writing *Tomorrow Is Lovely Day* is to entertain by story, essay, epigram and poem. I try to share with readers the impressions I formed of places I have visited.

The title is from a number by Irving Berlin sung during World War II by Vera Lynn. It suggests faith, hope, courage and patience. Tomorrow is a new start, a fresh beginning, another chance to carry on as best we can. What we see from our lofty position on the top of a new day may be sunny dales and green valleys.

Today and yesterday were once tomorrows. Every day is tomorrow. Always, a lovely day.

I wish you many.

September, 2005
Ottawa, Canada

If today your heart is weary
If every little thing looks grey
Just forget your troubles
and learn to say
Tomorrow is a lovely day.

— Irving Berlin

A Touch of Loveliness

Behind the railway station, among the wild flowers, stood a beautiful Indian maiden. She was staring sideways towards the Atlantic Ocean. Behind her, the shaded mountains of the Gaspé Peninsula in Québec echoed the whistles of the approaching Gaspé-Montreal train.

Along the wooden platform some 20 other passengers, with their fine luggage piled high on the train cart, waited in the cooling sun. In contrast, the maiden, quite alone, carried only a bundle hanging by a belt.

She was beautiful. Her amber skin blended with the summer colours of her blouse and skirt. The ocean breeze teased her shiny black hair. Her face was placid and refined. She had a wistful softness about her.

I smiled her way and waved. She waved back and gazed through me. I hoped she felt something of my admiration and my eagerness to assuage the pain of centuries.

I last saw her standing by herself up near the first coach. I never saw her again. For all I know, she may have been only a vision travelling daily on a lonesome trail of her ancestors.

In moments of quietness, I see her again and pray for her.

A Chance Meeting

No one man could ever claim her beauty. It belongs to all people. I first saw her in the mall. She was impervious to my adulation.

Her dress was the colour of wild flowers and her strawberry hair had a golden sheen.

An impish smile suggested a roguish heart. When the stranger introduced us, I fell. I spoke of her beauty and I invited her into my home that very evening. She made no resistance. And we are together, now and always.

I call her "Angel." Officially, she's #HN3313 — "Summer Breeze," Royal Doulton.

A Just Reward

A J. Cronin, a medical doctor in Scotland, and the creator of the detective Sherlock Holmes, once told a nurse in Glasgow she was worth twice the salary the hospital was paying her. "Your work is outstanding. Obviously the administration is not aware of your true value."

And the nurse countered, "Thank you, Doctor, but is it not a fact that most of us who take our work seriously are undervalued? If they paid us more, they'd have to pay the poorer workers less. We carry the load for the rest."

And the doctor said, "Is it possible that God is the only one who knows your true value?"

And the nurse said, "That's the way I see it. If God knows our true worth, that's good enough for me. He'll reward us as He sees fit."

The Love in My Old Dog's Eyes

If Clancy, our Border Collie, could have talked near the end, he may have said something like this:

"I can tell sadness. I've heard the big guy sob and Marilyn, too. I know sadness because I've been there. Back on the farm, the children hit me. My brothers and sisters were picked earlier by buyers. I guess I was left because I wasn't much good. And then the big guy and Marilyn came along and just like that I was in my new home. I also understood sadness when the suitcases were put on the bed and the clothes come out of the closet. I knew I would be without Marilyn. I didn't like that.

These days have been really sad. Everybody I meet is crying. I am patted and stroked. The kids get down beside me on the floor near my head and they call my name and I look into their eyes and they cry and I don't know why.

My pain is bad. I can't walk. I can speak a little. I'm not hungry. At night it's worse. I wake up yelping and Marilyn says, 'Clancy, it's okay.' And she gets up and runs her hand 'round me ears and along my back. And soon I settle down beside the bed and dream again.

I remember then the romps in the country where I would run in the open fields between Marilyn and the big guy, the swims in the river, and Marilyn and I walking every day around our neighbourhood. And I remember the time I escaped from the backyard and went alone along our usual route at the usual pace. I remember running for sticks and balls and knocking the kids down and going into a rage over the postman and failing at puppy school three times. Marilyn was upset about that schooling. I started fights there, broke ranks and bit the instructor.

I guess I pushed Marilyn pretty far. But she never got too upset. Never shouted. Never tugged the leash too hard. She loves me. I could always tell. It shows in her eyes. Everybody in the family was good to me. Even those damn cats.

Over the years I've seen many changes — Cathy, Mary, Tom, and John leaving home, and then the grandchildren coming and helping rid me of my fear of those bad children back on the farm. I can lie among them now — I'm like one of the boys, or girls.

One person I miss is an old man named Poppa. He lived here off and on for eight years. He had some of the same problems I have — trouble walking, blindness, poor hearing. I'd lie beside him at the table or by his chaise in the backyard or I'd run to his room and call him to supper where he'd slip me food when the big guy wasn't looking.

Last night was tough. I suffered. I can't move. The big guy gave me a dish of ice cream. I got it down. I'm miserable. But, I have Marilyn.

One morning the big guy took me to see the doctor who gives me needles. I used to be able to jump clear up onto the table. But not this time. The big guy lifted me up. Then he and the doctor talked sharply to each other. The big guy wasn't happy. I just kept quiet and watched. Then he took me home.

But not for long. Everybody was upset. Marilyn kissed and hugged me. I showed her all the love I had. My eyes never left her.

Then John, Marilyn's son, carried me to his car and the big guy came and kissed me and cried. I put my head down and looked up at him. He's really not a bad guy. I like him.

Then John and I drove around for a while and John talked to me and I felt happy to be with him no matter where we were going. He's my pal.

At the clinic, John carried me to the table and held me as the doctor took out one of those damn needles. I looked into John's eyes as the doctor jabbed me. I was happy. I thought I was the luckiest dog in the world.

As I fell asleep I thought of Marilyn. Our love for each other will never die. We could see the love in each other's eyes."

The Precious Few

I certainly don't begrudge God knowing all the evil people in the world, but I *am* envious of His being privy to all the good ones.

I'd love to know them. Just to say I met them would be enough. The diversity of perfection must be indescribable. Suffice to say, I must be content with the many good souls He sends my way. They are a treasure. I savour their presence. I thank God for them.

Getting to Know You

If we are going to help someone in need, we may have to share the pain. A famous monk, Tom Merton, who supported this theory, explained his position with an analogy. A forlorn person stands frozen with fear in a fast-flowing river. On shore, a good Samaritan decides to risk wading out to help him. He reaches the victim and leads him to safe ground.

Merton says helper and helped must work together. Both must get their feet wet. A bond of trust is vital to any solution.

In any process of healing, both sides must hurt a little, sweat a little and cry a little.

Two souls meet — out of the catharsis comes peace.

A Highland Romance

Balmoral Estate in Aberdeenshire, Scotland, is 600 miles north of London and 50 miles west of Aberdeen City. Its 62,000 acres by the River Dee have been the summer holiday site of the British Monarchy for 156 years.

The principal reason for my visit there in the summer of 2001, was to see Balmoral Castle built by Queen Victoria and her Prince Consort, Albert, in 1855.

As I took in the place, it didn't take long to realize that while seven generations of royalty from Albert to Harry have holidayed there, none had given Balmoral its winsome character more than the pert German princess and her handsome husband.

In fact, Balmoral Castle and its grounds are a shrine to Albert and Victoria. Everything about the place is a testimony to their love for each other.

The couple first came to Balmoral in 1848. They were both 29, married eight years and the parents of six. Here they had their first real home away from home — a "small, pretty" 200-hundred-year-old refurbished mansion.

Seven years later they built the present Balmoral castle near the original site of their first home. This new structure mirrored the personalities of its founders. It was simple, unpretentious and uncomplicated.

There, in the intimacy of wooden glens, granite sentinels and secret linns, a romance evolved that stands as one of the greatest of all time.

There, they treasured the breezes from the sea and Grampian Mountains. Victoria's diaries say they found the atmosphere "refreshing," "dry" and "pure" and the scenery "delightful," "peaceful" and "free."

There, the royal hair came down. Away from the peeping eye and acid tongue they were themselves. They blended into the simple life. They developed a bond with the Scottish crofters. In due course they became more highland than the highlanders.

At Balmoral, the Royals dined in their neighbours' homes and danced at their flings. They shared whisky and recipes. They rode trails and picnicked together. Victoria even invited them to games and dinner parties at Balmoral.

As for employment, the locals were given work on the estate. They built larders, stables, sheds and cottages. They helped raise the deer and red Scottish cattle. They bred white ponies and capricious dogs. They cut out plantations in the glens. Upon the top of Craig Cowan above the southern part of the estate, they built their owners a hut where the Royals roughed it.

Victoria was particularly well-suited to the Scottish culture. She was straightforward, kind and just. She had its toughness, resiliency and sense of duty. She had its mystery of character. She was her own woman. She was a survivor.

With the passing years, Victoria became more and more attached to Balmoral. With the death of Albert and her mother in 1861 and that of her close friend and mentor, John Brown, in 1883, Victoria turned to Balmoral for peace and comfort. And Balmoral did not fail her.

I like to think that it was in fact Balmoral's serenity that carried her through. Among her close friends there, living and dead, she found the courage to go on. There, she came to grips with previous deaths, particularly the loss of two children, the humiliation of her playboy sons, the dislike from the English public and seven attempts on her life.

My visit to Balmoral Castle was made especially memorable by coming upon the River Dee. The Dee holds Balmoral grounds in a four-mile-long embrace. Never more than 50 yards wide here, the Dee narrows by the Castle and then quickly sweeps north-east to Aberdeen City. Shallow enough for boots-on salmon fishing, its amber stones reflect the cool sunshine as its white caps trill away the day.

Along one stretch by the water, a walking trail hugs the southern shore. The path's inner side has stands of trees donated by admirers from all over the world and, in addition, copious wild rose bushes that sweeten the air. My special spot along here was a short section of the path directly behind the west end of the Castle. It faces the Dee and the mountains to the north.

At one point, where the walkway sinks to afford privacy, I found an old green bench facing the west and the rushing Dee. I became pensive. In those dappled waters, I saw the serenity of my life. I concluded that life had been good to me. I felt quietly elated.

Soon I dozed off and an hour later felt even more refreshed. I vowed then that if I lived nearby I would come to this place tomorrow and tomorrow and never grow tired of it.

What made this retreat so sacred was the bench's accessibility and privacy. Victoria had probably sat there many times. In fact, I felt her presence. On that seat, by that dusty way, she must have often rested for countless hours. One day, Albert would sit with her, then a child, or John Brown. Other days, she would come alone — perhaps to read, knit, dream or cry.

Surely Victoria must have had other favourite nooks around Balmoral — the rose gardens, the orchards, the cairns to Albert and John and her favourite dogs, certain vistas in the dells, perhaps some tree under which she and Albert had kissed. Yet, somehow I believe this resting place by the Dee was by far her most beloved, especially in the sunset of her life.

Although, this tiny lady ruled one quarter of the globe for 64 years, mothered nine children, and had the world's adulation, she viewed her love affair with Albert to be the greatest triumph in her life. And it all began at Balmoral!

The Last Days of Fall

The chickadees are at the feeder — always two together. Like the sparrows they fly in roller coaster fashion as if trying to see where they're going. The blue jays come at mid-morning and before dusk. They must have a set route during the day. When they arrive, the cardinals are not far behind.

Across the street the sycamores are on fire with colour, reminding me that years ago the woollen factories in the small towns used sycamores to fuel their ovens. The wood burned slowly giving off intense heat. Locals cut down the sycamores and hauled the bundles off to mills.

The pesky black squirrels have been about all year. Yesterday I saw three black ones having a tiff. One ran straight at another who sidestepped in time

SURELY

The other afternoon in the country two wolves were standing in an open field of frozen gray at a loss to know which way to go ... to face the wind in search of fare ... or retreat to the bush, a cozy lair to share. One wanted to go on, but the other admonished, "No, come this way, we'll find food another day...."

No more was said — across the drifting white dunes, they trundled in a row; surely they'd survive these cold nights, and with the first warm puffs of spring begin life anew.

to allow the first one to collide head on with one coming the other way. In general, they spell trouble. They hang upside down over the bird feeder and gorge themselves. This is infuriating. It's a game to them.

Last summer I caged 17 and relocated them in a forest about two miles away. As I released each one, it roared from the cage and took the first tree to the heavens. One tore to the top of a 50-foot pine and went off the point straight up.

The squirrel and I have one thing in common: we both forget where we put things. Sometimes we never find them.

I saw a raccoon in the shadows last evening. One night this summer, five frolicked on our roof. They eat through screens and garbage lids. Their claws are prehistoric. Wouldn't you know — I forgot to close the garage door that night and the garbage was everywhere.

The sprawling oak next door has reddened the lawns, but every year some leaves won't let go. Some hang on all winter, only to be pushed away by the new growth. Oaks are dirty, tough and durable but not bad looking as trees go.

An old lady asked me the other day why the red and orange maple leaves didn't blush this autumn. And she was right. They hadn't. Perhaps it was due to warm nights, a hot, dry summer, too much moisture at once, or just a quirk of nature. It was a shame though. The bright colours are a last hurrah before the drabness. I wonder how many missed their display as we did.

At bedtime, I hear the wolves. I imagine the pack — their hair mottled, their bony haunches, their restless cries. They are the true nomads — living off the land. For them the survival of the tribe means everything. I admire them.

Around the area we have four rabbits, maybe more. They stay all year. They're cocky. They eat the flowers. They ramble around on various properties to stop and stare and hop. The last you see of them is their white rears bobbing under a tree. They're likeable pests.

A skunk comes every night, but the groundhogs have been less frequent. Thank God for the sparrows, my little friends!

Nature is rolling up its carpet.

All the Same

My wife and I had taken Christmas presents for the 12 cloistered nuns of a convent near our home. With several Sisters present, one of whom was the Mother Superior, I said baitingly, "Mother, naturally you will be responsible for distributing the gifts. However, I would like you to know that one gift is a beautiful black shawl. May I suggest it be given to the *least* of your group? Do you know who is the least among you?"

One Sister, standing off to the side, shyly but pleasantly responded, "We are all the *least* in here!"

Iona

That the Island of Iona in Scotland has always had a reputation for holiness and mystery cannot be denied. In June of 2001, a Scottish gentleman in a Scottish hotel said to me, "I heard you say you're going to Iona. You'll love it. A very holy place. Everyone on the island whispers in deference to its spirituality."

Years before, I had read that even Iona's sands *whisper* in the wind and that on certain nights they intone the soft chants of the monks of old.

In *Macbeth*, Shakespeare called Iona "sacred." Dr. Johnson saw it as an "illustrious island" and felt any visitor's "piety would … grow warmer among the ruins of Iona." Barnett, a writer of Scottish history, called it "the holiest place in Scotland" and added "only love, memory, knowledge and a mystic's dream can unlock this secret of the Isle of Dreams."

Iona is a small island in the Inner Hebrides. Some call it a jewel. Thirty-five miles west of the Scottish mainland, its 3½ by 1½ miles is lapped by the Gulf Stream. Its temperate climate, especially from November to April, is the envy of Britain.

In early summer, plentiful sunshine bathes the yellow bogs, cotton grass, clover and wild flowers. A white sand dappled with volcanic rock lines the island's blue and green lagoons. The heather, fruit trees and sacred cairns on the hillocks invite walkers and painters.

On Iona's east, one mile away, the towering tree-lined mountains of the island of Mull cool the morning air; on the west side, the ocean runs straight to Labrador; and to the southwest, it's open water to Donegal, Ireland, 80 miles away.

Unfortunately, the day my wife and I chose to visit Iona, nature did not cooperate. The ferry left the coastal town of Oban, Scotland, under black clouds. But later on, the day did brighten and the rain held off and the air freshened.

While dark days do little to enhance Iona's natural beauty, they can be helpful in trying to capture its ethereal side. For example, the shadows of a foul day in medieval times, as in our own, certainly suited the arrival of 60 royal funeral processions. That's the number of kings of Scotland, Ireland and Norway buried beside the monastery church by the shore overlooking Mull.

They interred King Duncan there, murdered by Macbeth, in 1040. In 1057, they buried Macbeth himself after he was killed in battle near Aberdeen.

Macbeth, the last king placed there, was carried a long way — some 250 miles across Scotland through the Grampian mountains to Oban and then over to the island of Mull by boat. The journey continued by land to a small port on that island from which they crossed the one mile to Iona. On Iona, they followed the crest of the hill along a street called the Street of the Dead.

Imagine the sacred pomp of it all — the flags and banners, the galleys in the bay, the military dress, the ornate coffins, the drums, the chanting monks, the intonations, the best that royalty and church could afford. Is it any wonder that nature might shed a tear or two?

Somehow, too, a sombre day fits the wild raids on Iona by barbaric Danes in the ninth century. In 806, they stained the sands of Iona with the blood of 68 monks. Monks had been there for 250 years. The Danes stayed off and on for another 400.

The choice of Iona as a burial site for kings was obviously due to the holiness of the place, a holiness instilled largely by a man of royal blood, an Irishman named Columba.

In Ireland, Columba was a scholar and a founder of some 300 monasteries. His crest depicted a dove over his head. He was tender and forgiving, cried easily, talked with angels, had visions, loved horses, dogs, seals, bees and birds, and was never happier than when sitting in an orchard or walking his hills.

Iona's tragic history suggests Columba's other side. His very name means wolf. As a member of the fighting O'Donnells of Donegal with a lineage back to the all Kingship of Ireland, he was not above being disobedient, light-fingered and ready to bear arms even though they be clerical ones. Put out of Ireland by the King of Tara, he came to Iona at age 42 in 563, only 60 years after St. Patrick had died. He became the greatest Christian leader of the time. He even won over the Picts, the very people the Romans refused to attack.

Just how many monks does it take to make a place so sacred that pilgrims in the thousands have come to Iona for 1500 years? The answer is: all of them.

Some would say that Columba's fierce dedication to Christ alone could have done it. Perhaps. But I think that every monk and nun who toiled there and every pilgrim who walked there has left his or her own magic. If we can understand this, then maybe we can "unlock the secret of the Isle of Dreams." Iona is part and parcel of them all. Their spirits are everywhere.

As I stood on the Street of the Dead and later lay on my back resting beside the renovated church, I felt the sad silence that pervades Iona, a silence that one would expect to be found at any such place on earth where sacrifice and honour held sway.

I imagined Columba and the monks moving 'round the island as they once did. I could see them catching supper off a rock, thatching the huts of wattle, or grinding flour at the mill. I saw them draining the bog and pruning the fruit trees.

Soon they will gather for prayers in chapel and then go to the refectory for supper and after that take a turn or two around the cemetery or along the shore.

I see Columba among them, of handsome features with long hair and a tonsure ear to ear. He waits for the old to shuffle in at supper and stands stone-like before his warriors for Christ. Then, in his high-pitched voice, this holy Abbot intones grace and blesses the food.

That's the secret of this Isle — the goodness of Columba and the monks and pilgrims who came after them. I too left something of myself — there, on that sleepy hallowed place. For the next tourist.

Ozzie's Secret

Ozzie Smith's acceptance speech at Cooperstown, N.Y. on the occasion of his entry into Baseball's Hall of Fame in July, 2002, gave the world the reason for his success.

He said that as a boy he had looked within himself and discovered "that absolutely nothing is good enough if it can be made better." He knew that working on his character as best as he could was the only way to go.

He said, "I sincerely believe that there is nothing truly great in any man or woman except their character, their willingness to move beyond the realm of self and into a greater realm of selflessness.… Giving back is the ultimate talent in life."

Clarence

Clarence had pretty well decided that the life of a Minister was not for him. While he had generally enjoyed his first year of Bible college in Saskatchewan, the discipline and rules of the place clashed with his maverick tendencies. So he told the powers that be he would be leaving. He checked over his jalopy, spiked his hair, and headed home by way of the United States to Toronto.

His journey ended abruptly in the U.S. when a boy ran a stop sign and totalled Clarence's car. The investigating police were not impressed by Clarence's appearance and even less by what they decided was his carelessness at the intersection. The other driver, a local boy, was exonerated. Clarence was stranded without money and car.

Now, it happened upon the day of the accident that a local gentleman came upon Clarence nursing his wounds at a coffee shop near the accident site. He had seen the pile-up and wondered what he and his family could do to help.

And help they did. Clarence was swamped with Christian charity. He stayed a week with them until the police decided the crash was due to error on both sides. Clarence was then free to go. The family bought his bus ticket and gave Clarence $300 to cover further expenses.

Clarence's stay with that American family changed his life. So impressed was he by their kindness (no doubt, he said, arranged by God), that he made up his mind to return to Bible college.

Not long after, he was graduated and became a minister. His American friends and he still meet. Clarence has tried to pay them back, but in that regard, has never been able to get the best of them.

Guess Who, Mom?

On the Island of Prince Edward, along the Canadian Atlantic seaboard, up where the lobster and mussel abound, lives a middle-aged lady of singular faith in God.

Her life has not been easy. Plagued by a genetic mental aberration that requires occasional hospitalization and absence from work, she has always had to struggle just to get by. All considered, she's done quite well. She married, had two children, divorced and remarried. Always appreciative, she credits God, the medical profession and friends with her survival.

Liking her requires no effort. She has a way with people. She is considerate of everyone's well-being. She has innocence. You can sense it. The kind that's close to God and deserves reverence.

She prays much. She has a chapel upstairs in her home much like a princess of old would have. With all the rain in her life she gets her pennies from heaven.

The worst tragedy for her, she maintains, was the day she had to give up her baby girl for adoption. It wasn't anybody's fault. That's just the way it was — she was just too sick to look after the wee thing. Yet, the event still haunts her.

For over 40 years, she had been asking the social agency concerned with the adoption to help find her child. But they had refused. The agency claimed that the mother's vulnerable health never permitted any serious bonding. Many rules exist for the protection of all parties. Nothing could be done.

Until the mother's health got better.

And better it got. Everyone's prayers were answered. With new medication, a happier marriage, and the personal interest of her doctors, the agency decided to help her. And it's at this point that this story really begins.

Eventually, after more prayers and progress reports and old-fashioned detective work, the agency found the daughter. She was in the United States, married with five children, and had three university degrees. Would she agree to talk with her mother?

As I prayed for a happy ending to this adventure, I became agitated by the possibility that the girl would reject the mother. That's all the poor soul needed — more hurt and tears. I thought of the mother's innocence.

One afternoon, I found myself saying a prayer that the girl would phone her mother. I'm not sure my heart was in it. I had doubts: "What good can my small prayer achieve?"

The next day didn't the mother phone us? She said that her daughter had called her that very morning. She would like to see her. They were to meet in a small hotel halfway between their homes.

What could I think? Had my prayer helped open the daughter's heart? Was it really heard and granted? "My God, my God," I cried out to myself. "What if it was? What if it was?"

Not About Him

The lesson in this story is left to the reader. Don Shula, Miami's great football coach, had just had his most successful year. His picture appeared in papers and magazines across America. Sports enthusiasts reached out to him wherever he went.

One summer in a seaside town in Maine this is what happened. He and his family had decided to catch a movie in one of the old buildings on the boardwalk. As they entered into its shadows, a small crowd inside began clapping and cheering. Shula was absolutely blown away by their adulation for him until one lady explained, "The manager said not enough people were here to show the picture unless more came. And here you are; bless you!"

Nature Can Be Thoughtful

One day in a wee village by the seashore in Eastern Canada, a local man was dying.

Born in the community, he had spent decades away from there during which time he became a master criminal. His target was the rich whose money he distributed among the poor. He became a legend. Only a few knew his identity. He was never captured.

In retirement, this Robin Hood had been back at home for a few years and now death was near. His only request was that they bury him near his parents in the graveyard of the parish church.

Unfortunately, a hard core of the church elders, suspicious of his notoriety, felt his grave would some day draw unsavoury visitors. So, on the night he died, they began the transfer of his body 100 miles up the coast where they laid it in an unmarked grave in a seaside cemetery above the ocean. So much for that legend, they thought.

But a strange twist of fate gave the good thief his final wish. Some 100 years later a fierce storm ravaged his burial site and soon all the coffins were floating out to sea. In fact, the whole hillside slid into the briny.

One day, several months later, the townsfolk of the man's original village saw a box bobbing into the bay. It stopped near the church. It was a coffin.

As was proper, the people buried it in the local cemetery. Because the coffin still bore the identification initials of the undertaker, people knew it was from around those parts. Gradually, over the years, the truth becomes known.

Nowadays, people come to see the grave of the person who returned to his village on nature's whim. The elders were right. He has become a legend.

Playing Along

The lane in which I was walking ran by the fenced-in playground of a day care centre.

Suddenly, a little voice said, "What's your name?" I looked up to see a charming little girl. "What's your name?" she asked again.

"Garfield. What's yours?" She did not answer.

By this time, a row of bare knuckles clutched the chain-link fence. One kid said, "She's Lola." Another kid said, "Lola says your name is Garfield."

"That's right. Garfield, like the cat! I have four legs."

The gallery somehow appreciated that idea. A few gasped. Not to be outdone in imagination, when I said, "Count them," one lad started up, "One, two, three" and another quipped, "One, three, five." As I walked way, amazed by their cleverness, I heard one voice say, "Six."

I was going to look down, but I didn't.

The Flower Lady

The very elderly Sister Jeanne loved her flowers. She saw God's beauty in them. She would hold each flower like some treasure, turn it in her hands — admire its wonder.

Her spiritual life transcended the ordinary. The other Sisters saw her as a role model for convent life. She became a flower, herself, and they marvelled at her holiness. After her death, many Sisters prayed for her spiritual intervention.

One day, a Sister in the community became emotionally distraught over a seemingly unsolvable problem. At a crisis, she thought she would take her problem to the old nun. So she went to Sister's locked, vacant room and with her head placed against the door prayed for ten minutes. Tears of petition called on Sister Jeanne to ask God for a release from her pain.

Suddenly, a peace came over the Sister. Everything would be okay. That afternoon, the problem became history. God's loving flower-lady was found not wanting.

Somewhere, God is admiring in His hand, His special flower — Sister Jeanne.

Sadie

It was 6:15 p.m. and the British Airways 747 waited in line for take-off clearance at Toronto International Airport. When seven more planes had left, it would be Flight 880's turn to nose down runway A5, eat up tarmac for 45 seconds, and follow the beacons non-stop to London, England.

By a window, Sadie was anxious to get going. Her mother was dying in the Orkney Islands and she wanted to arrive in time to say goodbye. Sadie felt that her mother, only 62, just had to wait for her only child to reach her side.

Sadie watched the other airships leaving one by one until eventually the time came for her departure. The pilot turned into the wind. And waited. The time was 6:25 p.m.

Suddenly, Sadie felt an awareness that her mother had just died. She wilted and at the same time grabbed her armrest for support as the engines' thrust pinned Sadie to the back of the seat. Her mother's soul and Sadie rose to heaven at the same moment. Sadie felt at peace.

When Sadie arrived next afternoon at Kirkwall in the Orkney's, her father met her.

"Your mother's gone, Sadie."

"I know, Dad, she came to me to say goodbye. What time did she die?"

"At 11:25 p.m." That was the exact time when Sadie looked at her watch before take-off.

That evening the winds from Norway whipped down the narrow streets of Kirkwall as Sadie and her dad walked home to their empty house, both consoled by the mother's visitation to Sadie.

The Rocket

Maurice "Rocket" Richard was a legend in professional hockey. As a member of the Montreal Canadians, he set the standards for hockey. He became an idol for the French Canadian man-in-the-street.

In the 1940s, families gathered 'round their radios, many battery-charged, to listen to the play-by-play of the Rocket's scoring feats. With the coming of television, they marvelled at seeing possibly the most lethal scoring machine ever to play the game.

On his skates he stood tall and solid, lithe and handsome. His sleek jet black hair and flashing dark eyes unnerved his rivals.

The fans loved him because he was his own man. No one pushed him around, on the ice or off. He refused to be a pawn of the administration and, with good reason, never trusted them.

The Rocket loved the game in a different way than did the top brass. For him, it was a way of life to be respected for what it was — a game that was part and parcel of every kid's life across Canada.

He brought self-sacrifice to the game, shied from adulation and played hockey for the right reasons. He brought finesse and fire as no other player has ever done.

An example of the Rocket's charisma is shown by one young lady's lifetime devotion. Her name is Frances, the youngest of 12 children from a family in rural Québec. In 1945, the Rocket was 25 and Frances, 7, just old enough to appreciate the awe her brothers and sisters held for the Rocket. It rubbed off. She followed his career and retirement right up to his death.

You see Frances had that same pluck and focus the Rocket had. At 18 she began the austere vocation of a cloistered nun and, believe it or not, took the Rocket as a role model. She loved God the way the Rocket played the game. Her goal was holiness.

In the year 2000, the Rocket died and in her Christmas letter to friends which contained the year's highlights of her convent life, Frances mentioned her sorrow upon learning of his death. She told us that in honour of the Rocket she had worn the number 9 (his number) sewn inside her outfits for 43 years. When things got her down, she merely looked at the number 9 for inspiration. I'm sure God didn't mind.

No wonder, then, that some people saw a light shooting for the heavens over Montreal the night the Rocket died. It was put there by the spiritual energy of all the Rocket's admirers such as Frances, who has been his friend for 57 years and still wears in his memory the famous number "9" on her person.

St. Andrew's

The eastern section of St. Andrew's Town, Scotland, is built on an ancient Celtic cliff known as St. Mary of the Rock. Facing the German Sea, its manicured ruins recall the grandeur of those days when St. Andrew's was the ecclesiastical centre of all Scotland. Now, the ghostly skeletons of St. Andrew's Cathedral (founded 1160), the Monks' Priory (1160) and the great Castle (1200s) attest to Vanity's curse and King Henry's revenge.

Long before St. Andrew's lost much of its political and religious clout, the seeds for its continuous survival and popularity were planted by the astute. This once royal burgh of saints and sinners, martyrs and murderers, eventually gave way to scholars (oldest university in Scotland, 1411) and to athletes (birthplace of golf in the 1400s). On the west of the town are six courses all owned by the Burgh.

The small hotel where my wife and I stayed in March, 1968, still faces north on the street that runs to the castle. Two hundred yards west is the first tee of the Old Course and beside it the most famous golf clubhouse in the world, the Royal and Ancient Golf Club. East is the ocean shore.

I remember those March nights as being cold. The shore's light grey sand whistled in the windy blast from the northern sky. The owners of the hotel kindly gave us heated bricks for our bed.

While at St. Andrew's, we experienced a small happening perfectly suited to the colourful history of the place. We had driven down to Edinburgh on Saturday afternoon from St. Andrew's in our leased Vauxhall. On our way home, we missed a turn and found ourselves well on the way to Dundee. Since we had intended to visit with an old relative in Dundee, we thought we might as well go on ahead to see her.

After our visit, we headed back to our St. Andrew's hotel. We arrived about 1:30 a.m. to find the front door locked. We rang the bell again and again to no avail. So we drove into the town to the police station where an officer said not to worry: hotel owners often don't tell their clients that they lock up early. He said that he and his partner would meet us there. Unfortunately, our Vauxhall would not start. "No problem," said the officer, "jump in the back of our paddy wagon and we'll straighten out this situation."

At the hotel, one officer raised a small window at the side, squeezed through and opened the front door. The three of us piled into a two-passenger elevator that inched its way higher! Following the officer's big torch, we entered our bedroom. The bricks, needless to say, were not warm. "Are ye alright, now?" smiled the policeman.

The next day I phoned the car agency in Glasgow. The personnel couldn't understand how such a "reliable vehicle" could break down — never had trouble like that before, they claimed. On Sunday morning they drove up another car. That evening we had to be back at the Glasgow agency to return the car before 5:00 p.m. Our flight left at 6:30 p.m. I called the company at 4:30 p.m. — we're coming, I told him.

Well, we arrived at 4:45 p.m. The place was closed. So we drove the car to the airport environs, put a note on the window and literally took off. We never heard from them again.

After such escapades, somehow we felt we had left our mark at St. Andrew's: the warrior Bruce had once consecrated the Cathedral, Cardinal Beaton had been hung out to decay on a rampart, Jack Nicklaus had won the British Open there, Mary, Queen of Scots, had played golf there, and three famous Protestant martyrs had died at the castle. Now, the Ogilvies had ridden in a paddy wagon and along with two police officers seemingly committed a crime of break and enter.

Not bad for one day on the road.

IN THIS CORNER

One old timer said to the other, "There's going to be a big crowd at the arena next Saturday. Bishop Sheen is coming." To which the other said, "Yeah, who's he wrestling?"

Colin

Nine-year old Colin was playing as a goalie in a championship hockey game. The whole team played well, but in the last minute, a winning goal slipped in off an opponent's skate.

Colin was feeling badly in the dressing room. He thought he'd let the team down. He cried a little in the corner. Then his father came over and cheered him up. His Dad told him about the many goals he had saved in the game and how the players looked up to him and how much he had set an example.

Before they got home, Colin felt better. He knew then that sometimes things happen and that there's nothing anyone can do. Do your best, he said to himself: that's what his Dad had said. That's all that matters.

Some years later, Colin came upon his father sitting in an armchair. He was upset. Someone close had died. He was crying. He seemed alone, tired and worn out.

"What's wrong, Dad? Do you feel that you let your friend down? And that you weren't there *enough* for him? Didn't listen sometimes?"

"Yes, I do, Colin. How did you know?"

"Well, I'm not so dumb. I keep my eyes open. Dad, you've got to stop blaming yourself. You can't control some things. They happen and you can't do anything about them. I'm proud of you, Pop. You taught me to do my best and not worry. I learned that from you. Now, let's get out of here and throw the ball around.

Who Knows?

During the spring and summer of 2001, the behaviour of sharks around the world became erratic. The biting of humans by sharks became more frequent. Coastal areas, usually empty of sharks, became inundated with them. Small children, only knee-deep in the ocean, were attacked. The sandy ocean resorts of the world were in jeopardy.

As I grew up, I had heard how catastrophes were often predicted by the behaviour of animals. For example, the unusual agitation of ants and termites has been known to predict a coming earthquake. Battles of birds, as in Ireland, have been known to preface times of great sufferings among the people. Rats and cats abandon doomed ships. Family dogs often die just before their masters. Cattle in the field show the coming of rains and storms. Before the Vikings came to the British Isles, weird happenings in the northern skies were recorded for 100 years.

As these shark attacks took place more frequently over that summer, the possibility of there being some connection between their behaviour and some great tragedy to come became a strong possibility. Fifteen-million-year-old beings don't change their personalities in the space of a few months. Is it possible that they know of calamities coming to this planet, the awareness of which is shut out to the planet's younger members?

All summer I would ask my friends, "Why are the sharks behaving so much out of character? Why are they so agitated?" Some laughed and accused me of senility.

But no one had an answer. The answer came on September 11, 2001.

A THIN LINE

It's a thin line between crazy and sane
It's a thin line between pleasure and pain
It's a thin line between freedom and none
It's a thin line between the pen and the gun
It's a thin line between sleep and dreams
It's a thin line between the seen and unseen
It's a thin line between hatred and love
It's a thin line between below and above
It's a thin line between hello and goodbye
It's a thin line between living and dying
It's a thin line between day and night
It's a thin line between wrong and right
It's a thin line between sick and well
It's a thin line between heaven and hell.

— the Author

The Smile

This is the story of how one smile directly saved one life and indirectly took another.

In December, 1828, in a small pioneer village of Upper Canada, a burning home lit up the winter night. Before any neighbours could reach the scene, a mother and four of her children lost their lives. The survivors were her husband and the youngest child, aged three.

The husband's explanation of what had happened seemed plausible, and soon neighbours gathered 'round to help the poor "quiet," "sober," "industrious" widower. The surviving child was taken in by a lady from the area. A semblance of order returned to the struggling Scottish community.

But not for long. As the little waif gained more command of his language and thoughts, he started muttering about how his daddy had hit his mommy. His new guardian become so alarmed, she went to the police.

A coroner's inquest was held, and eventually the husband confessed to beating all five to death and igniting the log house to cover up the deed. Apparently, the previous post-mortem examinations of the burned bodies had been partially incriminating but not enough to warrant further investigation. It was the interrogation by a military-trained settler of the region that fragmented the killer's story. In August, 1829, the pioneer was hanged on the gallows. His body became an ornament for the curious and to this day no one knows if it ever received proper burial.

It came out at the trial that jealousy had driven this usually normal citizen into a rage. Had he caught his wife with a lover? Were some of his children not his? Had the gentleman become so demented by jealousy that he tried to destroy everything he loved? We shall never know the truth.

But we have one answer for sure, and it's like a crack of lightning on a hot rainless day. When the coroner asked the father why he didn't kill the remaining child, he said he couldn't: just as he raised his hand to batter the child, the boy smiled up at him and the father couldn't do it.

Imagine, in spite of the carnage that night and all the screams and blood and moans, that little child still managed a trusting smile. The power of a smile stayed a slayer's hand and melted down a killing frenzy.

Shortly after, the child was sent to another home in Canada, never to know anything about the family tragedy. This story was attested to by a descendent of that settlement who, though not born at the time of the murders, knew the chief participants, including the prosecutor. This man's name was McGregor, a principal of Almonte High School, Ontario.

MAKES SENSE

Why is it that some people mourn their pets more than they do their relatives? A minister once told me how his old Aunt answered this question. She said, "Someone asked me once why I cried more over my dead parrot than my brother. And I told him, 'I shall see my brother again, but my parrot has gone forever!'"

> ## REPAYMENT
>
> We are never alone
>> When someone cares enough
> To take our part in pain,
>> And asks God to come to us
> And help us stand again.
>> Then when we are well
> And long to know
>> How best we can repay,
> We learn to take on another's pain
>> And help him stand again.
>> — the Author

The Lady in Blue

Next to me in an aisle seat sat a man of great size and presence. He must have weighed 320 pounds. When he got up to adjust his shrieking hearing aids, he stood well over six feet. A whopping wide-brimmed sombrero shadowed piercing eyes. We were waiting for the curtain time of a Noel Coward play at the Shaw Festival at Niagara-on-the-Lake, Ontario. The stranger was excited. In fact, he was in his glory.

He was, as I found out, a literary genius. He had written some eight books at the University of Notre Dame in Indiana from which he had just retired as Head of the English Literature Department. Any doubts I had about his literary expertise were dispelled by an oral treatise he gave me on some 15 giants of English literature, none of whom I knew.

With the first dimming of the lights, he toddled down to the empty front row, still fiddling with his hearing aids. There he removed his hat and waited in breathless expectation.

As the play developed, he became very involved. You'd swear he knew all the lines of all the parts. He applauded, anticipated and squirmed. He was obviously crazy over theatre. He told me that this play was his seventh that week, with another on the morrow. He had money as well as brains.

Later, as he came up the aisle on his way out, I happened to notice an attractive, middle-aged woman follow him up the steps some four feet back of his right shoulder. She wore a not-off-the-rack business suit topped by a Napoleon cadet hat with a veil that reached just below her eyes. From head to toe, she was cobalt blue.

As she passed, she turned her head ever so slightly towards me. As if she didn't mind my seeing her. As if we shared some common knowledge. She smiled as I nodded hello.

She looked tired, but poised. She had difficulty with the stairs. For her, being at the theatre was more of a chore than a pleasure. Her pale blue eyes were solemn and penetrating. Her bearing suggested refinement. She was a lady.

Yet, there was a mystery about her. Her face was different. It did not look real. It had no solid structure; it was a collection of misty layers: dull, pasty, blue and grey. The dark veil helped hide it.

Next day, I met the professor outside the same theatre just before the afternoon's performance. He spoke of his family, his permanently-hospitalized mentally-ill wife, and how deathly sick he himself had recently been. He talked of tragedies and miracles and victories. He had faith, this huge intellectual from the Midwest. Before parting, I asked boldly, "Professor, are you travelling alone?" "Oh, yes," he said. "I'm used to it."

Later that afternoon, at the play, I was not so sure of his last statement. This time I was sitting on the other side of the theatre when the professor passed me on his way down to the front. And there, discreetly behind him, off his right shoulder was the same lady in blue — same suit, same colouring, and the same smile cast my way.

Immediately I sensed she was *with* the professor. Her resigned look told me so. Duty and love directed that she be with him. Somehow from his past, he had a lady companion who loved and cared for him so much that she took on a ghostly form to be with him. At the front of the theatre where she supposedly went to sit during both performances, she was nowhere to be seen. He always sat alone — so he and I thought.

For some unknown reason (perhaps it was my infatuation with the professor), she had let me see her. Who was she? The ghost of his mother? His real sickly wife, bi-located? Or a resident spirit in that theatre who felt comfortable in the professor's presence?

After the performance, in the sunshine of Niagara, I saw the professor standing with a group. The lady was not there ... *not that I could see.*

NEVER TOO LATE

The soft smile on her face did little to lighten the sledge hammer blow ... yet, it said to me, "I did not suffer ... a holy lady took my hand and I was not alone...." I straightened her and held her in my arms off the cold floor ... and I kissed her more than once and told her cold ear of my love ... too late, too late, perhaps, perhaps ... and then two men came and carried her away ... and the silence in the house screamed.

THE ONLY WAY

Without the storm
  We'd never love the sun
Without the pain
  God's will would not be done.
After the rain
  The skies are blue
After sorrow
  God's love shines through.
Sorrow and rain
  Storm and pain
Into every life will fall.
  Yet, they are the only way
We come to know
  The mercy God has for us all.

— the Author

A Wild Rover

Never in my 74 years have I known anyone so brilliant who suffered as much as my friend, Earl.

He wandered in his wilderness, knelt in his Gethsemane and withstood his Calvary. Yet in spite of many personal hardships, his intelligence and sensitivity carried him to a heavenly plane where in his own way he conversed with God.

His theological views were strong. He saw evil for what it was — a force from hell. As for goodness, he felt it could deflect evil. By surrounding ourselves with a circle of God's grace (which he called goodness), evil could not touch us.

My friend, Earl, loved justice. He hated meanness. He admired loyalty. He hated hypocrisy. He disliked blarney. He loved malarkey. He was shy about being praised and equally reticent about articulating his love for others. Hiding his emotion was a way of survival. But his actions gave him away.

Earl instilled admiration. He stood tall for family, friends, young people, and the sick. He was an able dealer: no one coerced him; no one did his thinking; no one pushed him or his friends around. He stood up to unfair bosses, tried to start unions and did as much as he could to get to the heart of all problems. Earl hated the padding and phoniness in the market places of the world! As a principal, teacher and school trustee, he avoided politics and kept the welfare of the child uppermost.

Earl, my friend, was the truest Irishman I ever met. If Sarsfield needed a man to blow up a train belonging to William of Orange, he would have chosen a man like Earl. His dedication could be fierce — he was an Irish Rover. Like the true Irish, he loved to sing, dance, brood, laugh, tell a joke, write poems and play games with people's minds. He read profusely. He could talk on any subject. He believed in giving children freedom to seek and fulfill their own dreams. He was a melancholic romanticist.

Earl, my friend, never recovered emotionally from the tremendous effort of trying to save two babies from drowning in a city pool. He dove in and searched the bottom until he was spent. The children died and Earl was heart-broken.

Last week he "dove into eternity" looking for God. It was something over which God gave him no choice. God called him. God wanted *him*. He said, "Earl, you have had enough suffering for any man. Come to me, my friend. I am here. You will never suffer again. You will be with me. You funny Irishman."

The day after I learned of Earl's passing, a baby bird sat on the edge of our sliding door. It looked frightened. It stared at me. With my movement of the inner door and outer screen, it never moved. I thought it was injured. It was red-capped, with young black and white feathers, its wings folded close to its body.

As my wife reached for it, it flinched and flew up to a nearby window, still staring at us. As my wife reached again, it flew away.

In 44 years in our house, no bird had ever come to my window that way. Was it Earl saying he was all right? I like to think so

Earl was never far from heaven in life. In death, he will never be far from earth.

Earl, I still see your grimaces. I feel the gaze of your big puppy-dog eyes. I hear your guffaws. On another day, we'll once again do our crazy dance routines to a jazz band. On another day, we'll sing "Swanee" and "Bill Bailey" and the "Black Velvet Band."

When again I hear your voice piping "Danny Boy" from some great pinnacle beyond the winds, I'll know I'm on my way to where you are and where I want to be.

"God, I Have to Go Back"

Dorothy felt uneasy in her hospital room. The birth of her seventh child had not gone well. She had required patch-up surgery and as a nurse herself, knew the probability of a complication.

Sure enough, Dorothy began to haemorrhage. She pushed the nurse's alarm button and passed out. Everybody came running to save her. And they did.

About two weeks later Dorothy was in for a check-up with her doctor. "How are you feeling, Dorothy?"

"Not too bad. And the baby is well too."

"We almost lost you that evening."

"Yes, I know," answered Dorothy. "I heard and saw it all."

"I beg your pardon. Did you say you heard and saw it all?"

"Yes, Doctor. I saw you run into the room. The nurses were already there. I heard you sounding orders. I heard you shout, 'She's dead. She's dead.' I heard your wild swearing, your condemnation of the nurses, your hopeless ranting."

The doctor became uncomfortable. All that she had said was true.

Dorothy went on, "You see, I was standing above the bed in a great shaft of light, the bottom of which covered the bed and the top ran straight up in the shape of a funnel beyond the room. From where I was, my lifeless body on the bed looked only the size of a doll.

"Above the bed, I was fully aware I had no body with me. I was a spirit. But I could see and hear and reason and feel. I knew then that the soul has its own body and mind.

"When I heard you shout, 'She's dead. She's dead,' I remember saying to myself, 'I can't die. No one would help my husband care for the children. God, I have to go back. I can't die.' I then felt myself re-enter my body."

By this time, the doctor was crimson. He said, "Dorothy, I can deny nothing. You were officially dead and now you are not. But I'll tell you one thing — if ever I lose a patient like that again, I'll keep working to bring him or her back until they have to pull me away."

Dorothy today is still in good health. As for the baby girl born that night, she is now 39 years old, raised by a mother who turned down heaven for her family.

Better still, this Irish girl, Colleen, is my godchild.

COINCIDENCES?

When the world needs military leaders, God sends babies:
* In 1769, Napoleon was born and so was Wellington.
* Hitler was born in 1889, Eisenhower in 1890 and Charlie Chaplin in 1889.
* Stalin was born in 1879, MacArthur in 1880 and Roosevelt in 1882.
* Two other boys sent to help mankind were: Churchill, born in 1874, and the great composer of inspirational war songs, George M. Cohan in 1878.
* Communism came in 1917, Pope John Paul II was born in 1920.

Martha

Tommy Joyce grew up on a farm in County Galway, Ireland at the turn of the twentieth century. His family had little money since their land was marsh and rock. But the Joyces had good food, fresh air, space, and a river by their home.

As the oldest, Tom could have inherited the farm in time and made a comfortable living. But he was more ambitious than that. He wanted to see the world.

Around 1909, he went to Canada for a couple of years and returned home with the idea of taking up an apprenticeship arranged by his father. When that idea fell through, he went to England with money supplied by his grandmother. Tom must have been a regular guy because everybody wanted to help him. Lucky for him they did.

In pre-war England, he met his future wife, Beth. They postponed their marriage until Tommy finished with his tour of duty in the British Army. In 1919 he returned wounded from Europe and married Beth.

In 1920, they went to British Columbia, where Tom joined the Canadian Navy. Five years later, Beth died giving birth to a baby girl.

Tom managed for two years, but when a sudden sickness threatened the life of his girl, he wrote home for someone to come and help. Not long after, his sister, Martha, the oldest of four girls, travelled 6000 miles by boat and train to give her support.

Soon Martha became totally enamoured with her niece. For 15 years she cared for her brother and his daughter. But not without difficulty.

For example, Tom wanted no part of Catholicism for his daughter or himself while Martha insisted on her niece being raised a Catholic. Martha even put her job on the line to enforce her feeling in this regard. The result was a stalemate. The daughter's welfare kept Tom and Martha together but the daughter's religious upbringing drove them apart. Such enmity is all too common today in homes everywhere.

Around 1944 Tom married. Martha, then 50 years old, lost her job and home because Tom's new wife didn't like her. She left. For the first time in her life Martha had to be a housekeeper for strangers. About this time Martha's niece entered a Catholic convent to become a nun.

Sitting in her upper room at her new residence, quite alone and forgotten, Martha must have questioned her decision to leave all she had cherished in Ireland for an unappreciative brother in a foreign land. Had it been worth it? Would she do it again? Yes, it had. Yes, she would.

Love had made it worthwhile. She had helped two people in difficulty. Her niece was everything. She carried that thought through the years left to her.

One night Tom had a call from the hospital telling him his sister was in critical condition. She died before he got there.

At Martha's wake, Tom came to pay his respects. He had returned to the Church about a year after his daughter's religious profession. His daughter was there too, Martha's best friend. It was she who sent me the above story. It is she who still lives in the convent, forever mindful of Martha's love.

Her name is Joyce. Joyce wrote, "Martha's life of sacrifice was not in vain. Martha and I had prayed unceasingly for my father. She taught me to pray for him from the time I could understand. That night at the wake, Dad and I prayed together — this time for Martha. She would have liked that. I know I did. Thank you Martha, for everything."

The Hug

Any Scottish relatives I have or had, came from Glasgow, Scotland, to Verdun, Québec. Their patriarch was one Fred Robertson who had spent three years in a German concentration camp in the First World War. In spite of imprisonment, traces of yellow gas in his lungs, and shrapnel in his knees, he had the strength to bring his family to Canada in 1920. My father who had been raised as a foster child by the Robertsons in Glasgow until he was 12, met up with them again in Verdun. In time my mother and I came to know these wonderful people who had been so kind to my Dad.

What pleased me most about the Robertson men was that they always called me "son." Back on the farm in my summer holidays, my Irish relatives referred to me as "the little man," "bucko," or "Jack." But with the Scottish, I was always "son." And I liked that — I felt wanted and appreciated.

Years later I met an 84-year-old veteran from Edinburgh and I mentioned this "son" business. And he said, "Aye, I still use it myself, but only with those I like." This news made me feel even more comfortable with the term.

I was recently in Glasgow for a second time. Thirty-three years before, I had visited my father's school in a suburb called Denistown. The janitor took me through the school called Haghill. I saw the First Grade classroom where

ANOTHER START

The white blossoms of the apple tree swirl 'round the tulips ... from the top of the oak, the seldom seen Baltimore oriole welcomes the morn ... the dew sparkles on the greening lawns and in the fountains a pair of red-winged blackbirds bathe ... the peonies are out and the lilacs blush against the hedge ... a southwest breeze is refreshing ... the sun is warm ... the geese are farther north ... the baby robins and sparrows test their wings ... another day has come ... the woods are fresh and the pastures new ... another day to spend with you.

my father sat at age five in 1912. Since my dad was dead only 15 years at the time of this visit, my seeing his early haunts of home and school in 1968 moved me deeply.

My second visit was different. I was older and so was Glasgow. Haghill had aged badly and the tenements around it were bleak. I also felt sad about seeing Scotland perhaps for the last time. That feeling may have left me jaundiced. I thought of all my dead Scottish relatives, not just from around Glasgow, but from Dundee, Aberdeen, Airlie and Drum. I was there to say goodbye to them all, and to thank those who had stayed on in Scotland for having kept the Ogilvie name alive and strong.

As for Glasgow itself, it still has that neighbourhood feeling. Never rich, it has struggled to feed, clothe and educate its children. It carries in its environs the wounds of its struggle.

A grey wash covers the seven hills and valleys — the Clyde is dirty — the traffic noisy — the clutter is cluttered — a sombreness has settled on the land.

But the people, thank God, are the same. They see themselves as part of a great Glaswegian family. They pull together. There's always a sparkle in the eye, a strut in the gait, a smile, a quip. Old ladies on buses still go google-eyed over the bairns of Glasgow's young mothers. Waitresses go out of their way to serve the old their pension-paid, Saturday-night dinner. Admission to museums, parks and botanical gardens is free.

Never too rich and never too poor, the Scottish carry on.

A wee story before I close. Our last four nights in Glasgow were spent at a fairly fancy hotel. Every morning at breakfast, I had a chat with the head chef. His name was Jimmy Steele — a solid chunk of a man with rugged good looks and an easy charm.

One morning I said, "Jim, with that white hair, you must have been a chef for a number of years."

"Only five, I drove a bus for twenty-five."

Thinking he must have gone back to chef's school to get such a job in this swanky hotel, I asked, "Where did you learn to cook, then?"

"From watching me mother cook for us bairns."

When the final morning came, on the day of our departure, a small event happened that made the whole trip worthwhile. It was as if Jimmy, the chef, was chosen by God to say goodbye to me for all of Scotland and in particular, Glasgow.

What Jimmy said assuaged my sadness. We were standing together at the end of the counter of bacon, blood pudding, kippers and haggis, and I said, "Jim, we're heading out today. I want to thank you for being so pleasant. My wife and I wish you every happiness."

I guess Jim felt my emotion. He said, "You know, Gar, I'm a Glaswegian. I grew up in Denistown just like your father. It's still a wonderful place — a little Glasgow, in a way. I think I know how you feel."

He then stepped out away from the counter, wrapped me in a great bear hug and said, "God go with you, my Son."

And I whispered in his ear, "Jimmy, you don't know how much that means to me."

"I do know," he said. "I do."

On Being There

Snippets of information handed down to posterity by *those who were there*, often convey best the depth of mankind's greatest tragedies.

War

Father Dillon Cahill, an Oblate of Mary Immaculate Missionary, who taught at my alma mater, St. Patrick's College, Ottawa, once told his students a fact which brought home the heart-wrenching nature of war. As a Canadian chaplain stationed in Europe in the 1940s, he had buried over 230 Canadian soldiers and written to all the families.

Famine

In Ireland, the calamity of the potato famine in 1847, '48, '49, was best described by a Father Kavanagh, a curate appointed to St. Mary's Church in Westport, Mayo, Ireland. In his diary, he wrote, "Every morning before breakfast I went to visit the dying, and every morning I gave the last rites to 50 parishioners."

Loss of Family Among Pioneers

I never properly understood the difficulties my Irish ancestors had in trying to survive in Canada between 1824 and 1920 until I read a notation written by a parish priest of Corkery, Ontario, in his official book *Parish Funerals*. The year was about 1900. He wrote, "Buried one Maurice Tynes this day, predeceased by his wife and eight children. He was the only one left."

Pioneer Medical Shortage

Edith married Bill, a Home Boy from England, around 1927. Bill had been taken in by a Canadian Irish family about 1910 with the proviso that he receive security and acceptance in return for his work on their farm. When Edith became part of that family, she dedicated most of her life to both Bill and his guardians.

When I asked Edith in her 90th year how it was that some families were offered Home Boys by our government and some weren't, she said that the needs of the applying family had much to do with eligibility. "In the family where my husband lived," she said, "the reason was that this couple couldn't have children. There was no help on the farm."

And then she said something that showed the inadequacy of medical care in the pioneer days, "It was hell! The lady in question had seven pregnancies, all of which went full term. The tragedy was that all the children were born in body parts."

Isolation

The inhabitants of Blasket Island, 12 miles off the west coast of County Kerry in Ireland, knew from experience that weather can push people to the brink of despair. Winter storms, from Christmas to St. Patrick's Day, could cut them off from the mainland for dangerous lengths of time.

One safeguard that showed the depths to which their depression could plummet in such extended isolation was the practice each family had of putting away a bottle of whiskey to be used only when life on the island became unbearable. Usually, at the end of three weeks of pounding wind and sea, they released its spirits to take the edge off their depression. They had a special name for these bottles, but it escapes me.

Poverty in Canada

The Irish Catholic immigrant to Canada, for the most part, never received good land from the British. Around 1900, Michael and Kathleen Hogan raised eight children on marginal land in the Gatineau Hills of Québec. Anybody who knew them vouched for their devotion to each other. The hardship of the times only strengthened their bond.

Michael's mettle in the face of family tragedy was best illustrated the time he lost two children on the same day: Joy, six, and Allen, four. Distraught because he could not afford proper tombstones, Michael went searching among the hills for suitable natural stones to act as markers. He found two. Imagine the sorrow as he sculpted the stones down to size and chiselled Joy's and Allan's names, ages and date of death.

When Kathleen came to see what Michael had done, her appreciation had no bounds.

The Depression

My first cousins, Clarence and Allen, age six and five respectively in 1936, lived with their parents and a sister on a hundred-acre farm. The world Depression already in its fifth year had left people *cost conscious*, and the Williams, although not poor, had to cut back like everyone else. Frills were out. My three cousins remember that their Christmas presents for the year 1936 were two oranges each.

War Fatalities

At a restaurant, one evening, a Mr. Gordon told me: "In 1939, I was one of 170 members of the Edinburgh Flying Club who enlisted in the RAF. Our wing command was called the First Squadron of Scotland. We were a brash bunch — the world was our oyster. At the end, two of us came back."

Annette

During elementary and high school days, the death of a classmate can be a shock. I remember Mike O'Brien who died of polio, Jimmy Grace who had leukemia, Albert Finn who collided with a train and Sylvester Corkery and Tom White who had cancer.

Their deaths affected the entire school.

I heard recently of such a loss which took place in the city of Montreal in 1932. The staff and students of St. Stanislaus School on Rue de Laroche were heartbroken by the passing of a 16-year-old girl named Marie Annette. Her story has come down the years from Agnes, her younger sister. Agnes was eighth in a family of eleven and Annette the eldest.

Naturally, Annette, being the first child, was called upon by her mother to help with the ten children all under sixteen, a challenge that Annette met with extraordinary sacrifice. By 1931, already in her final year at high school, this pretty, talented and popular young lady appeared well on the road to a successful life.

But that year life changed for Annette. Her mother, whom she adored, developed angina and within a few months went to hospital. Annette was very upset when she heard her mother would be in hospital for an undetermined length of time. But she made up her mind to run the house as best she could. And she did.

A few months later, however, Annette's own health gave way. No one knows the cause — worry, overwork, a virus, other natural causes. What we do know is that she was overly sensitive and intelligent, that she loved her family, particularly her mother, and that she worried about the welfare of the children if her mother died.

When Annette's condition worsened to the point of her entering hospital, the family and community became more concerned. The possibility of Annette's dying triggered many prayers for her cure. Then came the bombshell. Annette raised the stakes when she announced that she planned to die in place of her mother. This intention to substitute her death for her mother's death was clearly expressed by a message given to her friends through the parish priest: "I have made the sacrifice of my life to save my mother's. God has accepted; blessed be His name … the family needs Mama. I could not do the work."

Then, the messages became more cryptic: "I will love you in Heaven as I loved you on earth. I beg for the prayers of all those I have known and loved. I have left you in tears, but be consoled. Though separated, we are still united."

With her schoolmates spreading this news, needless to say, the petitions to God were beyond estimation since, as Agnes says, "She was admired by everyone."

But Annette did die.

After Annette's funeral, which her mother could not attend, many in Montreal began praying to Annette to intercede in heaven. According to Agnes, countless testimonies of Annette's answers to prayers came into the possession of her family.

Not surprisingly, Annette's mother regained her health. She even had another child. She died in 1979 at 85, outliving her husband by eight years.

Some say it was Annette in heaven who instilled in her sister, Agnes, the desire to care for her parents in their senior years. Unable to stay in the religious cloistered life due to poor health (she tried three times in the early 1950s), Agnes decided to stay home. For over 25 years, she ran the household. In 1986, at age 56, Agnes entered a cloistered convent where she has lived happily ever since.

To this day, Agnes feels that her sister Annette is a saint. At St. Stanislaus School and Church some still remember her. They recall a self-possessed, unpretentious dark-haired beauty praying and setting good example.

Agnes remembers her penetrating eyes, her pronounced eyebrows, her lily-white neck and her exquisitely formed mouth with its gentle smile. She was tall and thin and straight of carriage. She had flair.

She recalls the story of Annette's sacrifice for God and family. She says that her staid gentility was just a front for the fire of love that burned in her heart, a fire so great that she died that another might live. Just like her Master and our soldiers and missionaries.

Annette died at 3 p.m. on Good Friday, March 25, 1932, the Feast of the Annunciation of the Virgin Mary.

The Good with the Bad

If we don't learn to accept the small failures in life, how can we be expected to survive the big ones? Today in education, for example, students with bad grades are never held back. They proceed according to their age. Granted, their school reports show they are doing the best they can, but the fact remains their self-image is being falsely buoyed up. At the end of the educational road, some hit a dead end. They may well have a ready disposition for work, but have no talents or certification with which to make a living. Facing such a reality at that time is difficult.

Shielding children from life's sorrows is also not recommended. The death of a favourite animal prepares a child for the loss of a parent or sibling. *Booting* a ball in a game builds character. So does missing an answer in arithmetic. Bullies in the schoolyard must be personally dealt with because later on in life, they're everywhere.

Everybody is born equal, but some more equal than others. A rough sea trains the mariner. Without the wind, would the sapling ever grow straight?

The way it is, we have little say over the cards we're dealt. Daily living has a way of kneading us into shape. We must learn to survive on our own. Only sacrifice and discipline help build character. Too much praise, mollycoddling and false grades have a purpose, but so do a spanking, a reality check, and a good dressing-down. A sentence to the time-out room can really work.

I knew a wonderful, talented girl who never had many serious rejections in life. She sailed through school and enjoyed many friends. Having a good mind, a pretty face, and sweet charm, opened doors. One day, while working in a big city, she was rejected by a suitor. It just happened that way. She was alone. She couldn't handle the loss. Too proud to ask for help, she caved in. One morning, they found her dead in her father's Mercedes in the family garage.

TOO LATE

Hell is full of people who left it too late to change their ways. They died professing their self-indulgent habits. They followed their own code all the way to darkness.

The Wagon

Just after daybreak on Saturday, February 10, 1810, the portress of the Visitation Convent at Georgetown, Washington, D.C. heard a rap at the front door. To her surprise, when she opened it, no one was there, nor were there any footprints in the fresh snow. What she did see, however, was a girl, bundle-in-hand, entering the convent gate from the street. She waited for her. Seeing that the girl was exhausted, she quickly invited her to come in and sit down.

"Can I help, my friend?" asked the Sister.

"My name is Margaret Marshall. I have come to live and die with you."

"You are welcome, Margaret. My name is Sister Frances. Of course, you know that you must have a recommendation before you may enter our Novitiate."

"I have no recommendation, Sister Frances. My parish priest back in Warren County, Pennsylvania, refused to give me one. Since my mother is not well and I am the only girl in our family, the priest told me I should stay at home with my mother, father and brothers. Even one of my brothers who was permitted to join the Jesuits was against my leaving home. I have disobeyed everyone by coming here."

"Well, Margaret, you must at least see our Bishop Neale and receive his approval."

"Sister Frances, I have already travelled two hundred and fifty miles. I don't mind going on.

"But you don't have to go far. He lives across the street," said Sister Frances.

The Bishop saw her that day.

"How old are you, my child?" asked the archbishop.

"I am nineteen years old, your Grace."

"And your name?"

"Margaret Marshall."

"What makes you think you have a vocation to the sisterhood?"

"I feel God has been calling me."

"Do your parents agree with your decision?"

"No one I love agrees with it. Perhaps I should have stayed at home and helped my sick mother. I feel guilty."

"When did you leave home?"

"Last Sunday, on a stormy morning. I threw a bundle out the window, stole across my parent's bedroom and slipped into the night. I never said goodbye. My heart aches for them all."

"They tell me you have travelled across the Allegheny Mountains from north-west Pennsylvania, a great journey. You must be strong physically as well as mentally to do that. I find it amazing."

"Yes, your Grace. I came through the gorges. Strangers showed me the way. I rested in shacks and huts by the roads. I heard wolves, fought snow-drifts, walked in dense forest, and suffered frostbite on my hands and feet. But suddenly God sent me an angel and here I am, ready to serve God."

The Bishop for the moment ignored her remark about the angel. "Well," he said, "we could use a good postulant. There are only eight Sisters. Sister Josephine Barber, the Superior, told me she likes you. I also have two nieces, Eliza and Henrietta, who will join the order in the next two years. Mobile, Alabama, is looking for the Order to go there. The future has no bounds for God's missionaries. But continue with your story and the bit about the angel."

"Well, your Grace, back home, my parents probably would not have been concerned at first when they found me absent. They would have thought I had gone to early Mass. So afraid was I of their chasing after me when they realized I had gone, that by the end of their Mass, I was seven miles away. By evening, 20. All through knee-deep snow.

"But, in truth, without my angel, I'd never be here. It happened this way. I had made it to Maryland and was enjoying a stop at a resting place. As I left, I saw a wagon standing at the door. I asked the driver where he was going. 'Georgetown,' he answered. And I said, 'May I put my bundle in your wagon?'

And he joked, 'Not only your bundle, Madam; but if you wish you may ride yourself.'

"I got on the wagon, your Grace. We drove all day into the dusk with hardly a word spoken. In Georgetown, I asked him to drop me off in front of the Catholic Church where services were being held. You know it to be Trinity Church. I planned to seek lodging there and go to the convent the next morning.

"The wagon stopped. The driver said goodbye. I threw my bundle on the snow and got down to reach for it. Your Grace, when I turned to thank the driver, the wagon, the team of horses and the driver had disappeared. 'Twas my Guardian Angel helped get me here."

This story about the angel, coupled with the mysterious knock at the convent door, helped convince Bishop Neale to admit her. The next morning, exactly one week after leaving home, Margaret began her life as a Sister.

She did indeed live and die with those Sisters. She is remembered for her goodness, resolution and courage. She went to Alabama where she founded a convent in Mobile. Wherever she was posted, Sister Margaret was useful and inspirational — worthy of a miracle to get her where God wanted her to be.

EXASPERATION

The parish priest got tired answering inane questions on his telephone. When one lady called and asked the cost of baptisms, the priest blurted: "Ten dollars an inch."

Edward VII

The bon vivant Edward VII finally became King of England in 1901. Up to the time of his coronation, he had made England his playground. He gambled, followed the horses, joined the hunts, drank his fill and openly courted several mistresses. Naturally the press and parliament belittled his disregard for morality. But the Prince paid no attention. He defied them all, state, church, press and people.

His attitude to wagging tongues is best illustrated by words he wrote on the wall of a small restaurant on the southern coast of England where he and a lady friend once dined. This is what he wrote: "They say! What say they? Let them say!" Those words are still there today as defiant as ever.

Not bad advice for those who worry about people talking behind their backs.

A WINTER NIGHT

The locomotive puffed away into the winter night and I began my five-mile trek to grandma's country home … as I moved out of the town, the woods ahead beckoned, the wind picked up and the snowflakes whirled … my gait quickened as a heavy dampness penetrated my bones….

Then, I thought of grandma's lion's-paw stove, and her scones, jam and tea … and I plodded on with renewed spirit … on that winter night so long ago on that white road that led me to her warm embrace.

A Tribute to Hughie

I met Hughie several years before he died. I respected him as a classic Scottish gentleman.

Of quality and goodness, Hughie had abundance. And charm too. When Hughie talked, I listened. He spoke as a teacher and I was his student. He knew the ways of the world. He held my attention. He'd lean forward in his chair and punctuate his points with flair. His lessons on justice, honesty, and loyalty were easy on the mind.

Hughie was both gentry and ploughman. He could be gentle and polished — he could be rough. He played by rules honed in hard times.

You have to admire a man who suffered the early loss of his parents in Scotland, the dispersion of his siblings, and long years in an orphanage. Here was a city lad who had come at 16 as a Home Boy from his beloved Scotland into the isolation of a Canadian farm. There he worked full out in the depressed 1930s. Later on he settled down with a Canadian wife and raised a fine family.

Hughie ran deep. He had scars. Yet, he never complained. He felt he had been lucky. He had nothing but respect for his relatives, the administrators and teachers at the orphanage, and his adoptive family in Canada.

He kept a diary in his memory where he carefully stored selected facts on characters and everyday life. In his writings and speech he seldom spoke ill of anyone. He saw good intentions in another's behaviour. He was merciful. He used empathy for others to take the bite out of life.

Hughie believed God "walked and talked" to him. How else, he said, could he have been so fortunate? He prayed in his own way. He had a worn-thin Bible. He was more than a Sunday Christian.

In 1919, three small boys were growing up in the grime and noise of Glasgow's environs. They lived in tenements, and ate porridge three times a day (sometimes they got meat and the top of an egg). After school they scurried off to play in the fields of rhubarb scattered throughout the city. They enjoyed soccer and rugby, wrestled, went to the circus and flicks, and once in a while feasted on fish and chips or rock candy.

They all eventually left Glasgow, but never could get it out of their minds. They never lost the brogue. They were hospitable. They loved to sing and dance. All three played the piano. They had hearty laughs especially at their own expense. You could warm your heart in their presence.

They're all gone now: my father, Tom, who like Hughie married a Canadian farm girl, Alf Wright, everybody's favourite vet, James Herriot, and my friend Hughie who went to his reward four years ago while singing his rendition of a Celtic song at a St. Patrick's Day party.

Lucky Pennies

Challenging Mother Nature is not done without risk. Open water rafting is precarious, freefalling can be deadly, and mountain climbing can have a finality about it.

Man also pays a price for tempting Mother Nature. The price is human lives. Man built the Titanic to break speed records on the Atlantic. The liner became a coffin. The success and safety of the American Space Programme was routinely accepted until one day six astronauts were blown away. Supposedly-safe bridges collapse in rubble, miners lie buried in ore, oil-laden tankers break in half. Such tragedies are testimony to man's greed for gold, glory, and power.

Pre-twentieth-century man was more sensitive to his precarious position whenever he put grandiose demands on Nature. Fleets were blessed and feasts and sacrifices held in honour of the gods or God who controlled the weather, crops, yields and conquests. People praised and thanked the unknown. They were solicitous of the good will of God. They never took Mother Nature for granted. They respected her.

The Celts of old held similar convictions about Nature. Potato pickers often left a final row unpicked. At meals, morsels were left untouched on plates as a way of giving thanks.

The Irish also had a custom known as the lucky penny, for example. The owner of a threshing machine would receive payment from the farmer for services rendered and then return, as a sign of appreciation, a small coin or two to the farmer. The same procedure happened at sales of cattle, property, horses, cars and boats — always that giving back of the lucky penny as a way of sharing good fortune.

We can see the theory of the lucky penny in our present society. Church goers pay tithes. Casino winners tip dealers. Those who receive service in restaurants, train stations, hair salons and the like, pay gratuities.

Even donations to the poor, the orphans, the sick, and research, can fall under the lucky penny superstition.

Giving back a little of what we receive, being thankful for good fortune and not tempting God with indifference, are good rules to play by, at any age.

The Rope

A certain gentleman went to the first night of a parish mission only to find the speaker's material "old hat" and his style "porridge plain." On the second night, not surprisingly, as he took his place in the back left corner, he found the attendance somewhat down.

The sermon before Mass was again quite ordinary and the evening service moved routinely along. Suddenly, however, just after the Eucharistic Consecration, the priest stopped his regular prayers. He wanted to tell a short story, a story so powerful that he had to ask the parish priest for permission to relate it. The gentleman in the corner said to himself, "Anything would be an improvement!"

This is the gist of what the priest said: "Some months ago a young lady came to my rectory in Florida. She was very troubled. She had so many burdens, she didn't know where or how to begin. In fact, she wasn't sure that she wanted to share them.

"After a few weeks of counselling, we got to know each other a little. I tried to structure her experiences and determine the major causes of her grief. We relied heavily on the Holy Spirit for counsel. One evening we decided to involve Jesus more directly in our meetings. We would take Him at His word and transfer all her burdens, one by one, to His care.

"I asked the girl to believe Jesus was present in the room and that He fully understood her problems and would take them from her if He wished. I told her that much depended on how much faith she and I had. Then we prayed and prayed and began.

"I urged her to imagine each major difficulty as a rope around her neck. Let's say, for instance, that the burden was an early childhood abuse by her father. The process was this: we would both think deeply on the abuse and hurt, shame and the resentment it engendered; and then I would ask her to release every feeling she had about it and give it over to Jesus. This was accomplished symbolically by her taking an imaginary rope (which represented the abuse) from her own neck and giving it to Jesus who placed it around his own. This hurt was then gone forever. And so it went with the others problems.

"As we proceeded, the electricity of God's grace permeated the room. The catharsis was volatile. At times we wondered if it was too much for us. But we had to go on; turning back was impossible. Finally, the fever of the transition peaked. Tears gave way to a sense of peace. Jesus had indeed taken to Himself all her grief of mind. A miracle had occurred. She was free."

At this juncture, the priest continued with the service. But somehow the church's atmosphere had changed. You could feel it, an energy of spirit, a silence so sacred no one even looked around. It was as if the Holy Spirit moved everywhere and angels were singing for only souls to hear. Even the priest spoke more softly.

The gentleman at the back was overwhelmed by the holy hush in the church. Its origin was a mystery. The priest had spoken simply, like a child. The message had been interesting, but certainly not mesmerizing. The gentleman decided *the presence* had come from God through the holiness of the priest, the girl, and those present that evening in the church. The Holy Spirit was definitely at work.

The tension eased as the parishioners came forward to receive communion. The choir sang. The priest suggested that everyone give over his or her worries after they received the Body of Christ. And everyone tried. After communion, the priest went to his presiding chair to meditate.

It was at this moment that the atmosphere took on an unworldly dimension. In the corner, the gentleman asked Jesus to accept all his worries and cares.

Then it happened. He experienced a miracle of sight. He saw Jesus walk up the aisle from the tabernacle and enter his body from the left side. He knew beyond doubt that Jesus had physically entered his person. It was so natural. He accepted Him graciously.

Then, the crowd began to disperse. And the gentleman, with His friend within, slipped quietly into the night.

HELEN

Helen Hayes, the queen of Broadway Theatre, said her husband (whom she adored) spent all his days walking backwards through life. He relived his failures, constantly pining for what could have been. His past shaded his whole life.

We cannot change what has been written. Sorrows and regrets, guilt and remorse, hurts and failures must be cast aside.

Every new day is a fresh start ... like a dolphin bursting from the sea or an eagle soaring into the blue.

We should never look over our shoulder. Tomorrow is a lovely day.

A Tough Little Island

Through the mists of a spring morning, the ms *Noordam* rode the strong Atlantic currents into the 32-mile-long Strait of Gibraltar. Ahead was the Mediterranean Sea, battleground for the powerful, playground to the rich and garden centre of the world.

Some miles in where the Strait widens, the ocean liner's great black prow swung north. And straight ahead in the early morning light loomed the sulking shadow of the great Rock of Gibraltar. Masked for war, it looked every bit what it claimed to be, a strategically placed limestone fortress that has defied the ages.

At the inhabited south end of the Island where we entered, a crippled Corvette from the Iraqi conflict lay moored. Near these shipyards, an international airstrip winked a welcome to the night flights from Central Europe, Africa, and the East. On the Island's north-west side, we could see the beams of early morning traffic on the long bridge over the isthmus between Spain and Gibraltar.

The Greek historian, Herodotus, spoke of Gibraltar; he called it one of the Pillars of Hercules. The Moors came there; so did the Italians, the Spaniards, the Africans, the Carthaginians, the French and the British. It has been British for the last 300 years. It was Eisenhower's headquarters for the Second World War.

It is a privilege to stand on top of Gibraltar. To the East, the greenish-blue Mediterranean beckons; to the southeast, just eight miles away, the silhouette of Africa runs as far as the eye can see; in the West, the Atlantic churns; to the North sprawls Spain and right below on the southwest of the great rock, just a mile away, is the tidy two-and-a-half square miles called Gibraltar.

Below, the seas are teeming with one of the greatest concentration of mammals in the world. Baleen-feeding whales weighing up to 200 tons enjoy the meeting of the warm Mediterranean and cold Atlantic. The tides are minimal and the amount of protein-rich organisms beyond imagination. Here, the walrus and seal come to play and on a good day the tourist can see the arched backs of the dolphins and the markings of the killer whales.

What famous navigator or naval hero has not looked with awe upon Gibraltar's Rock? Vasco da Gama, Columbus and Champlain were there. So were Drake, Nelson, Alexander, Napoleon and Wellington. And perhaps even Charlemagne and Constantine came by.

On its sunny top, 70 feet short of the Empire State Building's 1472-foot television tower, the breezes swirl. It's worth the $75 taxi ride up a donkey trail for a road.

There the taxis park askew allowing just enough space for loitering tourists to move around on the uneven plateau. The guide will tell you that the Rock has ten miles of tunnels, many dug by Canadian miners in the Second World War. The tunnels hold food, water, ammunition, offices, living quarters for the military, even a hospital. So effective in war are these entrails that as early as 1779, the British withstood a three-year blockade by both Spain and France.

But the top is not just for humans. The oldest animal inhabitants of the Rock are there: the Barbary Apes, six tribes of them making up 160 members who live in the caves above the city. They are Gibraltar's true ambassadors. They've been there forever.

The apes act like they run the place. They're full of devilment. They sit on tourists' shoulders, reach in pockets and steal purses. Watch out. This is their territory.

Legend has it that the departure of the apes will signal the end of British rule over Gibraltar; so the Brits feed them fresh vegetables to augment the vegetation they eat on the cliffs.

What a Camelot is this island! A pugnacious air surrounds it. It has more fire power for its size than any other similar island in the world. Vibrant, menacing, ugly, independent, proud like its people. Its secrets belong to the gods.

Five hundred years from now, the Rock will still stand guard and Britannia may still rule its waves. More strife will come its way but no doubt it will survive.

The Barbary Apes, too, will play on, no wiser than they ever were. Just like the world's leaders who make history and learn nothing from it.

TRUE CHARITY

A visiting American congressman at a leper colony in Africa said to a missionary who was cleaning a leper's wounds, "I wouldn't do that job for all the money in the world."

And the nun replied, "Neither would I. I do it for God."

Three Good Sons

It didn't take Abraham long to realize that God's promise to make him "the father of many nations" was in jeopardy the day that God ordered him to offer "his only child" in sacrifice. But, Abraham overcame his doubts about God's word. He went ahead and made ready for his son's sacrifice.

He and his son Isaac were commanded to travel to a certain hill in Channan. When they arrived, Abraham was told to build an altar upon which he was to arrange the wood Isaac had carried. He then tied up Isaac and laid him on the bier and unsheathed his own knife. Isaac's blood was to be drained and splashed over the altar and the wood ignited with the fire Abraham had brought from home. At the last moment, God stayed Abraham's hand.

In this biblical story, Jewish scholars make much of Abraham's trust in that it shows Abraham's suitability as the leader of Israel.

But what of Isaac? Did he not also show courage and faith and he only a boy knowing nothing of God's promises to his father? According to Scripture, he raised no objection, although he did wonder, at one stage, where the animals for sacrifice were.

Yet, he did what his father bade. He was, indeed, the proverbial silent lamb being led to slaughter. He trusted his father, even when the knife was drawn. He said nothing. *Isaac was a good son.*

Centuries later, another Son was sent by his Father for sacrifice. He, too, carried His own wood to a hill where He was prepared for death. The difference from Isaac's situation was that he knew His Father would not change His mind.

Even though He could foresee what was coming, Jesus too trusted His Father. He believed in the Resurrection. He had done what he was asked to do: pay the ransom for mankind's sins. It was the only time in history when a Shepherd became a lamb to be sacrificed for the good of the flock. *Jesus was a good Son.*

Two thousand years later, in the small town of Aylmer in Québec, a ten-year-old boy watched his father, my friend, struggle with cancer. The boy's name was Chris.

Chris had three siblings, but no mother. A dump truck had fatally pinned her against the wall in her driveway.

Chris worshipped his father. The cancer had come two years before. Now in its final stages, Chris could sense his father's agony. The pain never relented. They both knew tomorrow brought no hope. Physically, the emaciation was cruel.

One day, out in the car, father and son were talking when Chris said something that few fathers ever hear. He said, "You know, Dad, if I could, I would gladly suffer and die in your place." *Chris too was a good son!*

Thoughtfulness

Thoughtfulness is best explained by example. When my mother was living, a mutual friend sometimes drove her home from our house. Since she lived alone, he would wait in his car until she was in, had turned on the indoor lights, and had come to the door to wave goodbye.

Thoughtful deeds are almost unnoticeable: a card of sympathy, a phone call, a small gift, holding the door, or helping the handicapped.

Thoughtful deeds are not planned. They are spontaneous and ready-made for unexpected occasions. They can come from complete strangers. They are special deeds for special moments.

A homemaker sends home-cooking to a recently bereaved family. A forlorn lady receives a stray compliment on the beauty of her eyes. A little child clutches a chocolate bar from a neighbour. A friend cuts the lawn for a sick neighbour. A farmer feeds a neighbour's cattle when the latter is away. A judge spares a convicted prisoner a lecture for the sake of his mother present in the courtroom.

No book written tells us how to be thoughtful. Even people who practise great charity *may never learn* the art.

It's a gift given from pure hearts.

A PRIORITY

A friend commented to another, "I understand that your ill husband doesn't know you anymore. That must be very difficult for you to accept."

And the wife answered, "Not really! What's important is that I still know him."

A Man Named Walsh

I was walking one August evening along the main street of a seaside village called Dunfanaghy (Dun-fan-a-he) in Donegal, Ireland. Along its Atlantic shoreline, miles of golden sand beckon riders, walkers and clam hunters.

The village has beautiful churches, two fine hotels run by the Arnolds and Robinsons, a post office, a dry-goods store, and numerous apartments arm in arm on the sidewalk's edge.

Naturally, the village has pubs. As I passed one of them, the roar of imbibers invited me in. Standing for air at the entrance, a rosy-faced gentleman stepped aside for me as he said, "Welcome to the finest bar in all Ireland."

The physique of the gentleman allowed for no disagreement. I managed to say, "Yes, and it must be the noisiest as well." To which he shouted, "As you can see, there's not much space."

Now there was an understatement. Not more than 14 feet wide and 18 feet deep, it could easily have been the smallest bar in the world. Everyone shuffled like penguins up and down the room.

The drinking frenzy was such that two bartenders could barely keep up. The crowd was oblivious to the proximity, the heat, and the noise. Everyone seemed deliciously happy. It was a Friday night. All was right in Ireland.

Holding up his Guinness to avoid it being jolted, my new friend continued, "My name's Walsh from Cork. I come up here for 16 weeks every summer. I have a caravan by the sea among the dunes where I live the life of Riley, away from it all. This area is wonderful in the summer."

I couldn't help but agree. It certainly did wonders for Walsh. His face held the light of sunsets. His blue eyes shone like a calm sea. He had a smile that could beguile a donkey. He had no cares there in that wee bar on the top of Ireland. One sweet man in a fairyland.

Cocktails Après Beach

Andy at first wasn't going to go down to the beach. The wind had swelled the ocean and the surf pounded. Undertow warning signs were up. But at the last minute, he decided to go. He hadn't come to Mexico to sit in his room. Besides, a walk along the shore would do him good.

Not far into his gambol, he thought he heard cries for help above the wind. Eventually he looked out towards the ocean. Two swimmers were in distress. They were being slowly pulled out to their deaths.

As Andy dove in, he tried to remember the procedures for rescuing swimmers. Thirty years earlier, as a trainee in the Royal Canadian Mounted Police, he had learned how. At that time, he had thought little of the hours spent training for lifeguard duty. He felt that the chances of his being called on for such an emergency were slim.

The swimmer farthest out was a woman. Andy fought the waves to reach her. He could feel the downward pull and the sucking motion out to sea. But Andy was powerful and soon he was by the woman's side.

However, in his hurry, Andy forgot the first rule of such a procedure: never get too close to the victim. The proper way is to offer the person an arm and when he grabs it, wrap that arm under your side and head for shore. Instead, the woman clutched Andy wildly and began pulling him down. Andy then remembered the manual. He could make her let go by taking her to the bottom. With a thrust of power, he dove to the bottom where he felt her release. Quickly, he resurfaced and dragged her to shore.

But Andy had no time to dally. The other person, the woman's friend, had already been taken out beyond where the lady had been. This time, Andy made no mistake. He swam out. His extended arm was grabbed and Andy swept the weakened body under his shoulder to safety.

For a long time the three sat among the dunes, the victims seemingly unaware how close that they had come to death. That's the way with drowning — it can caress you.

That evening Andy and his wife had cocktails with the young couple at the resort. They discussed the day's events. In his room later that night, Andy thought about the coincidence of it all — his former training — his being in Mexico at the same time as the victims — his going down to the beach after he had changed his mind. Was someone pulling the strings? Or was it all just luck, a fluke in time?

Since that day, Andy has never heard from the couple. In fact, Andy recalls that he and his wife had to pay for their own cocktails.

Frances

Margaret held Frank close that summer day in 1915 in Ottawa. He was going to war. She said she would wait. He promised he'd come back. At the end of the lane, he waved. It took Margaret all her strength to stand. And then he was gone.

On the train to Halifax, Frank met Edgar, a fellow member of the Princess Pat's Infantry. They became fast friends, trench buddies, and soul mates. Frank never tired talking about Margaret and Edgar kept assuring Frank they'd make it back.

The two fought side by side for three years. Both proved themselves worthy of the Princess Pats. The end of the war appeared near. Frank's heart ached for Margaret. Soon they'd be together.

But two months before the war ended, somewhere in Germany, their chief officer called for yet another attack across the muddy fields of no man's land. Edgar and Frank went over the top. All hell broke loose.

As they moved forward, Edgar noticed Frank was not beside him. He turned slightly and shouted. Then he shouted again. This time Edgar looked down. Frank couldn't answer. The upper part of his body had been ripped open by machine gun fire. Edgar knelt by his buddy, said a prayer, removed his personal belongings and may well have wailed into the abyss. Edgar then turned and again took up his weapon. With his broken heart raging, he fired over and over into the white night until his passion was spent.

Back home, after the war, Edgar immediately looked for Frank's relatives. When he found them, he asked about Margaret. He had pictures for her and stories of Frank's bravery and love for her. Well, Edgar soon found Margaret and she was everything Frank had said. And Margaret saw goodness in Edgar too and soon they were married.

Now Edgar and Margaret had decided that if their first child was a boy, they would call him Frank. If a girl, they'd call her Frances. And so it came about that in the spring of 1921, Frances Faye was born. From where he watched, Frank couldn't have been more pleased.

Frances became everybody's darling, including mine. I first met her around 1938. In 1940, she was my Grade Five teacher. She could do no wrong as far as I was concerned. I was crazy over her.

In 1943 she married a wonderful gentleman named Albert. I served as an altar boy at their wedding. Frances was radiant.

Margaret and Edgar must have thought of Frank on that wedding day. And Frank would have been pleased. Without Frank, there would never have been Frances, Albert would never have enjoyed such a beautiful bride, and I would never have enjoyed such a good teacher who just happened to be my first love.

Frances, at age nine, I was smitten with you. 65 years later, I remain so.

Thanks, Frances. Thanks, Frank.

RIGHT ON

The Roman soldiers who discovered the great stone rolled away at Christ's grave rightly concluded that it was an inside job.

The Girl in the Clinic

Is it possible that after death the soul leaves its original mind and body, and takes on a *new* mind and *different* body?

How else can we explain mediums seeing and hearing the dead or the near-death experiences of those who look down on their bodies or see lights and tunnels and ancestors?

And what say we about the many documented reports by ordinary people of strange sounds and sightings, about drum rolls on Culloden moors in Scotland, the clank of steel on the Boyne River where William of Orange defeated the Irish, a lone piper's shrill at Gettysburg, Pennsylvania, or a child's cry by a Cornwall cove in England?

Christ had a different body after His resurrection. Yet Thomas put a hand in His side and Mary Magdalene saw and talked with Him. Shall we be the same after death and at earth's end receive our first bodies back?

My interest in such a possibility of events was stimulated by the title of a book being read by a pretty young lady seated next to me at a CT scan clinic. The title was: *Does the Soul Have Its Own Mind?*

Before she left, I asked her, "Excuse me, but *do you* believe the soul has its own mind?" She answered politely, "I do." And I said, "I do too."

The pleasant person I met that evening has already found the definitive answer to that question. Seven months later, I saw her picture in the paper beside her obituary. The CT scan must have been positive for cancer.

Paul

From where I stood beside the open grave, I could see the crowd of mourners spilling from the church. With hundreds already outside, they formed a single line that moved across the cemetery in measured gait.

Like the Moors on the brow of a desert dune or soldiers lined across the field of battle, they came sombrely to bury their popular pastor. In some way, all had been touched by his good works: the infirm, the young, the family heads and the school children.

Soon his coffin sat inside a great circle and the silent grey of the afternoon was filled with the prayers of 60 priests and a thousand other friends.

His name was Paul Baxter, a tall, lithe, dark, curly-haired lad with the emotional and physical energy of ten men. It was this intensity I remember best. It permeated everything he did: teaching, coaching, conversing, but, most all, preaching.

In the pulpit, he was Rockne in a Notre Dame dressing room, a Marc Antony in the market, an Olivier as Lear. His eyes flashed, his shoulders hunched, his voice cracked, his fists closed. He pierced everyone's soul. Yet he never judged or condemned. But he did throw challenges in your face. His was a fire that never burned out.

When he preached, there was no place for the parishioner to hide: he had a way of singling everyone out. In the pulpit, he entertained, cajoled, encouraged, demanded, laughed and teased. He had the power to stir the living and wake the dead. He got into everybody's mind. He was a sergeant-major, we, his troops. Life was a battle, heaven was the goal.

"Come," he said. "Do as I ask. Promise me you'll *live* better and pray *harder*. I know you'll not disappoint me. I've seen so much goodness among you. I know you can do it. Love God more! Be kind to one another! Live like Christ! Then I'll be happy."

At the finish his voice would drop, and as he leaned out over the pulpit, he would plead in the most endearing way, "Will you do these things for me? Will ya? Will ya? Will ya?"

And I for one felt like standing up and shouting, "I will! I will! I will!"

IT'S WORTH IT

The world we are living in
Is mighty hard to beat.
Sure, we may get a thorn with every rose,
But aren't the roses sweet.
— Found in a friend's old birthday book.

A Grain of Sand

One day in the backwash of time, the White Hare, the greatest spirit of all the Spirits, looked upon the desolation around him and decided to call all the animals of the forest to a general meeting.

When they had settled before him, he asked if there was anyone present who would dive to the ocean's bottom and bring back one grain of sand upon which they could build a new world.

The lone volunteer was a black muskrat who quickly slipped away into the murky depths in search of the grain.

After three days with no sign of the muskrat, the White Hare went looking for him. A long way down the shoreline, he found his floating body. He had given his life in search of the sand. The White Hare was disappointed and sad.

Suddenly, a sparkle caught the eye of the White Hare. Between the paws of the muskrat was a single grain of sand. The White Hare shook with emotion.

He once again called his subjects to a meeting. When all that walked and crawled and flew had assembled, he raised up the grain before them and said, "Upon this grain of sand, brought to us by the lowly muskrat whose memory we must preserve, we shall build our new nation. Go forward from here and rebuild your homes, as only you know how. We shall succeed."

As the subjects passed the grain to one another, it gave them strength.

Not long after, in a new age, the White Hare admired the land, forever mindful of the humble black muskrat that made it all possible.

— An adaptation of a Mic-Mac Myth, Gaspé, Nova Scotia

The Rock

When I told a young tour director on our train that my wife and I were going to Percé Rock for a week, she grimaced and said, "What are ya going to do there for a week? The rock is beautiful, but once you've seen it, that's it. A rock is a rock!"

When the train arrived at the town of Percé, her American tour was met by a bus. They spent the afternoon in Percé and took a trip later that same day to see the whales. Next morning they headed for greener pastures. "Enough of Percé," the director would have said.

But as we found out, Percé is not a place to be so idly dismissed. Percé Town is on the Atlantic Coast of Canada near the mouth of the St. Lawrence River. A fishing village from time immemorial, it is now a tourist town. Once, sailing ships from Jersey, France, Portugal and Norway came for cod, halibut and whale. Displaced by the British from their European lands, the Scottish and French also settled there and in turn forced the Indians backwards into the deep lumber-rich interiors.

The once rough-hewn dirt roads along its Bonaventure Bay are now neatly groomed. Where small boats once emptied their catch on the filleting tables, a boardwalk invites; where once working horses drew heavily-loaded carts to smoking sheds and drying nets, now there are park benches for the old and swings for the young; where once barefoot children built castles in the sand and played in pastures above the sea, lovers now walk and quaint homes rest.

There's fascination in Percé. Sit along its shore and watch the sun come up over Ireland, hear the gulls play and watch the gannets dive, feel the northern breeze from Hudson Bay and follow the touring boats bobbing out to Bonaventure Island in the Bay.

And then there's the Rock — a great mass of shifting colour and imagery — three football fields high, a New-York-City-Street-Block long — shaped like a hippopotamus. There, since well before Abraham, the Pharaohs, and Christ, this sleeping giant weathered the millenniums, welcomed visitors from air, sea and land, and befriended the thousands upon thousands who came to live near its shadow.

After everything has come and gone around Bonaventure Bay, after all the sorrow, work and play have been lost in time, after the rods, harpoons, nets, knives, sails, pitch and curraghs have been swallowed up, a great peace remains. It's a serenity left by the goodness of those who once lived there, who accepted their lot, who lived in tune with Nature, who laughed and frolicked, who treasured their faith and family, a people whose spirits today stir the waters and trees and move 'round and over the great Percé Rock.

Percé, truly you are a treasure!

A SCOTTISH COMPLIMENT

I met a man at church one Sunday. A cane and a slow pace suggested he'd had a stroke. Yet, he stood tall and robust, with good colour and fine features. His accent was Scottish.

I said to him, "That accent is music to my ears."

He retorted, "It should be, Lad. I learned it in the finest country in the world. The name is Geraghty."

"My Dad was from Glasgow," I said.

"A lucky man, so he was," he answered.

"You're doing very well I see — still spry and on the town. And you're as handsome as you were on your wedding day."

Quickly he shot back with tremendous verve a compliment perhaps as old as the Grampian Hills: "Sure it's only a mirror of yourself you're looking at."

The Talisman

Our small sightseeing boat returning to the shores of Newfoundland was suddenly enveloped in fog.

For the next 15 minutes, waves of mist disoriented us. As passengers we could do nothing but put our trust in the man at its controls. He knew what he was doing and he had special equipment for such emergencies.

Elsewhere in life, we often find ourselves suddenly stymied by circumstances beyond our control. We are up the proverbial creek with no paddle. Friends may forsake us; jobs may disappear; the death of a spouse or child may drive us to our knees. We feel lost or abandoned. We don't know which way to turn. We are in a House of Mirrors.

Often, our only method of survival is to *wait it out* by putting our trust in the one at the controls. God knows what He is doing. Be still, and He will show us the way.

The Run Around

When I was seventeen, I thought I was in very good physical condition. I ran everywhere: to stores, school and church, after streetcars and buses. I worked on farms and road construction. I chased footballs, pucks, softballs, and cows.

One day, around that time, a runner named Roger Bannister broke the four-minute mile and I tried to imagine why this event was so enormous in the world of track and field.

So I went to a mile-track near my home, checked the time at the start and ran the mile as best as I could. When the watch hit five and a half minutes, I could barely stand. I never did finish. But the experience was fruitful because I had a first-hand appreciation of Bannister's record-breaking feat.

Sometimes, if the opportunity arises, it's best to try things out for ourselves so as to better understand and appreciate them.

Molly's Friend

Molly, an old friend, was reminiscing the other day about special kindnesses she had received during her 90 years. She said: "One time, decades ago, I was in hospital for my first child. Naturally I was anxious. One evening after a nurse had changed my bed. I spilled my drink and ruined her efforts. The nurse dressed me down very badly, 'I have better things to do than make beds over and over. With proper care, accidents like this don't happen,' she said. I became distraught.

"A few days later, on a Saturday night, the same type of accident occurred under exactly the same circumstances. Only this time a different nurse was on duty. When she saw my tears, she came over to me and put her arms around me and said words I shall never forget, 'If this dang old accident hadn't happened, you and I could have gone out on the town tonight and had one heck of a time.'"

Two identical situations, two different attitudes. One reaped despair; the other peace.

What a difference the appropriate words make!

My friend Molly died a few months ago on her husband's birthday.

A WASTE OF TIME

People are never impressed when they know you are trying to impress them. Better not to try. Save yourself all that effort, futility and embarrassment. Leave them to themselves.

A Broken Angel

The highlights of any journey have to be the wonderful people one meets. I met Margaret at the Sherring Hotel in Strathpeffer, Scotland. Her attentive husband was pushing her wheelchair into the dining room. I learned she had had a stroke and so far was making a good recovery.

When I first saw her my heart jumped. She had a radiance that any knight in armour would die for. Her manners were graceful and her words charming. I boldly took her lily white hand and told her how lovely she looked. After an exchange of informalities I wished her well. I said, "Margaret, I shall pray for you." And she answered, "Thank you. And I for you."

Margaret, I do remember you. I hope God's blessings are with you always and that soon one of God's broken angels will walk straight and tall once more.

Picking Yourself Up

As we grow older, we learn more and more that we all have challenges to face. The measure in which we handle these challenges often is the measure of our happiness. Trials are part of living.

First, we must realize that we are not alone in our struggle. Everyone is buffeted. No one escapes. One day, it's our health; another, problems in the family. One week, friends disappoint, co-workers cause trouble, the economy sours; on another, resolutions go astray, the weather runs havoc, people cancel, machines break down, our plans go awry. Such is life.

Another principle to learn is that we must turn our bow into the storms; it's how we tack the sail in the winds. We must not wallow in pity. We must go on the offensive. We must adapt, reorganize, restructure. We must not dwell on our failures — washouts demand bridges, roadblocks need detours, and deadlocks require compromise.

Wilting under worries is natural but so is fighting on. The falling down is not as important as the getting up. We must be like terriers and bulldogs, and "the Little Engine That Could." We must never stop trying.

Remember the song from the Broadway hit, *Thoroughly Modern Millie.* Part of it goes: "Pick yourself up, dust yourself off and start all over again."

A GUARDIAN ANGEL

A tractor trailer and directly behind it, a passenger car, pulled off a side-road onto a main highway. The driver of the car, an impatient man at best, became frustrated by the slow speed of the truck. With his vision of the highway ahead impaired by the bigger vehicle's rear end, he decided to edge out into the oncoming lane to check the advisability of passing. He set out to do so several times, but for some reason, his body would not respond to what his mind was telling it to do.

Suddenly, a vehicle from the other direction, obviously out of control, side-swiped his car and ran into the ditch.

Later the driver of the truck ahead of the car was quoted as saying that he had been driving slowly because the car coming at him was weaving all over the road. It turned out that the person in the car was drunk.

The impatient driver told a group of us that his guardian angel had saved him. To pull out into the other lane would have been tragic. He had wanted to but the angel just wouldn't let him turn the wheel.

A Matter of Kindness

Connie had always made her husband, Ted, very aware before and during their marriage that she would never attend *any* church, especially his. Every Sunday as the family filed out to church, she stayed at home.

One day Ted decided that he and his seven children would light eight candles every Sunday for the conversion of their mother. His trust in God was such that he felt only God could help.

This practice went on for 12 years. To no avail. If anything, Connie was more adamant.

Then, Ted developed cancer. His doctor gave him a year to live. To spare his family any suffering, Ted told no one until two weeks before his death. And only then, because he had no choice.

About a week after the funeral, Connie asked the family to make an appointment with the parish priest, a confidant of Ted. She announced that she was going to join her husband's religion.

"How come you changed your mind, Mom?" asked one child. And she said, "Any faith that can give my husband the courage to do what he did in order to save his family from pain is good enough for me."

Connie became a stalwart worker for the church and community. She took up where Ted had left off. And every Sunday, for years, they lit eight candles in memory of Ted.

NOT TO TARRY

"Mommy," said the boy, "I went to feed the rabbits out back and I can't find them. Do you think they escaped?"

"No" said his mother, "didn't you notice? I gave them away last week!"

A Ghost in the Library

Many years ago, the guest speaker at a gathering of priests in the diocese of Sault St. Marie, Ontario, stunned his audience with a never-before-told ghost story about an old priest of that diocese. The speaker was a priest from the American side of the Sault Diocese. The younger brother of a friend of mine was there for the sermon and this in general was the priest's story: (I paraphrase)

"Around the turn of the century, a priest was buried in a certain parish of Sault St. Marie. In addition to family and parishioners, the Archbishop and 60 priests attended the funeral, an exceptionally fine turnout.

"After the funeral, the clergy retired to the priest's house for lunch after which they sat around chatting. Now rumour had it that the dead priest had kept a fine upstairs library and a few priests thought they would go up to see it. The first ones to enter the room stopped in their tracks. There, seated in his favourite chair, was the deceased priest — very much alive. When the ghost refused to speak to them, someone said, 'This is a job for the Archbishop!'

"The Archbishop came and for two hours the two conversed. Then the Archbishop left and took all the secrets of the event with him. The topics of discussion were left to conjecture: perhaps guilt on the part of the priest, unfinished business, trouble in the diocese, premonition, the plight of the world, the church, etc.

"To this day, the nature of this discussion between the living and the dead has never been made known. A priest had come back from eternity to speak with his boss. That's it, plain and simple and downright mysterious."

INCHING ALONG

Taken by the yard, life is hard.
Taken by the inch, life's a cinch.

Mildred

When Mildred went on a pilgrimage to the shrine of the Virgin Mary in Yugoslavia, her friends were surprised. After all, she was totally blind, over 75, unemotional, and not religious. She was the last person they'd expect to make such a long journey.

Her enticement for this adventure started the day Mildred read about the appearances in Yugoslavia of the Virgin. Ever since that chance article in the newspaper, she had had a strong desire to go. She wasn't looking for a miracle or cure. She just knew she had to make the trip.

The first night there, she awakened at 2 a.m. and told her friend that she wanted to begin the climb up the mountain to the shrine.

The friend objected to no avail and away they went.

The night was blustery and the shingles on the path slippery. Yet the two, one leaning on the other, persevered to the top.

When they finally arrived, Mildred knew why she had been urged to come. At the top, the blind Mildred saw a bright light that gradually turned into a beautiful lady. She knelt in prayer. That night Mildred was not cured of blindness, but for a few minutes her soul had seen heaven. Her life never was the same and she told everybody what she had seen.

Marie

Thérèse Martin, a pretty, sensitive, spoiled girl, entered the Carmelite Convent in Lisieux, France, in 1888 at age 15. She died in 1897, completely unknown except to her sisters and her relatives.

Before she died, she promised to do her best in heaven to help those who prayed for *her* intercession with God. And she did, and her fame spread throughout the world. In the trenches of the First War, soldiers of France carried her picture. Her popularity was such that the Church declared her a saint by 1925.

As a boy, I used to attend Tuesday night devotions at my church in her honour. As I grew older, I never lost my ardour for her. Her simple, holy life of prayer and sacrifice was a great example to all who knew her especially during the Depression and the Second World War. I considered her a friend.

In 1981, I went to visit her grave at Lisieux, France, some 117 miles west of Paris. While there I went to her old convent, the churches and parishes she attended, the Basilica raised in her honour, and the house where she lived for 11 years.

Shortly before going I met a friend whose husband had recently died. I said, "How are you, Marie?" And she answered, "Not too well. I have cancer of the cervix and the doctors are deciding what to do about it." Being an experienced nurse, Marie knew the gravity of her situation.

"Marie," I asked, "Are you a friend of St. Thérèse?"

"Yes, I am," she answered.

"Well," I added, "I am going to Lisieux next week and I shall pray for you and I shall have a High Mass sung for you in honour of St. Thérèse at the Basilica. We shall ask her to cure you."

A month after my return I met Marie. I asked, "What did the doctors say?"

She answered, "Before they operated they wanted to see more pictures. After they took them, they announced with great surprise, 'Marie, your cancer has completely gone. And we have no explanation.'"

Only Love Will Do

(A Son's Lament)

> The mind has a thousand eyes
> The heart but one.
> Yet the light of a whole life dies
> When love is done.
> — Francis Bourdillon

"Hey, Tommy, are ya comin'?" Teddy Greer shouted up the stairs of the tenement house. "We're gonna be late!" he added, as he sat down on the steps.

A minute later, the old stairwell creaked as Tommy bounded past Teddy and took off up Mar Street. Teddy soon caught up and together they ran through lanes and alleys to Haghill Elementary School. The year was 1919 and the place was Glasgow, Scotland, in the suburb of Deniston.

The boys knew that once the big black school gates were closed, late arrivals were in for a strapping in the Headmaster's office. So they turned on the speed and burst into the dusty playgrounds with little time to spare. The handbell was about to clang as some 300 children scurried about making last-chance visits to the outside toilets, gurgling down water from the iron drinking cup at the well, or collecting up their lunch-boxes and school bags.

At the bell, they all lined up in order of class seniority waiting nervously for Miss Kent's signal to enter. A tall straight-backed lady in a long black skirt and printed blouse, her no-nonsense glare was enough to demand any child's full attention. She had been principal for four years during the time most men teachers were at war.

Tommy and Teddy were veterans too — of Haghill. They knew the ropes. They'd been there seven years. This was the year of graduation to high school. They had started at age five and now they were twelve. They'd miss the old school with the square space on the first floor that opened up three stories to skylights. Around the outside of each floor were the classrooms and offices, and, of course, the many stairs that joined everything. The classrooms were big. Some held 50 students, two to a desk. Assemblies took place on the shiny wooden surface of the ground floor directly under the skylight.

After school, the boys would horse around in parks, go to the Clydebank to watch the boats or play in the fields of rhubarb that interlaced the suburbs of Glasgow. On Saturday, they'd take in the flicks, play soccer and rugby, or watch local teams battling on the commons. Tommy's grandmother, Granny McCrae, owned two fish and chip shops and often the boys took the green tram from Deniston for a free treat at Granny's places in the Gorbels, a high-density, low-income area.

Tommy and Teddy lived in tenement flats, three stories high, all joined to form a block of homes. Deniston was not rich, but neither was it the stuff of Dickens. These flats were home to what were called working middle-class, industrial families. Some among them, not involved in blue-collar work, were known as the genteel poor. While nothing to look at from the outside, inside, these flats were presentable. A burly steel fireplace dominated the living room around which one or two recesses were cut in the walls for extra sleeping accommodations behind curtains. There was also a kitchen, a bedroom or two, and a lavatory.

The coalman came around weekly to fill the inside box and the milkman showed up every day but Sunday. Tommy and Ted ate porridge and oatcakes, bread, cookies and preserves. Once in a while they had kippers, blood pudding, part of an egg, a little meat and, of course, fish and chips.

In dress, the children wore good quality homemade hand-me-downs. The girls sported below-the-knee smocks and pinafores and pretty ribbons in their long hair. The boys wore dark knee socks, breeches, vests, and various styles of quaint sweaters and jackets. Everybody wore boots or shoes, at least those children in the front row of the group class pictures.

In those days of yore, just a hop and a skip outside the smoke and grime of the factories and shipyards, was the fresh-air freedom of the country. It was paradise for the people entrapped in the big city, especially for the children who would never forget those enchanting dales and hills.

Tom's dad, Fred Robertson, was a carpenter. He built sets for the big music halls of Glasgow. In such theatres as The Emporium, The Pavilion and The New Star, he met Harry Lauder, Gracie Fields, Charlie Chaplin, Will Fyffe and many other great singers, dancers and comics. A staunch Scot, fierce Presbyterian, and skilled craftsman, he dearly loved his family, especially after four years as a soldier in France, two as a prisoner. He carried bits of shrapnel in one leg and traces of mustard gas in his lungs.

One summer's day, after graduation, Teddy asked Tommy, "Do you feel well, Tommy? You sure look sick."

"I am, Teddy. I got bad news yesterday. I'm being sent to my Aunt Charlotte's in Montreal. She needs my help. She lives alone. She's my mother's sister. Two years ago she wrote for them to send me over, but submarines were near the Clyde and the plan fell through. I thought the whole idea was forgotten, and now this."

"Tommy," pined Teddy, "I'm gonna miss you."

"Aye, and I you, Teddy."

But Tommy had told Teddy only part of the story. To save face, he had kept back the more humiliating aspects of the situation, those that had turned poor Tommy's life upside down. The day before, Tommy's father had taken him aside for a word. He had said slowly, "Tommy, I don't know how to tell you this. It breaks my heart and your mother's. Aunt Charlotte, you remember her, she came to visit twice before the war, she wants us to send you to Montreal. And there's nothing we can do but obey."

Tommy looked at him as if to ask, "Why not?"

"Laddie, we can't refuse her because she is [and he stopped for a few seconds], she is your real mother."

Tommy's eyes fell to his boots.

"As a baby," continued his Pa, "you came to live with us. We had just lost our first baby, named Charlotte after your mother. Your father had disappeared and your mother was without job, money, or prospects, so Ma and I raised you as our own. Which you have been and will always be."

By this time Tommy had broken down.

"The law is the law, Tommy. We have always wanted to adopt you, but she would never hear of it. Ye must be strong, Lad. I know you can be. And no matter where you go, Lad, remember, you'll always be a Robertson … and you'll always be my son."

So it was, that Tommy in one fell swoop, lost his father, mother, two brothers and a sister. His biological father and mother had rejected him. He would also lose his university seat, which he had won by his marks. Soon his friends and the old neighbourhood would be just a memory. Tommy's life was in a tailspin. What he didn't know was that it was going to get worse.

Before Tommy left for Canada, he put flowers at his grandma McCrae's grave, visited some old haunts, and kissed his Ma and siblings goodbye. With a heart of lead and with the dearest man he would ever know, he travelled to Greenock, the port of departure. At the dock, the crowd milled about in muffled tones. The great liner's whistle boomed and a military band played "Memories," a song which was to become Tommy's favourite.

Fred Robertson couldn't say much. He knew he would never see Tommy again. They hugged and pulled apart.

Over the ship's rail, Tommy waved his cap to his dad and soon the dock was a spot and the terns came to play as the ship groaned down the Clyde. A lady spoke to Tommy as much as to assuage her own loneliness as his. Later that night Tommy had a sandwich and soup in third class steerage and soon fell asleep in his bunk. He perhaps dreamed, "I wonder what Teddy's doing tomorrow."

> If you had only held out your arms to me
> I should have forgotten everything,
> And come back to you,
> a repentant child.
>
> — Irene Butler

About ten days later, Tommy got off the Québec-Montreal train in Windsor Station. His mother, Charlotte, showered him with affection. But it was not to last. She hadn't told Fred Robertson the truth. She wanted Tommy with her so she could put him to work. She needed money to pay for her flat in the Scottish section of Montreal. Gone were the promises for school and piano lessons. Instead he found himself working a ten-hour day in a bed factory.

Eventually, Tommy became so upset he wrote to the Robertsons. He told them he was going to run away. The day his letter arrived, Fred said to his wife, "What a mess. Our boy in Montreal is miserable and here we are with our tickets purchased and trunks packed for Australia. Your sister lied. She doesn't even own a piano to continue his lessons as she had said. We should have known better."

"Aye," his wife answered, "we're partially to blame. The poor bairn, I wonder what mother McCrae would say."

"I know what she'd say. 'Change your tickets for Canada. Go to *our* boy, Tommy'."

So the story goes that Ma and Pa Robertson said goodbye to Scotland forever and with their family of three, all under 12, steamed to Tommy in Montreal. At their arrival Tommy was so happy he almost jumped out of his skin. But his real mother with whom he lived did not share the elation. He was soon paying more attention to the Robertsons and giving *her* only token companionship. She had to do something to re-establish her dominance.

She decided to get out of Montreal, with Tommy. She had heard of job opportunities in Saskatchewan and she went there. Tommy was 14 and the year was 1921.

It would be a long winter for Tommy. In Saskatchewan, Charlotte married a widowed Englishman. Tommy was obviously part of the dowry because his foster father put him to work on their farm. Nothing Tommy did pleased them. They worked him hard and even physically punished him. Tommy was in the salt mines. Charlotte's two new babies didn't help the situation.

One morning, his mother found Tommy's bed empty. He had stolen away. He had been watching the freight trains and had learned the schedules for Ontario and Québec. In the wee hours of a summer night, with his back against the wall of a boxcar, he munched on cheese and cookies taken from the kitchen pantry. He was just another hobo riding the rails. But unlike the hobo, he had a place to go.

Lucky enough to escape the railroad police, he arrived in Montreal as dirty as a waif. Law or no law he would never leave his first Pa and Ma again. Besides he was 16. For the next three years he worked and took courses. His life finally *seemed* to be going smoothly.

> O, love, love, and love!
> Love is like dizziness;
> It winna let a poor body'
> Gang about his business.
> — James Hogg

Tommy soon had many friends in Montreal. Most had come from Scotland. One day, a friend from back home told Tommy that his biological father had been of a different religion than his mother Charlotte. His father had wanted to marry Charlotte, but Charlotte's mother, Grannie McCrae, who ruled the roost, said such a marriage was intolerable. For some reasons, Tommy then became interested in his father's religion. In fact, very soon afterwards he changed. Pa Robertson thought Tommy had made a serious mistake. According to Pa, no good Presbyterian ever gave up his religion. Out the window went love. Not even all that Tommy had endured, swayed Pa. He threw him out.

Tommy headed for Ottawa, the capitol of Canada. He got a job repairing typewriters and addressographs. He worked hard, saved money, and even chanced the odd letter home. He was on his own at 19.

It was one night about two years later, that he first saw her in his boarding house, a sweet Irish girl, a knockout with a bit of the flapper about her. Her name was Evelyn.

Now, in spite of his heartaches, Tommy remained a charmer. He was handsome and clever with the blarney. He enjoyed a party, loved singing, dancing and playing the piano. Evelyn fell victim to the young Scot's proposal for marriage. The year was 1929. In 1930, in a cold sacristy of Ottawa's St. Patrick's Church, they married.

Love was all they had to offer. The wedding party was four. The next weekend, they went to Evelyn's parents for the wedding feast. They travelled 30 miles by train and 5 by buggy and finally landed in the lap of poverty, an Irish farm.

That day Tommy renewed his friendship with Evelyn's sick father, blind uncle, two handicapped brothers and her younger siblings. But the person he especially wanted to see again was Genevieve, Evelyn's mother. Genny doted on Tommy. She loved him like a son.

Tommy later used his summer holidays to build sheds, wagons, stairs, verandas, doors, and other items for her. They were grateful they'd found each other. Their warmth and humour filled the 80-year-old farmhouse. Tommy was happy.

By 1935, Tommy had a son, a bungalow built by himself, a car, and a steady job. His two new loves, Evelyn and Genevieve, never got tired of appreciating him. Even the Robertsons eventually welcomed Tommy and his bride back into the fold and Tommy once again cuddled up to his dear Ma in Montreal, eating her fish and chips cooked according to the old recipe of his Glaswegian grandmother.

The years of wandering had ended. Tommy rejoiced in his new friends and the return of the old. His real mother came twice to visit in Montreal where she also saw Tommy and Evelyn. But she never went to Ottawa.

Now Tommy was a very sensitive person. Abused children usually are. This manifested itself in his inability to accept losses very well. He hated to see his foster parents age. He disliked the thought of dealing with their deaths. *Maybe he had already lost enough.* In Montreal and on the farm, his loved ones were in their seventies. Could he bear to see them pass away? He never found out.

In 1953, at age 45, Tommy died in hospital of a heart attack. His wife and son were with him at the end. He looked at them both, smiled, and died. And the tears of his three ladyloves, Evelyn, Genevieve and his Ma, Margaret, flowed as a river. Two years later Genevieve died and his Ma shortly after. His birth mother of whom he never spoke, died several years later.

And so it was that little Tommy Robertson of Montreal and Ottawa by way of Glasgow, Deniston and Mar Street went to his reward. Was it probable, as darkness descended over his bed in that sunny hospital room, that Tommy was again running over the Scottish hills with Teddy at his side both working up an appetite for Grannie's fish and chips? And Teddy was saying, "It's good to see you again, Tommy."

"Aye and you, Teddy."

"Anything new?"

"Not much!"

THE SQUALL

The squall hit and I ran under the leaves of a poplar bush ... sheets of rain slashed the river's edge ... sailboats leaned for home ... soon shafts of sun lightened the green and a scent of mist came down ... and I stepped into the open to watch the sun setting in the evening sky.

Chester

In recent times in my old neighbourhood, the Firefighters' Association had a luncheon every Wednesday attended by local cronies. At one such luncheon, I met an old friend of my parents.

As a young lad, I had always enjoyed his coming 'round. He had a way of stirring things up. His wit shadow-boxed with your brain. The big smile, the eager handshake and ready charm were there, but so were the digs and relentless baiting that could get a rise out of a stone. He always came straight at you. His voice was raspy and intimidating. His seal-like eyes sought you out.

Chester had a strong build. His shoulders sloped like a fighter's; his arms were stovepipes. His grip was merciless. When he spoke, his face came up close to my nose and I always listened.

I admired Chester. He was self-made man. He went overseas as an infantryman, married a British girl and returned to our old neighbourhood in Canada. He scrimped to build a fine home. He raised and educated four children. He was the perfect Canadian citizen, proud of his family and country, and the freedom he had helped preserve.

At a luncheon he showed me a photograph album that he had brought. One section had pictures of the 25th anniversary celebrations of World War II's end. There, taken on the Champs Élysées, was a full page shot in living colour of a giant tank covered with Canadian veterans and French citizens. As the tank came towards the cameraman, you could see Chester standing up in the command position of the open turret. He was waving a Canadian flag. His face was electrifying. Winning had meant everything. He felt that he represented every Canadian veteran. It was his finest hour. A tough kid from my old neighbourhood was showing the way.

A few months later, I heard that Chester was in the hospital. He had lost a foot to diabetes. Circulatory problems prevented him from ever walking again. His wife had left him. Only one child ever came to see him at the Veterans' Hospital. Any other man would have broken emotionally. But Chester was Chester, upbeat and hopeful and unsinkable.

Why anyone would ever abandon this fine man in his need was beyond me. He deserved so much respect.

The other day I saw a newspaper picture of one of Chester's sons. He is CEO of a huge, thriving business — big bucks, big job, big man, big success. In earlier days, Chester had spoken often of this boy's advancement. It meant much to him. Like the biblical father of the prodigal son, Chester had continued to love his son. Unlike the biblical son, this prodigal son never came home.

Was Chester alone when he died? Did anyone hold his hand? I hope so! I hope so! Perhaps an orphan child he had saved in France.

FATHER GILLIGAN

The Catholic Church teaches that the Eucharist is the Body of Christ.
As such, the priest often brings this body in the form of bread to
shut-ins. Receptions can vary.

Father Gilligan once took communion to an old codger in a manor.
He knocked on the door and went into the room to find the man
reading the paper.

The pastor bid him well and mentioned he had brought "Our
Lord" to him.

The old bird looked up from the paper just long enough to chirp:
"Put it over there on the table and I'll take it later."

Home Again

The long days of late June are perfect for visiting the towns along the north
shore of Scotland. A temperate climate coupled with more yearly sunshine
than any other part of Great Britain marks this area between Inverness and
Fraserburgh as one of the world's best kept vacation secrets. By 4:00 a.m. the
sky above Arctic Russia is already awash in colour. The clarity and freshness
that follows is a painter's delight.

This region, some 10 miles deep and 100 miles wide, is the flattest in the
Scottish Highlands. The lengthening rays of the June sun resist the darkness.
Pastures and early growths of barley and corn sweep to the sea. Smog-free
clouds are near enough to touch. On the green sea to the driver's left, fish-
ing trawlers roll and dip against cobalt blue. Such beauty makes it difficult to
keep one's eyes on the road.

Driving east, the tourist crosses tinsel-like rivers that rush from the great
Grampian and Cairngorm mountains to the north. Finally free from chasms,
moors, linns, marsh and forest clumps, the rivers offer trout and salmon and
a mineral-laden water that helps create the most popular whisky in the
world. Even the rivers' names conjure up the legendary mystery of this
stretch of land: the Findhorn, Lossie, Nairn, Spey, Deveron and Meldrum.

Believe it or not, the Highlands of Scotland were one of the last frontiers
to be opened in our modern world. The hostility of its geography and inhab-
itants maintained this isolation. In the 900 years after Christ, marauding
armies and navies in that domain, had to contend first with dense forests,
wild rivers, and vast mountain ranges. And, as if those weren't enough, they
subsequently had to face the Celts and Picts. So mean were these tribes that
the warring Romans, Vikings and other Teutonic nations dared not disturb

their suicidal antagonism. To the civilized world in general, they were known as mindless savages.

In the new millennium, despotic kings like Alexander, David, Duncan, Macbeth and Malcolm strove for independence as did the Highland Chiefs who followed them between the 1500s and 1750s. Eventually, Anglo-Saxon greed removed the stronghold of the great Scottish families. Such clans as the Macleans, Macleods, Frasers and Macdonalds threw in their kilts.

The English, as ever, were thorough. Homes were burnt, peasants banished, and sheep put in the pastures. The rich and famous from afar made sport on the land. The foxes were hounded, the pheasant and grouse nipped on the wing, and the lowly deer dropped in its tracks. After a shoot with the well-stocked game on the estates measurably reduced and the smoking guns racked, the participants, bathed and refreshed, would come down to a ten-course dinner at the manor house in the dale.

What had once been the playground of ghosts and witches — full of intrigue, double-crossing, secret societies, and self-styled executioners — became a theatre of sport for gentlemen. For the most part, the peasants began to live in the cities and the nobility on the land. Every burgh off the main road has a story.

Go, why don't you, to see Pennan's 27 homes built in a row on the North Sea's lip 600 feet below a cliff. Watch the fishing boats coming in at Fraserburg. Walk the sea walls at Macduff. Visit the legendary towns of Cawder and Forres spoken of by Shakespeare in *Macbeth*. Catch the ruins of Elgin's cathedral once called "The Lantern of the North." Take in a summer circus. Enjoy a picnic at a Portsay common.

At Nairn, my wife and I parked near the dunes beside some ten buses. Several games were in progress on a seven-acre field. It was a Saturday afternoon — bright and sunny with a cool wind off the sea. It was also a "beach day" for the people from surrounding towns like Keith and Huntley.

Along the dunes, facing the fields, the picnickers had divided off their territory by means of different coloured wind-bleached canvas joined together by poles driven in the ground. Between two poles and in front of each canvas, out of the wind, sat the members of a particular family. They enjoyed their lunches, drank soda and tea, and constantly chattered. The children frolicked and the dogs yapped. No one seemed in charge. No one needed to be.

For three hours, including rests, an eighteen-piece pipe-and-drum band marched up and down in front of the sitting people. Strains of music rose and fell on the stiff breeze. Their playing was inspiring. Their tunes were the stuff of Scottish history, battles, celebrations, victories, defeats, gatherings and dispersions. Kids walked with the band — some at its sides — others at the back. Up front, a four-year-old scampered full out to stay in the lead. So absorbed was he that he didn't notice the musicians had already turned around. Some 30 yards out of range, he found himself quite alone.

I spoke to a weathered-looking gentleman resting in the driver's seat of his grand touring car. He had grown up in the area and was back for a look-see. Seventy-five years ago he had played on that field and boarded at a nearby still-standing school overlooking the sea. Later as an army cadet, he had trained to be a commando on these same dunes. He spoke of a testy sergeant whose ranting drove his troops up to the bluffs and down to the sea. It was a proud moment for this gentleman to be there again.

Oceans put me to sleep. While my wife went walking, I lay down on the slanting dune. The band played on — the sand whistled by — the children squealed.

I felt I was at home. Not more than 30 miles from Nairn, the Ogilvies had settled around 1100 between Buckie and Banff. I felt at peace.

I woke an hour later to a wee dog licking my face.

Doreen

Back on the farm, Doreen had been a loving big sister to four brothers and sisters. So close was she that years later these family members always kept in touch with her. Whenever they sought out her friendship and advice, Doreen readily responded.

One day Doreen married gentle, reliable Norman. She had always wanted her own family but soon found out they couldn't have children. Seven years later they decided to adopt. Over a period of three years, they adopted two infant girls and the family life Doreen wanted was partially realized. But, she still felt something missing in her life.

One summer's day, when Norman and she were visiting Doreen's father and mother on the homestead farm, Doreen let it be known to her mother that she wanted to adopt a boy who would be older than her girls.

That evening, an hour after dinner, Doreen's father received news of a grave tragedy. The phone dropped from his hand. His other daughter, who was his second-youngest child, his son-in-law, and two of their sons, had died in a head-on car crash. One child survived but remained in a coma. His name was Ricky. He was seven. Doreen once again found herself in the position of keeping everyone emotionally and physically together.

The next day, Norman and his father-in-law drove 400 miles to identify their loved ones. While there, they visited Ricky in the hospital. He was still unconscious.

Everyone prayed for Ricky. After three weeks, word came that the boy had recovered consciousness. Norman and Doreen were overjoyed and set out on the long drive to the hospital.

When Ricky saw them, he ran into Doreen's arms and said, "Aunt Doreen, I want to live with you!" As Doreen held him close, she exclaimed with unimaginable joy, "Ricky that's just what Uncle Norman and I want." And then she added these magic words, "You shall be our son."

No Strings Attached

In spite of all the sacrifices parents make on behalf of their children, some can turn away without reason. No amount of expertise can prevent these splits. They just happen. Beyond control. A mystery in themselves.

In the same way, a released kite will go where it wills, soaring and diving, completely oblivious to the strings that once steered it.

Parents can only pray for the day when their strays return with open hearts. Meanwhile, they must not blame themselves.

IN HER EYES

As I bent to kiss her goodbye
She turned her head to the light
And I saw in her lovely blue eyes
A touch of paradise.
Happiness was there too
And love that will never die
For us, it'll always be, "Hello," "Hello"
And never, never, "Goodbye."

— the Author

The Record-keeper

Have you ever passed along the same street for years completely unaware of a certain house until the day comes when you notice it for the first time?

It is the same with the Bible. We can repeatedly hear or read a certain passage with no particular appreciation, until suddenly out of the blue a phrase's relevancy literally jumps off the page.

I recently experienced such an awakening when I heard the parable of the Samaritan woman read at a Sunday service.

The startling words in question were uttered by this woman who met Jesus at the site of Jacob's Well near the Samaritan town of Sheehem.

He told her of His being the Messiah and that He was the Water of Life and that He came to save all sinners, even those outside the Jewish faith. Then to convince this woman of His authenticity, He performed a small miracle which so impressed her that she forgot her water jar at the well and rushed into town to tell the people. She said to the people, "Come and see someone who told me everything I ever did." (John 4, 29)

It was then that Jesus's words struck home.

Jazz

When Doug's second wife died, he had no recourse but resign himself to the humdrum confinement of retirement-home living. He hated its repetition, regulations, confinement and loneliness. He longed for the freedom of the road, restaurant meals, afternoons of fishing, and heated exchanges with society's young and restless. Any hope of change flickered away with each day. What did the future hold? After all he was only 94.

Not far away from Doug lived a widow named Estelle. She too was lonely. Her only son had recently left home. She needed someone to care for, someone to benefit from her kindness and understanding. She prayed to God for someone to love — outside her small world of crafts and religious works.

She decided to go to work. After a few weeks at a small gift shop, she began feeling better. Tourists came from all over to her seaside town to enjoy sandy beaches, lobster and mussels. She welcomed their questions about this beautiful area of Prince Edward Island, that she called home.

One day an event took place which changed her life. A well-to-do lady approached her in the gift shop and asked, "Do you know of anyone who could provide a good home for my dog? I live in Charlottetown and I am in the process of moving into an apartment where animals are not permitted." She stopped, obviously upset. "He's a good dog, a small husky with shiny coat and eyes of blue. I have him out in the car."

Estelle felt the lady's sorrow. She said, "May I see the dog, please. I might consider adopting him."

The lady perked up. "Come to my car. His name is Jazz. He's my best friend."

Well, the upshot was that the owner and Jazz went for a goodbye walk on the beach and then she gave him to Estelle. And soon Estelle and Jazz grew closer in their humble clapboard home on the top of Souris Town's only large hill. Surrounded by the Atlantic on three sides, Jazz took to the fresh breezes and healthy playground.

Soon Estelle wanted to share Jazz. She had heard about the positive results of animals visiting residents in retirement homes and long-term care hospitals. "Why not take Jazz to see these residents?" she thought. They would love him.

And so they did. Particularly one resident named Doug whose love for animals went back to his days in England where the British people if they could, would give dogs the vote.

But it wasn't just Jazz that impressed Doug. It was also Estelle. In fact, they fell in love and married.

And today Doug, Estelle and Jazz live in Souris, Prince Edward Island. Estelle has found herself, and Doug thanks God for her and the dear dog that lies by his chair staring at his ancestral North.

The Warnings

One evening my wife called out, "Did you hear those three knocks at my window — loud, clear and measured? What do they mean?"

The next morning as I walked in our garden I heard weird shrieking from the neighbour's backyard. I looked in. A big black bird sitting in a tree was screeching. It wasn't a crow. Crows don't sound like that.

I said to my wife that I thought the knocks and the wailing were warnings of her father's death. At that time he was in poor health in hospital. He was 104! Two days later our 20-year-old cat suddenly took ill and we had to have her put down. Another warning I thought. Two weeks later my father-in-law died. The loss of this illustrious gentleman was worthy of these two warnings, even the baneful cry of the banshee.

A CHINESE PROVERB

If there is righteousness in the heart,
  there will be beauty in the character.
If there is beauty in the character,
  there will be harmony in the home.
If there is harmony in the home,
  there will be order in the nation.
If there is order in the nation,
  there will be peace in the world.
— Anonymous

Hector

This story is about Hector, a Jack Russell terrier, who like all members of his breed was intelligent, independent, spirited, brave and incorrigible. We had a Jack Russell one time named Paddy. He drove our family crazy with his antics. One day he dashed out the front door to die later in the middle of four-lane traffic. We cried for days.

Hector however was more loyal than our Paddy. His master was the famous Scottish veterinarian and writer, James Herriot of Yorkshire, England. For 15 years Hector sat beside James as he drove his small black sedan through the dales of Yorkshire in the service of gentle but raspy farmers.

Both had their troubles. Herriot struggled to make a living in impover-ished times. Hector did his best to live with blindness that had struck him at age five. Hector was an example to Herriot that problems can be endured and overcome. They were meant for each other.

One evening Herriot and Hector made a call some 40 miles from home. The procedure upon arrival at the client's farm was the same on each trip. Hector would go for a run in a pasture and then come back and wait near the car for Herriot's return.

On this particular night, Herriot did something unusual. He drove home without Hector. He never noted his absence until he pulled into the laneway of his home. Quickly, he drove back through the darkness to find him. When he arrived at the farm, frantic to say the least, blind Hector was sitting in the same spot where Herriot had left him two hours earlier. He had known his master would return.

Once again Hector had taught Herriot a lesson: when faced with a dilem-ma, sometimes it's best to do nothing but put your faith in those around you.

The Hanky

A young man once told me that whenever he is afraid, he sings, hums, or whistles Irish songs. My wife receives assurance from a small chain and medal given her by a favourite aunt. A family picture on my office desk used to give me a "reason for living" feeling.

And so it is across the world that people use such items as pendants, beads, worry stones, rings, and paintings to help them through the long nights.

My friend Pat had a mother of inordinate emotional strength in times of trial. Many years ago on the day her mother passed away, Pat came upon a dainty, embroidered hanky of her mother's, the kind used at early twentieth century ladies' teas. She tucked it away and forgot about it.

Ten years after her mother's death, she found it. She was getting ready to attend the funeral of one of her sons when she came upon the hanky. She slipped it between her fingers before she left.

MARY JOSEPH

There are many tricks to falling back to sleep after waking in the middle of the night. Some read, some eat, some go for a short walk; others telephone a friend, listen to music, or take a bath. The methods are numerous.

My friend, Sister Mary Joseph, has her way too: she kneels by her cot, raises her arms outright and prays for the world.

During the unbelievably sad service she never put it down. Showing it to me, she told me why: "I felt my mother's strength in this small keepsake. She was with me, guiding me through this day of grief. It's amazing how such a small insignificant piece of cloth could help. Whenever I felt myself sinking, I'd hear my mother's voice saying, 'Straighten up, show everyone your courage, just as a child of mine should.' And I did. I got through it. I never thought I would."

BEYOND THE BEYOND

The saddest moment on earth is the loss of a loved one. Nothing can surpass the trauma. Nothing in the revolt of wind, water, earth or fire can equal such a loss. Not lightning bolt, tidal wave, atomic fusion, nor earthquake can match the depth of its ferocity.
Severed love shakes the universe.

Rosary Waves

Life sends us warnings. A few near misses in traffic may be enough to force us to improve our driving skills. Mild heart attacks may be signs for us to slow down, increase exercise and watch our diet. Small losses in the investment field may be lessons to stay clear of the bigger game.

In Ireland, the children going to the beach were always told by their mothers to watch out for the "rosary waves." Rosary waves were large waves among smaller ones that angels sent to warn the little waders they'd gone out far enough.

It's a shame to miss the "rosary waves" in our lives. Not taking notice of them can lead to catastrophe.

The System

A social worker in a downtown hospital once told me that the only way to work under a "system" was to beat it. Every system has been purposely designed for expediency. It sets and controls most possibilities for the benefit of the common good. It cuts down on red tape, needless expenditure and abuse of time. But it can be impersonal, cold and unfeeling.

This social worker was involved with a friend of mine sent to hospital for treatment of a stroke. The stroke was so severe that several doctors agreed very little could be done. Due to his financial situation, the system called for him to be sent to a country nursing home some 40 miles away. Care was cheaper there.

The social worker knew that such a patient without friends to visit would not survive for long in the country. So the social worker, with the help of two of the patient's friends, arranged for a showdown meeting with the hospital staff involved. At the consultation were three doctors, a physiotherapist, psychiatrist, head nurse, dietician, orderly and, for part of the meeting, the patient himself.

Three people were trying to beat the system. And they did. The powers that be decided the patient should be kept in the city in a premiere hospital setting. He would be well looked after for the rest of his days.

In this world, the rules of any system should only be guidelines. They are to be weighed in the light of the situation and the individual. No two cases are the same. Law schools and judicial libraries are full of *interpretations* of the law. Every rule and system is open to scrutiny. Justice walks a thin line.

SOMETIMES YOU CAN'T WIN

The new boarder wasn't too pleased. Each night when he handed his empty lunch-pail to the woman of the house he looked disgruntled.

Finally one evening she asked, "Are you not happy with your lunch, Lad?"

To tell ye the truth, Ma'am, I find one sandwich not enough to satisfy my hunger."

Next morning, the landlady put in two sandwiches only to meet that evening with the same unhappy look. Next day, she tried three and the next, four. But the increases still brought no satisfaction.

Finally, she went the limit. She cut open a whole loaf and filled it with meat, onion, tomato, lettuce and home-made pickles. She thought this size of lunch would satisfy him.

That night he returned home no happier than before.

"Surely to goodness," said the lady, "you must have enjoyed your lunch this time?"

The lad looked up and chirped, "Not bad, Ma'am. Not bad. But I see you're back to one sandwich again."

A Little Extra

Eddie Cantor, stage and movie star, grew up in the poverty of New York's East Side. Like many poor Jewish boys, he tried to make a dime doing odd jobs in the neighbourhood. Running errands was one way.

One job bothered Eddie. He could never understand why his mother and neighbours sent him out of the district to buy groceries from a certain merchant. He couldn't see any difference between the grocery stores near home and this other one a good distance away.

After a few weeks, he asked his mother what was wrong with the stores in their area. And she said, "Nothing really, But they don't allow for a little extra. Now, for instance, you take Benny Green whom you know to live outside our area. He makes an effort to please. He tries to show us his appreciation. He builds good will. He gives a little extra."

"But how does he do that, Mama?" asked Eddie.

"Well, Son, Benny needs the business and we need a break, financially. So he meets us half way. When we buy three bananas, he throws in four. Every dozen of cookies is a baker's dozen — one extra. That's Benny — an extra scoop of tea — a bigger turnip — a few candies for your father. Benny never misses his extras. But we sure would."

I remember a baker who was like Benny. We drove 25 miles out of town to buy his delicious bread, cookies and cakes baked in a cedar-burning oven.

Mr. Graham, the baker, always gave us a discount to help cover the cost of gas. That little extra went a long way. One sacrifice deserves another.

THE REAL BATTLEFIELDS

The important battles of this life are not fought in market places and ivory towers where quotas and profits measure one kind of success. The real struggles take place in hospitals, nurseries, classrooms, clinics, missions, convents and retirement homes where good people face their relentless trials as best they can.

Archie

"Archie," I asked, "do you mind talking about your early days on the farm in the 1910s, 20s and 30s?"

His blue eyes sparkled and he said, "Not at all. They were great days. I miss them. How shall I begin?"

I said, "Why not talk about those times just as the thoughts come to mind? Don't bother with any particular order."

We were sitting across from each other at his small kitchen table. Because of his bad hearing, I spoke loudly and pronounced each word clearly so Archie could read my lips. His memory was exceptional. I felt comfortable with him. He was as winsome as the day he was born.

"Well, I remember we did a lot of hunting: muskrat, coons, wolves, fox, deer and even bears. The minks would hide down in the rocks and we'd put our traps there. And we'd catch and sell them for $32 a fur. The wolves were more like coyotes, a menace to the sheep and turkey and geese. One year we shot 60 wolves.

"The collies would fight any animal, but not the bear. Just the sight of a bear and they'd hightail it home — even leave the cattle. We had a fella' living near us who was always running into bears. His name was Mickey. One day a bear kept him up a tree for four hours. We called him Mickey the Bear.

"A few Indians were still around in the 1910s. They were kind, helpful people. There were Crees and Blackfoot — with high cheekbones, black eyes, and jet black straight hair. Many of to-day's Canadians have these features since a good deal of intermarriage took place among the French, Irish, Scottish and Indian.

"Many Indians were good-looking. They say the Indians came from Northern Tibet and Japan. They crossed over to this continent by the Bering Strait. Then they came down the coast of British Columbia and into the American and Canadian plains. Did you know they never fought at night?

"By the way, we also hunted snakes. Our fields were covered with them — adders, water snakes, milk snakes, timber snakes, grass snacks. Some were as big as your wrist. They could kill a newborn calf. We caught a snake milking a cow one time. We had more ways of killing snakes than you could think of. Eventually, we got rid of them all. And good riddance, I say.

"We grew grain, corn, wheat, beans and turnips. We had a silo and good barns. As a treat for our 26 cows we'd mix molasses with the hay, turnips and corn. We mixed 60 gallons at a time. We ate plenty of molasses ourselves — the better grade, of course. We churned butter and made preserves. My mother made bread, cookies, cakes and pies. And we even made our own soap. We'd mix small mashed bones into maple tree ashes and send the lot to England. It came back as special lye. We'd add fat and then boil. The lye gradually ate away the fat and the leftover was set and cooled and cut into large chunks. The soap was used only for laundry.

"I'd bet you'd be surprised if I told you we grew our own tobacco. We'd cut off the leaves and roll them up when they were almost dry. We stored enough in the dry, attic hay to last two years. Since we young lads weren't allowed tobacco, we'd smoke shavings from the inside of bark — no one the wiser.

"What do you say to a cup of tea?" And up he got. The effect of the Tullamore Dew Irish Whiskey we had enjoyed earlier had worn off. "Time for another shot of energy," he quipped.

"A few months ago I met a lady in town who was once a member of the French underground. She'd meet the parachutists coming in from England. She said she was never afraid of the Germans because she knew she was smarter.

"Anyway, she later contracted cancer and I went to see her. As she lay in bed she reached for my hand. At my touch she said, 'You have the sixth sense, don't you?' I said I wasn't sure.

"Then I thought about my first encounter with a ghost. I was twelve. My friend Danny and I were coming home from a practice for the Christmas concert at a hall near the church. Danny had gone ahead.

"The year was 1920. The winter night was typical of the Canadian climate — plenty of snow — packed roads, frozen creeks — and for good measure, a two-inch layer of ice over everything. The full moon glistened off the ice for miles. And as always, the heavy silence of a cold night

"As I neared a neighbour's house I saw a small lady coming towards me across the fields. She wore a dark cloak with a hood. Her hands were by her side. Her feet, hidden by a cloud, floated just above the ice. Her face was inside the hood. She passed by me, never said a word, and never looked at me. She went through the small gate, up the path and disappeared into the brick chimney at the side of the house.

"I told my mother about her when I got home. She said she remembered her. The ghost had once lived in that house. Her name was Millie. Her mother died when she was born and an aunt raised her. She married a town boy. They moved away. He was a drunkard. She never came back. She died of a broken heart.

"My mother told me Millie had appeared because she needed prayers. The night still being young, and my being very shook up by the sighting, I set off for the priest's house across the fields and over the dam on Grant's creek, *some creek, 6 feet deep and 20 yards wide*. I had a dollar in my pocket and I gave it to the priest to have a Mass said for Millie.

"Another time, at night too, my grandfather, my brother and I were in a sulky on the way to town. A sulky carried three — two on a front seat and one on a back seat facing the rear. We had just reached the top of the big hill near Westport, Ontario, when a man carrying a lantern walked from right to left across the small road just within a whisker of the pony's head. He went into the ditch and disappeared. My grandfather remembered him as the person who had died from a broken neck when his horse pitched him. He had a history of drinking. All three of us saw him that night. The sighting never bothered the pony, but it sure scared us. I guess his soul is still restless.

"We always had plenty of work. We milked 26 cows. One day I had to do them all by myself — it took four and a half hours, morning and night — I spent nearly the whole day milking.

"In the winter we cut bush. The best part of that was making green tea on a fire: we used to buy Salada Green Tea by 25 pound lots.

"Every winter we packed the blocks of ice in sawdust from the wood-cutting saws. For fun we fished and played hockey. We slid down hills on big pieces of cardboard. If anyone fell into the creek through the ice, two buddies would lie on their stomachs on the shore, end to end, while other persons would lie on the ice, hands to ankle, all the way out to the victim. We never lost anyone in all my years.

"In the summer, in addition to our regular chores we filled the silos, kept bees, trimmed apple trees and planted a garden. Threshing was a big day in the fall and, of course, "work bees" for construction of buildings were a part of everyone's duty. They were tough years.

"In 1918, the Spanish flu killed friends and neighbours, but we escaped. Lots stayed away from church in those days to prevent infection. My mother, Alice, had many home-made treatments: ointments, castor oil, Epsom salts, sugar and, of course, mustard plasters. Before plasters were put on, Momma would grease our chests. The plasters were replaced whenever necessary. To hold in the heat, she'd put heated salt bags around our necks and shoulders and cover them with blankets. Every hour and a half she'd change the bags. My God, the treatment was worse than the cure.

"The therapy for cuts on the farm wasn't pretty either. My brother once sliced his foot up through a toe; a nasty cut it was. Well, my father pushed it together and bandaged it tight. The wound was kept clean and eventually healed. Four popsicle-type sticks taped together often set a broken finger. A person with a broken hip would be placed in a bed between bags of sand to let the hip mend.

"One time my uncle put a gash in his leg. He was alone but for his collie. The collie ran for my father. He kept jumping up on him and running back and forward in the lane. My dad went by sleigh. He put a tourniquet on the wound and later sewed it up. A doctor wasn't called. My dad, James, was something else, I tell ya'.

"I've had my sixth sense since childhood. I can usually tell if someone in my presence is ill. In my time, I have cured a few minor ailments, just like my great-grandfather. People recognize this power in me and ask for help or prayers. I do what I can. Often, people just need someone to talk to.

"I also get premonitions. After my wife had been in hospital for a while, I heard a noise one afternoon in the upstairs bedroom where she had slept during the first days of her sickness. I entered the bedroom and looked around. As I left, a rather large crucifix on the wall outside the door fell to the floor. The figure on the cross looked up at me. I knew then that she would die soon.

"She did and what a loss. I cried for six weeks.

"Funny enough, her spirit stayed around the house. In the kitchen, sometimes I knew she was standing behind me. I could see without turning my head. One time I whipped around quickly and I saw her for a fleeting moment. She didn't want me to leave her either.

"One night, I came home at seven p.m.… when I stepped into the hall, the hair on my neck stood straight up. Her presence was so powerful, it overwhelmed me. I knew she was in the living room, just out of my sight. Suddenly, the presence disappeared. She was gone for good. I knew it and she knew it. She has never been back except in my heart."

A few jokes later I left him until my next visit. He stood on his side veranda and waved. I left him all the richer for the stories he had shared.

OPPOSITES

It's not who you are
But what you are.
It's not what you say
It's how you say it.
It's not how much you know
It's how you use it.
It's not so much to be in love
As to know how to show it.
— the Author

Graetan

In the middle of the night a lone nurse was working at her station on the third floor of a hospital for chronic care in Ottawa. Suddenly, a *call* light over her head began blinking. Her pulse quickened; her breathing shortened. It was the *call* light for Room 3312, a room with no one in it. The room had been empty for a few days.

The former patient, a lady named Graetan, had gone to another city hospital, one that specialized in pneumonia, and the officials at the chronic care hospital had kept her room empty and available for her possible return. After all, the lady had been a resident there for 26 years.

But the nurse on duty knew as did the whole hospital, that the patient would not be back. She had died 15 hours earlier on the previous day at 12:00 noon, December 23. And now the light at the station and also (as was found out later), the light over the doorway of Room 3312 were blinking and the nurse was afraid to go and see why.

She asked a companion to accompany her and together they went down the dim corridor to the room with no one in it. They turned the light on inside. It was indeed empty. Yet just two minutes earlier someone had activated the calling lights.

The two nurses decided Graetan had returned. Word spread rapidly throughout the hospital. Graetan had come to say goodbye.

Everyone there knew her. She had travelled the halls in her specially out-fitted motor wheelchair. Unable to move her body after a spinal operation 26 years earlier, she drove her machine by blowing sequenced puffs of air into a small tube near her mouth. Her big eyes watched everything. She greeted everyone with a smile.

I used to see her in the lobby. Usually she was selling lottery tickets by pointing to them with her eyes. Occasionally she spoke. And then she would continue on her route.

So it was a sombre time around the hospital that Christmas Eve of the year 2000. Graetan had a presence that lingered. And everyone felt it. She had been inspirational in life, and now in death gave testimony of how much God loved her.

Somebody had activated the lights — an angel, Graetan or God Himself. As one seasoned nurse told me: "I didn't know much about her, but I know she suffered for some 40 years. When she passed by me in the halls, I always felt a surge of love."

Before I left, a nurse took me aside and whispered, "The best proof we have that Graetan returned that night is known to only a few. In her bed, Graetan had near her mouth a tube similar to the one on her mobile wheel-chair. By blowing a special code of long and short puffs, she could turn the call lights on. No other way exists, and no one else but Graetan could do it. Only she knew the code.

"Not only that, but the machine had lain idle for two days. It was Graetan who turned it on and used it. By the way, I forgot to mention that Graetan always contacted the desk about 3 a.m. for a drink of water. The time was 3 a.m. that night the light blinked."

MARJORIE'S GIFT

On a dull afternoon,
  Just across my room
I see the blooms from a dear old friend.
  They brighten my gloom
As the sun doth the moon
  And soon I'm ready to smile again.
I know very well
  When their freshness is spent
And the spot by the window is bare
  That the memory of the love she sent me
Will forever linger there.

— the Author

The Indian

And the speaker said, "Addiction is the same as jumping from a plane without a parachute. The only real fun is the experience *on the way down*.

"We must be extra careful in our approach to alcohol, drugs, gambling, sex, power. There's entrapment in them, an enslavement that can be our ruination. Their abuse can wring peace from your soul. We must know them for what they are. Any alliance with them is dangerous.

"No one can afford to play around with them. A certain Indian once found a rattlesnake trapped by a wire. The snake said to the Indian, 'Indian, be kind to me. I need your help. I urge you to free me and take me down in the valley where I can begin again.'

"'I do not trust you,' said the Indian. 'You are dangerous.'

"'Indian, I promise I shall not hurt you. You have my word.'

"'I cannot trust the word of a snake. I have seen many mothers' children die from your attacks. My parents have taught me that your kind never changes.'

"'Not so, Indian. I will change if you help me.'

"And the snake coiled in pain before the feet of the lowly Indian.

"Eventually, the Indian freed the rattler and carried him down to fresh water and green fields. But as he put him down, the snake bit him on the hand.

"'Snake, you promised you wouldn't bite me. I am dying.'

"'Too bad,' answered the snake. 'You knew what I was before you ever picked me up. You are to blame for your death, not I.'"

Mitkley

A beige horse with his mouth foaming from exertion pulled up one evening in the yard of farmer-blacksmith Mitkley. The rider panted, "Mr. Mitkley, come quickly, my father has cut his leg and is bleeding to death!"

Mr. Mitkley answered, "There isn't enough time." With that, he went into his log home and brought out a small black cord with seven knots. He knelt down in the yard and fingered the cord as he prayed. Then he rose and went over to the rider and said, "Take your horse and go home. Your father's bleeding has stopped. He will live."

Such was the power of this Irish immigrant to Bathurst Township in Central Ontario. For 60 years (1840-1899), Mitkley's (slang for Michael), pioneer contemporaries travelled hazardous miles to seek his healing.

One can still see his home behind three great maples on the present Old Westport road, named after Westport in County Mayo, Ireland. Nearby is Grant's Creek and beyond, not far away, the church, school and hall of a community called Stanleyville.

Across the road from his house, Mitkley had his blacksmith shop. There he shod the horses, tended oxen, affixed runners to sleighs and rims on wagon wheels. He attached forks and rakes to handles, and repaired harnesses. His many hours work with anvil and bellows and iron put a roundness in his back that grew progressively worse down the years. But while advancing age did curtail his blacksmith business, it never affected his curative powers.

Buoyed up by his wife Sally and four sons, he never turned away a wayfarer. His name was a household word in all the nearby counties until his death at the age of 99.

It is said that the shortage of doctors in the frontiers, God had given Mitkley and a few others like him, the gift of healing. In Mitkley's case, God's power came through a black cord with seven knots. Tradition had it that the cord came with Mitkley from Ireland and somehow was linked to the goodness of St. Joseph.

The following story comes from a 92-year-old great-grandson of Mitkley with whom I have spent several hours. This gentleman's father knew Mitkley for over 40 years and actually grew up in Mitkley's home.

About 1920, this great-grandson met a woman who said she had been cured by Mitkley around 1846. The woman was raised in a community called Huntley, Ontario, 50 miles away. From birth she had had severe headaches: the crown of her head had never closed and one could see her pulse beat. A friend named Conroy took her to see Mitkley who closed the space and ended the headaches. The girl was only 12. Later, the girl and her sister became expert milliners and travelled throughout Canada and the United States displaying and selling their goods. They even had a booth at the Chicago's World Fair.

Mitkley's contribution to pioneer life was remarkable. He touched the lives of hundreds. God called him as assuredly as he calls our present day doctors. And he gave him a gift very much like the one he gave His only Son.

Mitkley is buried in Stanleyville's Catholic Church's graveyard, near Perth, Ontario. If you go there and meet the right party, you may learn Mitkley's last name and get a chance to kneel over his remains. Mitkley was a holy man. He deserves to be remembered!

Muriel

Muriel answered the phone. It was her husband, Andrew, calling to say he'd be home from fishing in 15 minutes.

An hour later, Andrew had not arrived. Muriel went outside and paced up and down the laneway. Suddenly, she saw a white cloud in the middle of the road. It wasn't mist or fog or smoke. It was something she had never before seen.

As she stared at the *cloud* she knew instinctively that her husband had been in an accident. She rushed in to phone 911. As she neared the phone, it rang. It was the police calling to say her husband had been injured. Another car had run a stop sign and hit him. Her husband was in hospital. They said he would be operated on later that night. Muriel had no choice but to wait at home. She had no car and no babysitter.

At 2:30 that morning she heard several knocks at her bedroom window. A voice outside said, "Your husband is going to make it." Muriel knew it was her dead mother.

A short while later, the doctor phoned to say her husband would be all right. "What time was the operation over, Doctor?" Muriel asked.

"At 2:30 a.m.," he answered.

SOMETHING GOOD

The parish priest asked the congregation if anyone there would come forward to say a few words about Archie before they took his body from the church. No one volunteered.

"Come now," the priest urged, "surely someone can say something!" Still, no reply.

"Do you mean to tell me no one here will offer an accolade or two for poor Archie?"

Suddenly, a man stood up at the back.

"Ah," said the priest, "What say you about Archie?"

"His brother was worse!"

Miracles

We have all been touched by miracles. The world is full of them: the boy condemned to paralysis who walks again; patients with inoperable cancer who live on.

I met one such survivor working as a nurse in a hospital for those with incurable sicknesses. She told me that at age 26 she developed leukemia. She was told nothing could be done. She took chemo, died twice on the operating table, and suffered physically and emotionally beyond comprehension.

Then one day with no explanation her appetite returned and the pain disappeared. She began to get better. She said she had promised the Virgin Mary she would work with incurables if her health came back. Within two years, she married and raised three children. Twenty-six years later, the cancer has never returned.

The doctors offered no explanations for her recovery. The cancer had disappeared on its own. She knew she had been cured.

What better person could we get to work with incurables? What better person to understand the agony of the terminally ill? What better person to nurse an incurable than another incurable?

> ## A BLESSING
>
> May your pain never be too much to bear.
> May your heart never know despair.
> May your faith grow stronger with each day.
> May angels accompany you on your way.
> And, when it's time to say "Adieu"
> May God Himself come for you.
>
> — Anonymous

Mark

When Mark was old enough to realize the gravity of his muscular dystrophy, he read everything he could about the disease. His research told him he would die around age 35. And, sure enough, at 35, he did.

Considering his delicate medical condition, Mark cherished his family. He had a special love for his young daughter Karen. They were together at every opportunity: romping, reading, walking, playing games.

One day, shortly after Mark's death, four-year-old Karen asked her mother, "Mommy, where has Daddy gone?"

"He has gone to heaven."

"How do you get to heaven?"

"Well, you must die first!"

"You mean if I ran in front of a truck, I could be with Daddy."

"Yes, but why would you do that when we need you here? Don't think of such a thing. Daddy wouldn't like you to leave us."

About a week later, Karen and her mother were walking downtown. Karen, on the inside, suddenly said, "Daddy's here."

"Where?" asked the mother.

"Right here on my other side."

"Can you see him?" she inquired.

"No, but I know he's here because I can smell him!"

Della Reese, the star of the *Touched By An Angel* television series recounts in her autobiography a similar account of spirit detection by odour.

Coming out of her outdoor pool, Della walked into the plate glass door at the back of the house. As she lay in the glass with a large piece in her stomach, she realized that the glass on the top part of the door was ready to fall and decapitate her. She struggled to get up, but the pain from her wound hindered her. Suddenly she felt the presence of her dead mother, who Della claims physically pulled her free just as the pane fell. "How did you know it was your mother?" asked a friend.

"I knew it was my mother because I recognized her odour — a combination of Lily Ponds Cream and vanilla. It was Momma, all right."

NOT SO EASY

An old man's daughter checked her father's lottery ticket and discovered he'd won three million dollars. Afraid to shock him, she asked his friend, the Irish parish priest, to break the news to him.

"Ah, sure," said the priest. "I'd be delighted. Consider it done. Easy as pie, so it'll be."

Next day the priest met the old man.

"Charlie, you wouldn't get too worked up if I told you that you won a bit of money in the lottery. In fact, more than a bit."

"Not a'tall, Father. Not a'tall. Sure it's music to my ears. How much did I win?"

"Three million."

"Thanks be to God, Father. It's a miracle. Now I have a surprise for you."

"What would that be, Charlie?"

"Well, I'm going to give you half."

And the priest dropped dead.

The Frenchman

This story is 165 years old. In 1840, a Frenchman from France acquired farmland from the British in Bathurst Township, Ontario, in repayment for his fighting for Britain in the Napoleonic War. He planted corn and faithfully cultivated a vegetable garden. Although he could speak little English, he made friends easily.

One afternoon, as he was working in his garden on a hill beside a main wagon trail, seven McCann brothers, just arrived from Ireland, came by on their way to their new homestead.

Now, the Frenchman had placed a scarecrow in the wheat field near the road and the McCann brothers decided to make its acquaintance. Each one approached the scarecrow and with typical Irish song and dance shook its extended hand. The Frenchman enjoyed their frolic and when they had finished he decided to join in the fun. He shouted from the hill, "Allo, Allo, mes amis, that not me down there, me up here!"

And all eight laughed in the sunshine on that day long ago.

Getting Serious

When Keith got incurable leukemia in 1988 he asked all his friends to pray for his cure. He even put the bite on his fellow executives at the large Canadian bank where he worked. Members of his church prayed at home and around the world. He made no bones about putting all his faith in God's mercy.

When he finally overcame his disease, he hoped his cure would bring others back to God, especially the movers and shakers at his bank. As it turned out, they *were* impressed by Keith's testimony and his praise of God.

This story of Keith's sickness was carried in my daily newspaper. The article contained many quotes from Keith. One quote was powerful, and the writer chose to end the article with it.

Keith told us: "It's amazing what God can do when we get serious with Him."

Jocelyn

"I try to live my life around common sense. Some people call it wisdom; others, prudence. But whatever you call it, it's not easy to come by."

For my young friend, Jocelyn, the restoration of old furniture and good conversation go hand in hand. He can dovetail the two as easily as he can fit two panels in the bottom of a desk drawer.

He went on, "One way we gain wisdom is by trial and error. Our failures can teach us a lot. In fact, when we learn from our failures, they are not failures at all. They become failures only when we don't learn from them."

As he stood up from his work, he stared for a moment and said, "A mistake, error or failure must become a lesson learned. Lessons acquired this way, I repeat, are not failures. They are successes."

And with that utterance, he drove home a nail. Then, he added, "See, it's common sense that a nail goes there. The last time I did a job like this, I forgot this nail, and the leg fell off."

The Old Man

In the quietness of the night, two nurses talked about the old man in the bed. One said, "He'd have a chance, if he weren't old. Poor soul, he's spent. Too many years to hurdle." The other nurse agreed.

Suddenly, the patient spoke like some great bell: "I'm not old ... I shall never be old. I refuse to be old. I shall be ever young." And he paused. And the nurses moved closer. He lay on his back, his head resting on his pillows. His eyes were closed.

He began again: "I remain a child ... I wonder and dream ... I run with my school friends ... I play with my children ... my dog frolics at my feet ... I smile often ... I hum and whistle....

"Do not be mislead by my gait or hair colour or wrinkles ... that is not I ... for I live in a land of eternal youth where the valleys are green and the breeze fresh and my heart beats with the chase ... my memories are sweet ... they feed my soul, lighten my heart ... give me a lift, put sparkle in my eye ... do not misjudge me ... look to your own spirit and keep it full of hope and cheer ... as for me, I live in fields of flowers, full of joy and laughter."

Two Boys

Hockey was a quality game in the first half of the last century. The 150 players who played professionally in North America were hand-picked from poor, cold arenas all across Canada and the United States. They were talented, rough, underpaid, and unique. A chance to see them play was a treat.

One Saturday in 1941, I travelled by train to Montreal where a Scottish uncle took me to my first National League Hockey game. I was ten.

I remember being mesmerized by the hockey greats in the old Montreal Forum. Boston was playing the Montreal Canadians. I recall thinking the best player on the ice was the old smoothie Bill Cowley, an all-star centreman for Boston and a product of my hometown.

Fifty-eight years later, my wife and I were staying at a hotel in Toronto. Our hotel was near the new hockey arena of the Toronto Maple Leafs. Naturally a large number of fans from out of town were staying there.

On Saturday evening, about game time, I was in a descending elevator in the company of a young family. I asked the young boy, "Are you all off to the game?"

"Yes," he said.

I asked his sister, "Do you like hockey, too?"

"Oh, yes. I play in a girl's hockey league."

"Is this your first National Hockey League game?" I asked the lad.

"Yes," he answered.

"How old are you?" I enquired.

"I'm ten."

As the doors opened, I asked one more question, "By the way, who's the visiting team?"

And the father said, "The Boston Bruins!"

Little Things Mean a Lot

One summer day in Ireland, the caretaker of a sprawling cemetery that lies on a long hill outside Westport in County Mayo, spoke about the thousands entrusted to his care.

He said, "Enough tears were shed here to fill two oceans. Funeral processions from all around brought the victims of famines and epidemics. The hundreds butchered by Ireton and Cromwell lie here. In addition, Mayo has always been poor, the poorest of the poor. Some people had nothing but the mementoes we find buried with them. You can't imagine the variety of these keepsakes under the headstones.

"Just the sight of them would break you heart — pipes, rings, watches, trinkets, hankies, toy soldiers, brooches, coins, balls, spinning tops, rosaries, crucifixes, hair ribbons, eyeglasses, dolls, tie clips, pins, prayer-books, mugs. Each item has its own story. Each has been close to someone's heart. Each is all that remains of a mother's memory, a child's dream or a young man's devotion."

In truth, isn't much of mankind prone to keeping mementoes of people and events that touch their hearts? More than often, these items are sources of consolation and courage to those who treasure them. For years my father in Glasgow carried on his person a tattered yellowed letter written to him in 1917 from his father imprisoned in a German prison camp in France. My wife always wears a medal given to her 64 years ago by her godmother. A cousin carries a packet in her purse containing a tuft of hair taken from her dearest dog. A favourite photo of my mother and my wife with our first child is with me wherever I go.

Two stories from opposite poles of the social order prove attachment to such items.

Toscanini, the great Italian maestro, in 1936, at age 70, was invited by the National Broadcasting Corporation in the United States to record ten live radio broadcasts for worldwide distribution. At first Toscanini said he was too old — his health was delicate — troubles with Mussolini and Hitler unsettled him — it had been 22 years since he had conducted in the States — would he be remembered? His confidence was not as great as those who wanted him.

Anyway, he did go — in 1937. His New York orchestra, hand-picked from the best, awaited his first rehearsal. In his dressing room on a cold December morning he made ready. His anxiety was great. He had reached the point of no return. Suddenly the maestro went to his dresser and picked up a small crucifix on a silver chain that linked tiny pictures in metal frames. He caressed them, raised them to his lips, and slipped them into his vest pocket. A few moments later, outside the rehearsal room door, Toscanini raised his hands in prayer and then swept like a god into the homes of millions of music lovers. He stayed in New York 17 years.

The second example is about a society dropout who came under the care of Covenant House in Toronto. This young girl, a runaway from home, is one of 41,000 young people being helped by Covenant House across North America. Recently, the director sent a request for money. In her letter she spoke of the above-mentioned girl whom we'll call Alice.

Among other points, she mentioned that Alice carries on her person a small piece of cloth. The director said that one day she asked Alice what significance the cloth held. She replied, "When I am really alone and sad and don't know what to do, I rest my head on this cloth. Before I left home I cut it from the blanket that I used to cry on after my father had abused me."

A SUGGESTION

Madame Lilian Stiles-Allen, long time singing instructress of Julie Andrews, once gave Julie sound advice about overcoming setbacks: "Pray about it, and forget it."

In a similar vein when Julie was asked what we should look for in life, she answered, "We should look for miracles, for they are always there. We must become aware of them and appreciate them."

Understanding Mercy

A certain priest asked God to teach him the true meaning of mercy. Several months went by and the priest was none the wiser.

One morning he chanced to officiate at a funeral Mass in an out-of-town church. As he was distributing Communion, an older gentleman stepped up to within earshot of the priest and whispered, "I have not attended church in years. I have not been to confession since I was a lad. But I am truly sorry for my many sins. Father, may I be forgiven and receive Communion?"

The priest's mind raced. "What should I do? Perhaps bring him into the vestry later and straighten it all out there. The people are watching. I must act responsibly. There are rules to follow. What would Jesus do?"

Suddenly, the priest was overwhelmed with God's mercy. He blessed the man and said, "Your sins are forgiven! And then added as he placed Jesus on the man's tongue, "Receive the Body of Christ."

The man thanked the priest and walked away. The priest said he cried throughout the rest of the service and most of the day. He had received God's answer.

Mercy is a matter of the heart. Just like forgiveness. Just like repentance. Mercy captures the moment. It can strike anytime if the circumstances are right. We must not wait to repent. God doesn't wait to forgive.

Easy Does It, Sometimes

Once we realized our Border Collie, Clancy, had the genetic trait of trying too hard, we never challenged him unduly. His was a fearless nature — personal safety never entered his mind. He'd run too far and too long. He'd jump too high, swim out too far, and create a sandstorm digging for a groundhog. He had too much heart. We actually had to protect him from himself.

People can have Clancy's problem. We must be on the lookout for it in others and in ourselves.

Children in particular need guidance. Trying too hard can kill. Society doesn't help. Educators, entrepreneurs, the military, and parents have a way of *leaning* on trainees, children, students, salesmen, etc. They expect total dedication. Like overzealous sergeants and coaches they often coerce others to go beyond their capacities. They're playing the old "duty calls" — "it's a grand old flag" — "everybody pulls his weight" — songs. Make everybody dance through their hoops and they're happy.

Do we know of anyone who tries too hard for his own good? Has he created goals he may not or cannot reach? Is ambition ruining his life? Has a person reached his optimum stress level? Is someone on a treadmill and can't get off?

These people must be tagged. They need help and counselling. We must get them to slow down, look around and take time to think things through. Health is important — so is family — and God. We must stop their running — make them take a walk in the park, paddle a canoe, sit on a rock, buy a cone, take in a game, plant flowers, take a drive to nowhere — slip into church, lie down in a pasture, kick off their shoes, and throw away their cell phones.

We must save them from themselves.

So Long Maurice

The night the town priest went over to the local hospital to give 97-year-old Mary the last rites, a strange happening occurred. At the exact moment the priest uttered the final word of the formal prayers, Mary died. It was as if she had waited politely for the priest to finish. In his long life, the priest knew of only one other similar happening!

Elsewhere, in that small town, earlier on that same day, Mary's first cousin, Maurice, was standing alone in his kitchen when he saw a shadow behind him. He turned as sharply as a 92-year-old can and felt his heart bang into his ribcage. Whatever it was startled him.

A few minutes later, he again saw the shadow and again he turned and again his heart jumped. He knew then he was in a presence of some unknown power.

Next morning, Maurice heard about the death of Mary and realized Mary had come to say goodbye the previous day.

You see, Mary and Maurice were very close friends. In fact, Mary owed her life to Maurice. Back in 1920, Maurice had saved her from drowning. For years, Mary never forgot Maurice. She remembered him even on her last day on earth.

Irish

A gentleman friend I call Irish was reading at home one evening when he began thinking about a lady friend he hadn't seen for some time. So he called her up and chatted about anything and everything.

Blessed with a sympathetic intuitive nature and some knowledge of the human psyche, Irish has the ability to sort out human emotions in conflict.

Irish was talking with me about this phone call in order to emphasize how necessary it is for all of us to be cognizant of why some friends pop into our minds at unexpected moments. Apparently, just before she closed off that night, his lady friend said she felt much better. When Irish had called, she said that she was on her way to the bathroom to overdose on pills.

Uncle Joe's Gift

In the summer of 1944, my uncle Joe gave me a precious gift, a small cross. His sister, a cloistered Precious Blood nun, had in turn given it to him in 1930. She had received it when she made her profession. About two inches by one and a half, and made of solid bronze with ebony imbedded on its front, it contained relics of St. Theresa of Liseux who died in 1897.

For many years I loaned it to sick friends. The possibility of losing it never crossed my mind. It was always returned. I've had it now for 65 years. For my own protection, I wore it during the eight years I played organized hockey, whenever I was ill, and wherever I travelled.

In the spring of 1984, I was in Lourdes, France, on a pilgrimage to the shrine of God's mother where she had appeared to St. Bernadette in 1848. I had the cross in my pocket. It was a rainy Easter Sunday and I was standing outside the cave above which the Virgin had appeared. Inside the cave along the walls surrounding an altar was a group of Italian pilgrims holding a service. I spotted an empty chair.

Not long after, the person sitting beside me left and a young lady took the spot. She looked agitated; so I asked her how everything was going. She was a Pat Mallow from Ireland. She was in Lourdes for the weekend. She had come to the shrine to ask the Holy Mother to beseech St. Theresa to give her a sign about a business problem she was having back in Dublin. The beauty salon she owned was not doing well. The question was: should she sell it or give it another try?

She was frantic. So far at the shrine, Theresa had not answered her and she was going home the next day. I remember the moment so well: the tears, her elbows on her knees, and her face buried in her hands. Suddenly, I said, "Funny you should mention St. Theresa. I've been her friend for 40 years. Did you know St. Theresa's mother came to Lourdes with two other daughters — she had terminal cancer — it was 1873? By the way, I have this cross with me that contains first-class relics of St. Theresa."

And I showed her the cross.

She took the battered relic in her hand, looked at it and said the most amazing thing, "That's it. This is the sign I wanted. I will keep the company."

"Thank you," she said, and kissed me on the cheek.

Then Pat Mallow got up and walked out into the biting wind of Easter Sunday. She had her answer.

A Thanksgiving

Blessings are usually taken for granted until we are in danger of losing them.

Years and years ago, a Scotsman found himself lost in a Far East desert. He was saved but only after suffering without water to the point of death.

On his return to his home in Aberdeen, Scotland, his appreciation of water's importance led him to erect a drinking fountain in a park for public use. On it he placed the following inscription:

> "Water murmurs, water plays,
>   Water speaks, hear what it says:
> 'I came from heaven, through earth I spring,
>   To man the sweetest draught to bring;
> Partake, each traveller, ere ye go
>   And give Him thanks who makes it flow.'"

On His Mind

My retired friend, Gerry, told this intriguing tale. One afternoon, during a siesta, he began thinking of a lady with whom he had once worked. Why she came to mind was a mystery since he hadn't heard from her for years.

Thoughts of her persisted so much that he looked up her address in the phone book and drove over to the seniors' residence where she lived.

Persistent knocking on her door brought no answer; so he entered. There she was lying in a heap on the floor. She whispered that she had fallen two hours earlier and had been praying for help.

The ambulance arrived. His 80-year-old friend had broken her hip.

After two operations, she lives on, thanks to Gerry and the angelic messenger who came calling one sleepy afternoon.

THE OBLIGING CLERK

Many years ago a man walked into a tractor dealer and asked for the price on a gasoline engine. The clerk who happened to be my cousin said, "They're fifty-five dollars."

The man said: "Why I can get one down at D's for forty-five dollars."

My cousin said, "I'm sorry, Sir; since I'm not the owner, it's the best I can do." The man left.

Two hours later he was back.

"Any change on that price for the engine?"

"No. I guess it's final. By the way, I thought you went to get one at D's for forty-five dollars."

"I did," he countered. But they don't have any."

"Ah, ha," said my cousin. "We sell the ones we don't have for thirty dollars."

One Child's Wisdom

Little children have a way of understanding great truths.

Recently, in the City of Oakville, Ontario, I attended a unique wake. In mid-afternoon, a group of relatives and friends formed a circle in the funeral parlour to pay tribute to a fine young man named Eric, whose death had shaken them.

Along with the prayers, several speakers paid homage to his memory. One friend told this story: "At home last night, my wife and I were talking about Eric. My grief was very evident to my seven-year-old son. He said, 'Why are you crying, Daddy?' I told him I missed my friend who had gone to heaven and he said, 'You shouldn't cry. Even though he is not here, isn't friendship forever?'"

THE SIGNAL

God sends each of us our unique beam to follow home. He is the master controller of all our worldly travelling. We need only fix our bearings on His signal, and we shall arrive safe and sound.

The Shout

One slippery winter night, my wife went out to collect for the arthritis fund. About 20 minutes after she left, I heard a shout — one word of alarm it was — and I thought she had fallen on the ice. I looked out but no one was there.

I was about to get into the car to search for her when she returned. She said she had had a bad fall about half a mile away just 20 minutes after she left. "Did you shout?" I asked. "Oh, yes!" she replied.

The Meeting

I have always regretted that my father and my wife never met. I am so proud of both.

One day I mentioned this fact to my wife. She said, "Yes, I have longed many times to have known him. I attended his wake, you remember, and admired how young and handsome he was. But I must tell you about my dream.

"One night, shortly after our marriage, I dreamed of your father. I came upon him working in a garden. And I said, 'I know you. You're my husband's father. I have always wanted to meet you.'

"And your father said, 'And I, you! Aren't we lucky? We'll never have to feel that way again. Haven't we met just now?'"

Emily

Recently my wife and I took some holidays in the Lakehead city of Thunder Bay, Ontario. As a century-old rail and shipping hub for wheat, lumber and minerals, Thunder Bay remains a cosmopolitan, neighbourly, blue-collar city. It doesn't take long to relate to its colourful, hardworking people. It's that kind of town.

At lunch one day in a small local eatery, I spoke to a young lady cleaning the floor around the tables. "You look a little tired," I said.

"Is it that noticeable?" she answered. "Well, actually I am. I have three jobs: I drive a school bus, I work here and I am a single mother of three boys."

My wife and I chatted with her until she moved on across the room.

Later, as we left the restaurant, I heard a voice call out, "Oh, Mister," and I turned at the door to see the same lady coming over.

"Mister, I've been thinking about our meeting here today. Was it just a coincidence do you think?"

"No, I don't think so."

"You see, this is my last day on this job. I have to cut back. The three children are becoming more of a handful. My husband and I separated after ten years of marriage. He provides no support. My mother has cancer and my father is too busy running around with his pals to notice any of us. I wonder if I'm going to make it."

Earlier, back at the table, my wife and I had encouraged her. It was up to me now to say something positive. I looked into the soft eyes of that tall, strong, sallow-faced child and spoke words beyond my scope:

"Emily, I can assure you with the utmost confidence that you are doing a good job, that you will continue to do so, and that you are not to worry about the future. God will look after you and your boys. Always remember that." I held her hand. And we parted in tears.

The Three Visions

An old French parable from Québec tells of a certain farmer who tried to raise his three sons in accordance with Christian values.

Unfortunately, after two sons died in their teens, the farmer stopped going to church. It doesn't pay to be good, he thought.

One day when the farmer was going through the bush with a wagon and team, a stranger stood in his path and motioned to the farmer to follow him deeper into the woods.

At a select spot, the stranger showed the farmer three visions: one was a man hanging from a gallows, the second a man in an insane asylum, the third a priest standing in a pulpit.

The stranger explained the visions to the mystified man in this way: "Monsieur, you have no reasons to fly in the face of God for the loss of your sons.

"The first vision is of your oldest son; if he had lived, he would have been a thief and would have been hanged. He is in heaven.

"The other dead son is also in heaven — the second vision shows he would have ended up in an insane asylum; God spared you and your son much suffering.

"The third vision is of your youngest who will one day be a priest. He will be a great comfort to you and bring many souls to heaven."

And the farmer went away, subdued and reconciled.

Marcel

In 1922, the Dominican Order in Montreal was in dire straits. Unless their monastery of Notre-Dame-de-Grace received more seminarians, it would be "history."

As a last resort, it was decided to have a Rosary Crusade. Benefactors and friends joined the priests and brothers of the Order in asking the Mother of God to ask her Son to send vocations. In the first year, ten postulants arrived and, over the next ten years, 151 joined the Order.

Seventy years later, in 1992, a similar crisis hit the monastery. Research showed the Order would die by 2030 if new recruits did not come. It was then that Father Marcel-Marie Desmarais decided another Rosary Crusade was needed. He remembered the success in 1922-32 and how the Virgin had interceded. In spite of his 86 years, he started a rosary campaign. It also worked.

In only six months, four million rosaries were pledged and it wasn't long before the prayers were answered: eight men came forward and the number has continued to increase. Hope of saving the Order has been rekindled.

AN IRISH TIP

Three folds in my garment
    Yet only one garment I bear
Three joints in a finger
    Yet only one finger is there
Three leaves in a shamrock
    Yet only one shamrock I wear
Frost, ice and snow
    Yet all three are nothing but water
Three persons in God
    Yet only one God is there.

— Anonymous

In the Bread Section

In the grocery store late one afternoon, my heart suddenly opened to the burdens of those around me. And it came to me how prone I was to be critical of others.

For a few minutes in the bread section, I deeply sensed people's problems. I looked beyond their masks and saw them as players doing their best to get by in the game of life.

All those around me had their own personal cares and trials. They deserve my understanding. I must not think ill of them. They need consideration and cheer. I must be on the look out for ways to love them.

No Card

Have you ever stewed over a problem to the point of capitulation and then suddenly in an almost miraculous way find you have reached a solution?

The author, C.S. Lewis, experienced such an incredulous happening. Up to age 35 he wrestled with the divinity of Jesus. Until one day his brother took him to the zoo.

Lewis says, "When we set out in the car, I did not believe that Jesus Christ was the Son of God, but by the time we reached the zoo, I did. On the way I had not exactly spent the journey in any deep thought or feeling.

A friend had a similar experience. For months he agonized over whether or not he should quit his job for a career in the church. The problem got bigger and bigger.

One afternoon he went walking in a large country estate. He saw the trees and trails as a settling influence.

Now the estate had two gateways about a 15-minute walk apart. As he entered in one gate, he was as befuddled as ever over his dilemma. But during his stroll among the gardens, he grew less agitated. In fact, he seemed not to care one way or the other.

One can imagine his surprise when, by the time he went out the second gate, he discovered he had made up his mind to enter into religious life. He said he had no doubts about his decision. And he had no explanation. He heard no voice, saw no light. The decision was there. From nowhere. Just like that.

What triggers such an adjustment? What power bends the will so effortlessly and positively?

It's like a gift. Without any card from the sender.

Mystery in the Orchard

A few years ago, a strange happening as told by a friend, Father Ockwood, took place in Providence, Rhode Island.

Three children stealing apples in an orchard were interrupted by the figure of an ugly woman dressed in a gold-trimmed blue gown. She smiled in friendship and told them she was very powerful and could do whatever they asked. The children's story spread so wildly among the people that the archbishop of the diocese appointed a priest to investigate. Some people might think the lady was the Virgin Mary.

The priest chosen to do the detective work was a member of a missionary order whose monastery was only 18 miles from Providence. Now it happened that this same priest was giving a mission in the parish church where the three children resided; so he took the occasion to see what he could learn about the strange lady.

His examination didn't take long. He decided that the whole encounter was a hoax. These were his reasons: if the lady was from heaven, she should have been beautiful — according to the children, this woman was not; a lady from heaven would not have bragged about being so powerful; and a lady from heaven would not have appeared to children who were stealing.

The priest wrote out his report for the archbishop and mailed it.

That evening, the night before the conclusion of the mission, the priest decided to go home to his monastery and return in the morning. The winter night was pleasant, the moon full and the open highway before him. He was pleased; the mission was going well and his report sent off.

Not far out of town, his composure came to an abrupt end. His car suddenly headed for the ditch. Only by his wrenching the steering wheel, did the car straighten up. Not long after, the car lurched again. A third occurrence put the car in a snow bank. Beyond the bank was a cliff.

The priest, unhurt, walked to a nearby farmhouse. He phoned a mechanic who drove him home and towed the car to the garage.

As it turned out, the mechanic found the car to be in perfect condition. The car's behaviour was not due to any mechanical flaw.

The priest decided the devil was taking revenge on him. He had called the devil's work a hoax. The devil was furious that the archbishop, after reading the priest's findings, would send a letter to the diocese denouncing the appearance of the lady as being a fantasy. The devil was trying to kill the priest.

The priest now knew that his first report had not been entirely accurate. The visitor in the garden was the devil. Three factors enforced his belief: the devil is *not* beautiful, the devil *would* brag, and the devil *would* try to kill the priest.

Dennis

Jack Benny was at a loss to know which male singer to hire for his radio show since all the contestants at the audition were equally good. After some deliberation, he said to his wife, "Mary, you may think this strange, but I'm going to give the job to the Irish boy, Dennis Day. And do you know why? Because he's the only one who thanked me after his audition."

For decades, both on radio and television, listeners had the pleasure of hearing Dennis say after Benny's introduction to a song, "Thanks, Mr. Benny." And why not? It got him his job.

God's Chatterbox

Many people have shrines in their homes. They vary from a chapel to a single religious object on a wall.

A friend recently showed me an upper room in her house which she has set aside for prayer and meditation. A prie-dieu faces a small cross on an altar. Fresh field flowers colour the room. Around the walls are pictures of her family, friends, and favourite saints.

She has had her share of troubles — health, family and money — but she has survived — still naively wise, intuitively smart, and innocently mature.

I asked her the other day how long she prays in the upper room. And she elaborated: "I go there several times a day to pray. When I am not there, I am either talking to people or God — one or the other."

SCOTTISH ADVICE

A smooth sea never makes a skilful mariner; neither will a smooth and easy life lead to anything higher.
— William Johnson, Scotland, 1895

It All Depends

As I wrote earlier, a few years ago I had a serious operation. Since I was to be awake during the process, I hung a small wooden rosary on my right wrist to give me comfort.

After the operation, in the recovery centre, I was attended by a motherly nurse. Suddenly, when she spotted my rosary she rolled her eyes and twittered, "Now, you're making me nervous."

The Candle

A married couple was driving home from their cottage one Sunday afternoon. As they approached a small town, the wife said she would like to stop to light a candle in the town church. She did and stayed a while to pray.

Later that evening at home, they heard that their son had died that very afternoon. Upon investigation they learned he crashed his car at approximately the moment his mother lit the candle. As one light was snuffed out, another was lit. Perhaps her prayer opened his way to heaven.

A SIMPLE PRAYER

My mother's prayer was simple. Tucked inside her prayer book I found the words, "Jesus, someone who loves, You needs You."

The Dime

Some people give, some take. Those that have, often don't help — those that have nothing, give what they can.

Some are spenders, but only on themselves; others spend on charity.

Some fight for a nickel and give away a dollar; others scramble for the dollar and keep the nickel.

Some feel good by giving money to the needy — others need the security derived from saving.

An American navy veteran I met once in Bermuda told me he worked as a kid back in the 1930s at Yankee Stadium showing celebrities to their box seats. One Broadway star, known as "a top banana" of the *Lighted Way,* impressed my friend as a first-class cheapo. He always gave the same tip: one thin dime

As a result, nobody wanted to be bothered escorting the skinflint, and the word went out from Ruth's House across the naked city that the comedian was not such a great guy after all.

The widow in the Bible gave a mite — this millionaire, a dime.

BREAKING THE NEWS

McGraw phoned his younger brother in America.

"I've got some bad news for ya. Your cat is dead."

"No! No! That's awful," said the brother. "It is a terrible shock. Don't ye think you could'a been more careful how ya broke the news? Kinda easy like, in stages ... for example, you might have begun by saying, 'Your cat is on the roof and we're trying to get her down as best we can.' Then the next time I call, you could say, 'Your cat is at the vet — we're hoping for good news.' And then, finally on the next call, 'We did our best, the poor wee thing, but, but, she's gone.' You see what I mean, gently, Lad, gently, in stages. It makes bad news so much easier to bear. Do ya understand?"

"Of course I do. I'm sorry," answered the brother.

"Forget it," said McGraw. "It's over. By the way, how's mother?"

"Well, said the brother, "I regret to say that mother is up on the roof."

Attilio de Milan

While driving alone on a country road, my car was hit a resounding blow on its right rear side. I thought immediately of a deer or a flock of birds or perhaps a broken axle. I pulled over onto the apron and discovered that no damage had been inflicted. Behind me the empty road ran through the middle of green pastures. Next day, auto mechanics found nothing untoward

The cause of the hit has remained a mystery. One friend suggested a mini-tornado. And another caught my full attention with the words, "Sounds to me like some spirit is trying to get in touch with you."

Strangely enough, after the incident, I did immediately think of my sick friend, Father Attilio Klinger. Three weeks earlier I had spoken to him by phone as he lay recuperating in a New York City hospital. His operation for cancer was over. In a soft voice, he whispered, "Gary, my pain is gone. Thank God, no more pain. I am weak. I can do nothing for myself. But God's Will be done. He is in control. I follow. The room is dark. I am alone. Remember me as I you. I must go now. Smile! Goodbye, Gary, my friend." Content that Attilio was in no immediate danger, I decided not to bother him for a while. I would call back later when he was better.

I first met Attilio in the Bahamas in 1972. He had come there from Japan where as a missionary priest of the Salesians of Don Bosco, he had taught school for 20 years. In 1971, his Superiors sent him to the Bahamas to work with the Haitians and simultaneously regain his health which had proven unsuited to the Japanese climate. For the next 20 years, he was a true friend of the Blacks — in Nassau, Eight-Mile Rock, Bimini and Grand Bahama Island. Later from 1991 to 2002 he worked with the Spanish immigrants in Florida.

I wish I could find the words to describe this man's fineness. His humility of spirit was admirable. He owned nothing and desired nothing. An innocent reference to his holiness was met with rebuke.

He believed a person's goodness was known only to God. He would say, "Gary, only God knows who is good. Do not concern yourself with such matters. Reading hearts can be risky." As I write this tribute, I can hear him saying as he waves his finger, "Tut, tut, tut, what did I tell you?"

On the surface, Attilio was a very "ordinary man." He had no great charisma, no oratorical gifts. He was just a sweet, unassuming, genius who walked with the poor. He hid his attributes well.

He had grace and bearing. He was a gentleman of exquisite refinement, a student of literature, music and paintings, a linguist who spoke Spanish, Japanese, German, French, English, Latin and Italian. He had the *noblesse oblige* of his Italian mother and the wanderlust-courage of his German father, a corvette captain in the Italian navy.

This was a scholar who read avidly, wrote professionally, and phrased his thoughts like lyrics. This was a priest who never compromised his ideals, breeding or faith. This was a Samaritan who saw the good side in all, especially the uneducated, deprived, poor and unwashed.

Not all Attilio's humility of spirit came naturally. More than a little was forged by the trials in his life. Karsh, the world-famous photographer, put this trauma of spiritual development in another way. Using the analogy of the darkroom, he said that any person's improvement of character usually took place in times of darkness.

Attilio had his share of fire and darkness. Crushed by his mother's death when he was seven and orphaned not long after, he lived in the economic failure of the Mussolini era. He learned to go it alone.

Pain caused much of Attilio's chronic depression. He was intolerant of extreme heat and cold. He had allergies, malaria, back and stomach problems. He had operations on his heart, stomach, appendix, gall bladder and prostate.

He paced himself constantly. Energy was at a minimum. He'd rest all day just to be able to say Mass. He learned patience. He took his prescribed exercise and rest. He meditated and mused. He used tricks known only to himself to survive the long nights.

Yet, except for his last few years, Attilio's actions were not that of a sick person. He kept on the job, visiting schools and homes across his diocese. He was a master at begging — yet seldom asked for anything. He used the money that poured in from friends and tourists to clothe children, buy medicine, support educational bursaries, improve shacks and put food on the table.

Attilio had a big mailing list. Once a year he'd send newsletters with pictures to Japan, the United States, Canada, Italy — wherever people would remember him. The pictures he sent showed where the money had gone. As if to say, "Look at this. You're responsible for this house, this paved cement playground and this old jeep we use to get supplies."

One special enjoyment Attilio had, was to send to his friends those special pictures taken of himself with his children. How proudly he stood among them, the girls with their bright ribbons, skirts and bows, the boys with their coloured sweaters and new shoes — everyone neat and tidy and whistle-clean! The children eased his pain.

Although Attilio could be irritable and snappy under duress, (he admitted that he never could control his temper), he seldom turned on his parishioners. He had a Nelson eye towards their indifference. His patience was exemplary. Some of his morning Masses had no one in attendance. Often the very families he had once helped, snubbed him. But he didn't seem overly disturbed. He never became discouraged. He kept to his rounds with a smile.

How could there not be joy in the heart of a man who spent his life filling the minds and bodies of black, yellow and brown youths with moon-beams, sugar plums and lollipops?

The ending of this tribute is difficult to write. The very night of my car being pounded I called the Salesian Order's main house on Long Island, New York. "Do you not know Attilio died three weeks ago?" someone said.

Was it he who caused the blow to my car? I'll never know. However, a day or so later I was getting out of an elevator on the ground floor of a senior citizen's home, when a vase and its three fresh flowers went flying on their own across the receptionist's desk. "We're not alone," she said. And just yesterday as I wrote this story and was thinking of how Attilio may well have been contacting me that day in the car, a heavy calendar in my nearby kitchen broke from its nail and struck the floor.

The last time I saw Attilio at my home he pointed heavenward and said, "Until we meet again." So be it.

Personally, I have never met a man who suffered so much, gave up so much and loved so much as Attilio Gaetano Klinger. Caruso, Marconi, Lombardo,

DiMaggio, St. Francis were all great Italians, yet none more fine than Attilio de Milan, my friend.

Father Attilio told his Superior during his last hospitalization that he would not pray for a recovery — he would offer his death for the good of the Salesian Missions. He told his Superior that he had only one request of God — he wanted to die on the anniversary of his mother's death — May 3. And he did.

In God's Hands

John Corkery, a gentlemen farmer, recently helped save the life of a newly-dropped lamb. What happened was this. A nearby neighbour, his son Michael, had a ewe that gave birth to twins. As sometimes occurs, the ewe assumed no responsibility for the lamb born second. She refused to feed it and along with the other sheep began bunting it into eternity. John brought the orphaned lamb in beside his country stove and fed him by bottle.

Now Michael's two children, a boy and girl, concerned about the lamb, decided they'd like to sleep over at Gramp's. Before going to bed that night, they felt the lamb would benefit from a bedtime story. Seated on pillows by the fire, they took turns reading to the lamb from a book.

The girl began, "Once upon time, a rabbit lost its way in the forest. Soon he was cold and lonely."

"But not for long," continued the boy. "Along came a nice farmer, who picked him up, wrapped him in a big red scarf and brought him to his home."

The girl went on, "The man who brought the rabbit home was a grandpa. He made the rabbit all better and returned him to his parents."

Just then Grandpa said, "Time for bed, kids," as he reached for their storybook.

The book was upside down. The little boy was four and the girl was two.

The Little Saint of Montreal

The beautiful lines from a popular hymn, "He walks with me and He talks with me," indicate how close God can be to some people. One person who enjoyed such a privilege was Alfred Bessette, otherwise known as Brother André, the Wonder Man of Québec.

Alfred was the sixth child of 12 children born to poor parents in a community outside the city of Montreal. He had no education, bad health and few opportunities. Yet, by the time he was 60 in 1905, he was one of the most revered citizens of his day.

Sitting in a shanty-style shelter on the north-west side of Mount Royal in Montreal, this religious brother of the Holy Cross Order welcomed thousands who came there seeking the help of St. Joseph. My mother, aunts and uncles were among them. Every year I meet people who tell me about their ancestors' visits to this good man.

Not long ago an 80-year-old lady told me about her father's visit to Brother André in 1911. The father had an enlarged heart that pushed noticeably out in his chest. Brother André cured him. Years later, this father, McManus by name, by then the father of nine, returned to thank him. When Brother André saw him, he remembered, "I am happy to see you again, the man with the enlarged heart."

Two summers ago, while praying in the crypt under the great oratory built in honour of St. Joseph, I met a local man who spoke of Brother André in glowing terms. I asked him if he came there often and he replied, "Every working day at lunch. The little man is helping me." The truth of this statement shone in his eyes.

Recently on the Internet, I read about a lady who suffered depression and anger over her experiences as an abused child. She had prayed to Brother André. She wrote, "I began to feel the presence of Brother André; I could hear him speaking to me with most reassuring kind words. 'Calm down' and 'be at peace,' he said. And I did."

The story of another friend concerned her mother's sister who once took her sick baby to Brother André. Brother André held the baby, prayed and said, "There's nothing St. Joseph can do. Take this child home and give it all the love it deserves."

So how did it come about that such a scrawny kid born on the wrong side of the country roads became a miracle worker? Who, among his relatives and friend, would ever have thought it possible?

Orphaned at 12 and a foster-child for 16 years, he failed at just about every career he tried: farmhand, cobbler, blacksmith, carriage maker, caretaker, baker, church custodian and factory hand. For 13 years, he wandered from pillar to post in search of a livelihood. Up and down the Eastern Atlantic Coast he went. His lot in life seemed to be that of an itinerant labourer. Eventually, he says, by the grace of God and St. Joseph's guidance, he entered the Novitiate of the Holy Cross Order in 1870. He stayed 67 years and turned the Order on its ear.

André would be the first to say that finding his place in that Order was the will of God. His devotion to St. Joseph started early in life back at his country church. Friends often found him there in prayer before St. Joseph's statue. André had the example of his father, mother and parish priest who all had great confidence in St. Joseph.

As the years went by, André's relationship with St. Joseph deepened. In the name of God, through St. Joseph, André cured souls and bodies, read hearts and saw the future.

André's entry into the religious life was not easy. Some members of the Order (the same group that runs Notre Dame University in South Bend, Indiana) did not think he measured up. They saw a small wispy delicate man with not enough energy to do even the smallest tasks around the college. True, they had heard that André's parish priest had sent a letter with André saying to the superior, "I am sending you a Saint." But, in a practical world, his contemporaries felt, "What is a holy man's worth if he can't earn his supper?"

André's two years as a novice only strengthened suspicions that he couldn't pull his weight. He struggled with his assignments and his health got in the way.

If it wasn't for the Archbishop of Montreal, André's immediate superior, he might have gone back on the road. The Archbishop told André's Order in so many words, "Let praying be his vocation. That's good enough for me."

The Holy Cross Order had come to Québec in 1847 from France. It bought an old hotel across from Mount Royal in Montreal and erected a religious house and a private boys' school. A few years later, it built a sturdier complex that still stands.

In some ways, André's entrance into the religious life at this monastery was going from the pan into the fire. He suffered as before, but in a different way. In those days, religious orders were austere and the brothers were low on the ecclesiastical totem pole. The priests had no time for domestic chores. They had their teaching load, class preparation, marking, group prayers and supervision. The priests' servants were the brothers. The priests knew it and so did the brothers.

André festered under the bullying of confrères. Condescending, snide remarks raised his ire. He could not tolerate being merely tolerated. No doubt he cried out to St. Joseph to save him from those "who must be obeyed."

————

With the passing years, however, André was given more respect. He was not the wimp they had thought. As porter, a job he held for 40 years, he rang the wake-up bell for the school at 5:00 a.m. From then on, until 7:30 p.m. with the exception of forced rest periods, he was at everyone's beck and call. All visitors — cleric, delivery boy, doctor, and parent — had to pass through his little office.

He also had many chores to do. André's buddies watched in wonder as he washed parlour floors, cleaned windows, ran errands, cut grass, made communion hosts, and picked up and delivered laundry. They seldom "saw him sweat," but they came to know about his gastric attacks, weak turns and arthritic troubles. At 7:30 p.m., they'd see him retire to the chapel to fall asleep at God's feet.

Another factor kept André going. He had had a dream of building a shrine to St. Joseph across the road on the Mount. He had that vision from the day he arrived at the college. In the early days he put a small statue of St. Joseph in his office window so that the statue faced the mountain. That dream would become a reality.

Gradually, in the years from 1904 to 1922, André's religious life changed. He was allowed to spend more time on the mountain. More people came to see him. He became a guru. His fame spread to hearths and hearts. He eventually would have to live on the Mount to accommodate his many visitors.

The Order soon bought the property on the Mount as a real estate investment. Shortly after, André built a trail up the slopes where the Order set up, at André's request, a small open-air shanty. Along the way, André put a small statue and a dish in a niche, and called the path, *Le Boulevard de St. Joseph.*

Before 1905, the people had had difficulty seeing him. He would meet them in his office, in the school gym, on the lawn outside the college or in the pavilion across the street built by the Montreal Transportation Company to handle the pilgrims. The miracles of André, once confined to schoolboys and contemporaries, eventually reached into the city. So many people came that André was released from his household duties.

In 1905, the Order also built him a small wooden chapel (18´ by 15´) on a flank of the mountain. In 1909, a pavilion was added. In 1910, a restaurant, a restroom for the pilgrims, and a small office for André were constructed. The chapel had its sacristy extended; André got a live-in cell, a bell and a steeple. In 1915, a substantial crypt of some beauty was built across the centre of the Mount — with landscaped terraces, flowers, grass and trees. In 1924, the Order laid the cornerstone for the new Oratory.

Back around 1904, a lady living near the school, was quoted in the newspaper as saying, "I wonder how the old fool on the mountain is tonight." At that time, she had every reason to consider André nothing but a dreamer. She felt the man was old, and no doubt practising hocus-pocus in all weather on the top of a natural eyesore. She was at least right about the area. The place was nothing but a wild forest of oaks, birches, maples, fruit trees and pines.

But André was not an ordinary man. Today, what was once wasteland is a magnificent tribute to the ingenuity of the divine and human, a rendezvous of heaven and earth. The Oratory is a Mecca of healing. Three hundred feet above Côte-des-Neiges, it reaches out to the suffering. Another Montemarte of Paris, they say. Architecturally, its lines are open and simple, as unpretentious as its founder. It has a lightness inside and out. It is a sacred place built by the pennies and prayers of people from all walks of life and religions. The same peace as in André's little chapel pervades the place.

Upon his death, January 6, 1937, the edifice was unfinished. In 2005 it still is. No matter. No amount of further embellishment can add to the joy already there.

St. John quoted Jesus as promising He and His Father would come and make their abode with those that love them. André fits into this mould.

André truly lived with God. He never prayed alone, slept alone or ate alone. Jesus was there.

My favourite picture shows André standing outside his wooden chapel in 1907. His worn cassock shines. His white collar hangs loosely. Snips of unkempt white hair lie over his high forehead, his face is lined, his eyes hollow. A faint smile sweetens his lips. He hasn't got a dime. He owns nothing. He never made any promises. He has no army. Not even a gimmick. Nothing up his sleeve. What you see is what you see: a simple, dedicated soul who never held back anything from God. Soon, as the evening mists cover the mount, André will turn and slip into his cell.

Needs

Most living things have a built-in purpose for existence, the satisfaction of which brings them fulfillment. The bird has to fly and the fish has to swim.

But, what about the soul? It comes from God; it seeks to return. So what are its needs?

Brother André, the great healer from Montreal was a religious for 6 decades. In his old age, someone told him he should get more sleep and should not pray for so long. The Brother answered, "If you only knew the need that a soul has for prayer, you wouldn't say that."

Souls need to pray. They belong to God. When our soul feels satisfied, so do we.

John's Gift

One afternoon in March of 2001, a lone figure knelt beside a small white gravestone somewhere in Germany. A middle-aged lady had come from Canada to pay her respects to a man whom she never knew; yet whose death had been instrumental in her being alive.

In 1945, two months before the European war ended, John Casey, R.A.F., was shot down in his bomber. Back at home base, his best friend, Pat, the mechanic for John's plane, waited in vain. All Pat had left in remembrance was John's motorcycle and a few pictures and letters from back home.

I knew John and his father. The Caseys came from an Irish settlement called Corkery, Ontario, a place dear to my heart. I had been playing ball near John's house in Ottawa the day word came of his death.

It happened that Pat and John were from the same city and when Pat got home, he had little difficulty finding John's next of kin. But, tracking down John's girl, Connie, was another matter. No one could help him locate her.

As if by a miracle, one day Pat walked into a bank in another part of his city. As he talked with the teller, she said, "I know you. I've seen your picture. You're John Casey's friend. I was John's girl, Connie. And I *still* am."

The outcome was that Pat and Connie married and had a large family, one of whom was their daughter, Maureen, the same lady in Germany that afternoon in March, 2001. She felt that she just had to pay respects to the man who had been responsible for her being the daughter of Pat and Connie.

John had been a victim of war, but was also the cupid who brought together his friend, Pat and his girl, Connie, *John's last gift to Pat.*

Mrs. Andrietti

"Mister Mellor, my son says you are constantly picking on him. He should be enjoying your physical education classes, but he can't because you won't stop hounding him."

The occasion was the first parent-teacher meeting for the Grade 9 students and Mrs. Andrietti had come out swinging.

When she stopped for a breath, Mr. Mellor, the Director of the Department, tried to make some points: "Mrs. Andrietti, your son is a fine boy, but he makes up his own rules and expects me to play by them. His antics upset the other boys. Nothing serious, mind you, but all in all, rather unnerving."

"But he says other boys do the same as he does and you say nothing. Why is that?"

"Mrs. Andrietti, I will get to the others in due time. I'll straighten them up too. Right now, I am working on *your* son. You must remember it takes my time and energy to discipline your son. I could ignore him or give him detentions. But would he improve? Would he knuckle down to discipline later on in life?

"I *could* concentrate on the other boys and let your son drift. Which is easier for me: let him go or mould him? I choose to better his disposition and behaviour. I choose to give my time, my concern, my advice, my wisdom, my love. Isn't that what you really want for your child?"

"Mr. Mellor, you do what you have to! If he says one more word at home about your class, I'll show *him*. The spaghetti will fly!"

Brothers

In the beginning, Father Flanagan's Boys' Town in Nebraska, where Babe Ruth once lived as an orphan, was just an old run-down tourist home. One night a desperate mother asked the priest in charge to find room for her son. After the mother had gone, it was discovered the boy was a cripple. One of the boys offered to carry him to the dormitory. To Father Flanagan's suggestion that the boy was too heavy, the Good Samaritan said, "He ain't heavy, Father. He's my brother."

If the tourist visits Boys' Town today, outside the entrance he will see a large sculptured figure of a boy carrying a crippled friend on his back, and beneath it the caption, "He ain't heavy, Father. He's my brother."

On one pillar of Hercules, Gibraltar, the Barbary monkeys flaunt their heritage. If they could only talk, what tales they would tell!

Clancy's attentiveness at dog school did little to control his incorrigible nature. The open wildness of the Yorkshire dales always shone in his eyes.

The brisk freshness of the North Sea air from Nairn to Fraserburgh draws young and old Caledonians to the dunes and playing fields of Northern Scotland.

The star of the Hebridean Islands is Iona, home to Columba and his monks. Colomba based his ministry on the Holy Spirit and His grace.

The stark ruins of St. Andrew's Cathedral remain a beacon for travellers of sea and air. Many present-day buildings in St. Andrews were constructed from its stones. The first bishopric of Scotland was founded at St. Andrews.

A Roman beggar plies her trade at the entrance of the Church of Saint Marie in the oldest section of Rome. On this spot stood the first church in the world dedicated to the Virgin Mary.

The cement bricks of Capitaline Hill, Rome, come tumbling down.

The older sections of European cities tend to have the narrowest streets. These areas, such as the one shown in old Rome, seldom feel the sun's warmth. They are true cities of light and shadow.

Bill

Mickey Rooney once made a great movie about a mentally handicapped adult named Bill.

Bill was living at the time of the movie's shooting; so Rooney had opportunities to meet and study his character.

What Rooney mirrored was a gentle, innocent gentleman who accepted people as they were. Bill didn't worry about his popularity, he never tried to make an impression, he avoided confrontation, he spoke well of others.

Bill was a good listener. He never corrected. He never let his views get in the way of what others were saying.

But what I found most impressive about Bill was his friendly, easy manner of reacting to someone's advice. His friend Charlie who acted as his guardian was constantly giving Bill direction. You'd think such harping would bother Bill, but it didn't. Bill's response was always the same, "Charlie, I understand you perfectly."

Those words are magical. I feel good every time I hear them. How many people *never* hear them and never *utter* them. Just to know that someone agrees with us on some point or issue or topic is absolutely wonderful. To hear such expressions as, "I agree," "Why didn't I think of that?" "I like the way you think," "That says it all!" "Right on, let's get a copy made of that."

The use of such a technique in conversation with our parents, our children, our clients, our subordinates, and others, is truly a form of genuine politeness.

Bill, I understood you perfectly. And thanks!

Animal Sense

On Thursday, May 28, in the year 1914, as the luxury liner, *The Empress of Ireland*, prepared to embark from Québec City, an insignificant but strange event occurred.

Having been a working member of the crew for two years, a yellow tabby, aware that the ship's blasts meant imminent departure, decided to retire.

She timed her desertion perfectly. She bounded down the rising gangplank to freedom. Unfortunately for her, a deck-hand noticed her departure. The gangplank was lowered again and the cat retrieved.

But the feline was persistent. She bolted again and disappeared into the shipping sheds.

Soon the anchoring ropes were pulled in and the tugs nosed the 14,000-ton pride of the CPR around to face the St. Lawrence River. Sitting in the front of the crowd on the shore, the triumphant cat stared its farewell. The time was 4:27 p.m. The weather was grand and Liverpool just six days away.

Nine hours and forty-two minutes later, 205 miles down river, the liner sank in 150 feet of water. A Danish freighter had cut her open in thick fog at 1:55 a.m. Fourteen minutes later she went down.

Of the 1,057 passengers, 840 died, the highest number of passengers, excluding crew, ever lost in a maritime disaster.

Did the cat know something that afternoon in Québec? Can animals experience presentiments of death? Can they sense death's presence?

We have all known of pets who have died just before or after the deaths of their owners. In the first scenario, they cannot accept the coming separation and in the second, they waste away in mourning.

Tradition has it that the moment Franklin Delano Roosevelt died in Warm Springs, Georgia, his dog took off through the screen mesh of the summer door into the fields.

Recently, a friend told me about the death of a young person. Throughout his illness, his dog ate and slept in his master's room. At the time of death, relatives, clergy and the dog were around the bed. At the moment of passing, the large dog let out a bone-chilling howl that said it all.

The Tugs

True compassion allows for no desks, no curtains, no masks, no double standards and no excuses. True compassion can't be bought.

I noticed a lady crying quietly in church one morning. On her way out, she stopped to talk with a friend. The lady rested her head on her friend's shoulder and sobbed. Soon the friend was crying too. They held each other.

Another example of pulling together in difficulty occurred at the funeral of an elderly friend of my mother. On the way out of the chapel, the coffin was delayed at the front door. Behind it stood a grieving son and his wife. He was very upset. Through their tears, they smiled at each other.

As the procession started to move again, the wife pulled her husband close with her left arm and he did the same to her with his right. She was saying to this husband of many years, "We're in this together."

And she tugged him again, this time harder. And they kept looking at each other. And then some more tugs. Finally she rested her head on his shoulder and they walked out together.

I felt honoured to witness such devotion.

Faith and Logic

Measurement experts tell us that intelligence quotients seldom change after age 16. However, a certain broadcaster was an exception. His reasoning ability increased with the years to the point that he could prove beyond a doubt the non-existence of God.

In his younger days, he had been a successful minister in the Christian Church. His golden voice, good looks and genuine honesty made him a popular Canadian religious leader.

In his senior years, however, he became an atheist and since then has done everything to persuade people to turn away from God.

Recently, in a television interview, the interviewer asked him, "You, Sir, are on record as claiming there is no God. How can you be sure?"

His answer ran like this: "I know there is no God because my reason tells me so. I am an intelligent man and a thinker. Over four decades, many listeners to my television and radio programmes attest to my reason as do the thousands who have made best sellers of my 12 books.

"Look about you, if you would learn the truth. The world is in chaos. Does it look like the work of a Supreme Being? Famines, wars, refugees, genocide, torture, floods and fires — no God who *is* a God would permit such disorder and suffering."

THERE'S A REASON

For every pain
    that we must bear,
For every burden,
    every care,
There's a reason.
For every grief
    that bows the head,
For every teardrop
    that is shed,
There's a reason.

For every hurt,
    every plight,
For every lonely,
    pain-racked night,
There's a reason.

But if we trust God
    as we should,
All must work out
    for our good;
He ... knows the reason!
    — Anonymous

Where geniuses like Augustine, Milton, Bede, Arnold, Benedict, Einstein, Shakespeare had failed to explain God's existence by reason, this broadcaster had succeeded. Like Voltaire, Welles, Ruskin and Descartes (also geniuses in their own right), he closed the door on heaven and threw away the key.

Fortunately, for all of us, the revealed Word has proclaimed that God's existence is a mystery. It is in truth a matter of faith only revealed by Him to those He deems worthy. In fact, heaven is made up, in large part, by those who think as children. No amount of mental gymnastics can prove God's existence.

Uncle Alf

My cousin Margaret told me this story: "My Uncle Alf was some guy. When his father died, it happened that next to his room in the funeral parlour was a deceased old lady whom I had been nursing in a hospital.

"When I went in to pay my respects, I found the room empty of tributes: no flowers, cards or people. No one had signed the register. Before going home that evening, I casually mentioned the situation to my Uncle Alf.

"Next afternoon, I again popped into the deceased lady's room. I thought I had the wrong place. Flowers and wreaths were all around the casket; cards were in the container, and a beautiful bouquet on the coffin. I went over to the condolence book. There, under my signature, was the name, Alfred Robertson. I knew then that my Uncle Alf had shared his father's flowers and cards with this poor lady who had no one to mourn her."

An Instant Martyr

In my lifetime, I have heard of only one person who was a sure martyr for God.

A witness at Columbine High School in Colorado in the year 1999 saw a boy shooting up the school cafeteria. The killer came upon a teen hiding under a table. He asked her if she believed in God. She said she did.

And he blew her straight into heaven.

The Soul

We are all aware of the devastating pain inflicted by physical and emotional sickness. But there's another malady that's far more subtle and pernicious in the way it brings us down.

This sickness comes from the soul. When the soul is out of touch with God's laws, the whole being of a person is disoriented. A soul in distress must find its way back to God in order for the whole person to find peace.

The soul is not the mind or the brain. It is a unique creation. Formed by God and instilled at conception. It has a life of its own. It lives forever. We must not neglect it.

Right Way Corrigan

The Way of the Cross is a prayerful devotion practised by those who would remember the Crucifixion Day of Christ. A priest I knew, a Father Corrigan, was one such devotee. He was the Chaplain of St. Augustine's Seminary in Toronto, a counsellor to any one of 170 men who might need his direction. I was one.

In the late evening shadows of the seminary chapel, this holy old country priest could be seen stopping before each of the 14 scenes that commemorate the story of Calvary.

So enraptured was he that his body moved as if in a trance; his head would toss, his torso sway and his hands clasp and unclasp in intensity.

In today's modern parish, his country-bumpkin's ways would be only tolerated. But what a good man he was! On the surface so ordinary, but underneath a fierce apostle, like Christ's fishermen.

Society saw a plain old-fashioned man of average ability with funny ways of talking and walking. But to those of us seminarians who knew him, he was another Christ carrying his cross from station to station on his path to glory. Every night in the darkness, he made his "round of love." In the priest's graveyard near the Seminary, a small lonesome pine has completely covered his headstone — even in death, he hides from the world.

Years ago, a football player for Notre Dame actually ran the wrong way in a game. His name was Corrigan — so they called him Wrong Way Corrigan.

This Corrigan from the Toronto diocese, thank God, chose the right way!

There's talk now of his name being put forward for sainthood.

The Lacemaker

In behind the great Basilica at Lisieux in the summer of 1981, I stood over the grave of a Celtic lady of extraordinary character. Her name was Zelie Guerin, born in Normandy in 1831. In 1858, she married Louis Martin, a watchmaker whom she met in Alençon, France, where both their military fathers had gone to retire.

Her first choice of career proved disappointing: she was turned down several times for the religious life. Faced with the necessity of raising her own dowry for a suitable marriage, since her father's poor financial position offered no support, she stormed heaven for guidance. Could God resist helping this petite, poised, pretty 20-year-old Normandy girl who wanted to give her life to Him? Apparently not. While working quietly at her home one day, she heard a strong inner voice say, "Make Alençon lace."

And she did. She took lessons in lacemaking, a craft brought to Alençon in 1664, and soon was producing a much sought-after and very expensive "Point d'Alençon." She set up an office and workshop at home, assembled and designed her lace, organized workers in and around Alençon, contacted buyers and eventually obtained a ten-year contract with a Parisian firm. Her dowry grew. All that remained was to find a husband.

So again she prayed. She asked for a good Christian man and many children, "so as to let them all be consecrated to You." Seven years later God answered her. It was worth the wait!

Zelie was crossing a bridge in Alençon in April, 1857, when she noticed a tall, rather grave man approaching. She felt an instant attraction for him and again heard an interior voice say, "It is this young man I have selected for you." Her mother arranged an introduction and three months later they were married. Over the next 20 years left to her, Zelie successfully combined the roles of homemaker, mother and businesswoman.

Louis and Zelie brought nine children into a hostile France. In the late 1860s the black Prussians, flaunting their spiked helmets with imprinted skulls and crossbones, ravaged France. They bombarded Alençon, seized livestock, and butchered resisting townsfolk. As further settlement, they demanded 300,000 francs from Alençon. Then, 25,000 of these invaders roamed like bears through the town. Later in 1870, the French turned on their own in a civil war. The Archbishop of Paris and 64 priests were shot. The poor lost everything and the rich lived in constant fear.

The reason for Zelie's denial by God of her religious career became clear when the first three Martin children went on to be cloistered Carmelite nuns. (In all, five girls entered.) A fourth child, Helen, died at age five, not long after Zelie had buried two infant sons.

A Father Dolan, who had interviewed four of Zelie's religious daughters in the early 1900s, told of another of Zelie's *close encounters*. It concerned Helen.

He says that shortly after Helen's death, a scrupulous Zelie remembered a small lie Helen had once told. Convinced this transgression might delay Helen in purgatory, Zelie went up to her room to pray before a statue of the Blessed Virgin given to her husband by a saintly Alençon woman. I chanced to see this statue in 1981 on a visit to Louis's home in Lisieux where he had taken his family after Zelie's death. Later in life, this very statue had once supposedly smiled at Thérèse (the daughter who became a saint) during a serious illness from which she miraculously recovered.

Praying to Mary that day Zelie begged God to forgive Helen so she could go to heaven. Immediately, she again heard a voice, this time from the statue which said, "Helen is here — here at my side."

Until her death in 1877 at age 46 from breast cancer contracted ten years earlier, she was a truly successful lady. Her husband even closed his watchmaker shop to become her full-time salesman across France.

Her lifestyle was exemplary: Mass each morning at 5:30, many moments in prayer with her husband and children, and a good deal of hands-on kindness to the poor in her district. And all this in the shadow of sickness and death and the necessity to carry on. Zelie was a candle that burned out for God.

In the last stage of her life, another remarkable event occurred. She was sitting in an easy chair one evening pondering her situation. She knew death was imminent: tumours on her back, neck and breasts thrust "daggers" of pain through her frail body. She had made a difficult trip to the Virgin's Shrine at Lourdes, France, where God chose not to cure her.

Resting there that evening she felt sure that she had done her best in life. She would leave her house in order: her saintly husband would be cared for by two adolescent daughters; the sale of the business would help; Leonie, once a troublesome child, had settled down; four children were in heaven; her smallest child Thérèse, only four, had the help of four sisters.

Apparently, she then commented on how God couldn't expect much more than she was doing. And then feeling somewhat assured, she had just said to herself, "Not even the Devil could bother me now," when suddenly a force pushed down on her shoulders driving her body into the chair.

She immediately signed herself and whispered a prayer. The pressure disappeared. She knew then that the fight was not over and that God's grace would be needed to the end.

A few months later, God's little lacemaker from Alençon left everything she loved for heaven. Satan missed another prize. And deservedly so.

Danny

Experts say there are various levels of conscious reality in dreams, trances, comas, seizures, hypnosis, memory loss, and even sleep.

Recently an English-speaking friend under partial anaesthetic said all his old bedtime prayers in French with his French doctor. When he woke, he could remember the prayers only in English.

In hypnosis, the past comes forward into reality. People in comas see tunnels of light or relatives waiting on the other side. Saints have slipped into trances and appeared *in reality* hundred of miles away.

Recently I met a middle-aged man from Ireland who told me this story: "I grew up in a poor family of ten children. My father drank too much — my mother worked too hard. As for me, I was a rogue. I broke every rule ever made and it never bothered me. I thought I knew everything. Nobody pushed me around.

"The only person I loved besides myself was my mother. She and I fought a lot, but only because we were so much alike.

"After my father died, she took sick. And I was the one who nursed her. I sat with her for hours in the hospital. I said so many rosaries, I felt like I was a bishop.

"After my mother's health improved, I came to Canada. I worked at my trade, plumbing. Then I got sick. I was hospitalized many times with asthma, depression, and alcoholism. During all this, my marriage broke down and my only child had difficulties. Without my faith, I would have gone completely under. I prayed and prayed. I suffered so much I felt like Job.

"Then I had an experience that turned my life around. I was sitting one evening at my desk doodling. I was always a good doodler. In school, I was the best. The other kids gathered around to watch me doodle…. Well, as I said, I was sitting there doodling when I slipped into a sort of trance. I've had them before. I don't know what they are — I just have them. Anyway, I awoke later, still at my desk, still holding my pen. An hour had passed. I felt tired — so I went to lie down.

"A half-hour later, the phone rang. It was my sister in Ireland. My mother had died an hour before.

"I knew then where I had been in that hour: with my mother, holding her hand, consoling her. She would not die without me. And I wouldn't let her go without being there. We were so close. And still are. This intimacy with my mother especially during her last illness, has given me much consolation. It has helped my faith."

The Stranger

After Nellie's first marriage failed, she and her little boy made it on their own for a few years. Then, one day, the country girl Nellie met a new beau from the city with whom she chose to live but not marry.

Everything went along fine until Nellie found out she was with child. Still not willing to marry and her relationship with the child's father already on shaky ground, she became severely perplexed. Trying to cope emotionally and economically with the added complication of a new baby would not be easy. She even thought of ending the pregnancy.

One day Nellie decided to visit a favourite aunt. A change of scenery might do her good and maybe her aunt could give her some advice.

She did receive help at her aunt's, but in a very strange way. This is what she told me, (I paraphrase): "One night, while there, I awoke to find my bedroom full of a dazzling light. It permeated the entire room. Over the end of my bed stood a tall handsome dark-haired young man who looked at me in an endearing way. His mouth was moving in the shape of words but nothing came out. Then he moved closer to my person. Again he tried to speak, but again nothing. I pinched myself to see if I was awake. *It hurt.*

"Next the man bent over my form and again tried to tell me something. He was trying to help me. Then he disappeared.

"I can tell you I was really upset. I stayed until morning and without telling anyone anything, I went to see my mother and father on a nearby farm. I told my mother about the vision. She said, 'Describe him to me.' I did. 'I know who it was,' she quietly said. 'His name is Allan, the illegitimate son of the aunt you visited. He was born before her marriage and although he wasn't the offspring of her husband, the husband took him in as part of the new family. Allan was a fine boy. He moved away to Texas where he married. He died in the oil fields at age 25. A tragic loss!'

"'Why do you think he came to me last night?' I asked.

"'He came to tell you not to worry. He understands your situation. *He* turned out fine and so will *you* with your child. I can tell you that if your child is half the person Allan was, you need have no questions about going ahead with your pregnancy. Allan was no burden to his mother or adopted father.'

"Well, since that day I never looked back. I had a grand baby boy whom my family and I have never tired of loving."

WELL DONE, PATSY

Words heard at the funeral of a mentally handicapped adult: "Well, Patsy, life threw you more than a few curve balls, but more than once you hit them out of the park."

Barbara

Somewhere in heaven, Barbara watches over her husband and their two boys and a girl. She left them in 1995 in the City of Eugene, Oregon, under unusual circumstances.

It all began in the fall of 1993. Her doctors had good news: she was pregnant with twins; and bad news: she had chronic granulocytic leukemia.

The doctors gave her a choice: abort the children and begin cancer treatment immediately or go full term and with the help of chemo and bone-marrow transplants save her babies and prolong her life for three years

She chose the latter.

Six months after the twin's birth, despite radiation and a transplant, her condition worsened. Yet, she spent the last year of her life caring for them. They were "meant to be born," she said. She gave them life and the start they needed.

"To die that others may live" is an oft repeated epigram.

But every time such sacrifices do occur we cannot help but marvel at the persons involved.

George

A contemporary of the western ballad singer, George Jones, once asked why George's songs capture the heart of grass-roots America. I'd like to answer that question — George writes and sings for the soul, he draws on his own experiences, tells us that we are not alone, and that the world is full of heartbreak. He specializes in love. He sells comfort and understanding. He soothes the heart. He brings a tear and takes it away. He gives meaning to our confused feelings.

In short, he tells us how and why we feel the way we do. And for many, that's everything.

Force of Habit

After living for 42 years in the same bungalow, an elderly lady died there. The new owners began to hear strange noises after they had gone to bed.

For example, the key would turn in the front door and someone would move to a small cupboard and put a coat on a hanger. Then came sounds of a cup and saucer being taken from the kitchen cupboard and the electric kettle being filled with water. The person made tea and washed up. Then all the noises stopped. The couple never had the courage to walk in on their visitor. They assumed it was the ghost of the lady.

Once, however, they did venture out into the kitchen, but only after the ghost had gone. What they discovered unnerved them. The electric kettle was still warm.

Bobby

"Let his loyalty and devotion be a lesson to us all."
— Inscription on Bobby's Tombstone.

Monuments are one way society has of preserving history in an enduring way. While our forefathers usually honoured politicians, composers, inventors, explorers, and the military, they did not forget the exceptional offerings of mankind's artistic heroes and entertainers who inspired the masses.

Every bus driver pulling out of the main bus terminal in New York City faces a statue of Ralph Cramden (Jackie Gleason). In Dublin, you can sit and chat with John Keats' life-size sculpture beside a park bench. In London's East End, Charlie Chaplain's monument, as the Little Tramp, gives hope to the poor. While on Broadway, George M. Cohan presides over "the Great White Way." Across the world, our children admire similar memorials to honour such heroes as Florence Nightingale, Joan of Arc, Al Jolson, and Babe Ruth, and ask, "Who's that person, Daddy?"

In Edinburgh, Scotland, the city elders have taken such tributes further. They have raised bronze and stone remembrances to birds and a dog. They do not forget those mice and canaries that died while testing the deadly gases in the trenches and mines. And as for the dog, the city officials once commissioned a bronze statue of a Skye Terrier named Bobby who captured the imagination of Scotland and the world by his persevering loyalty to his master, Jacques Gray.

Bobby's bigger than life-size statue is up on a hill above Edinburgh's Waverly train station. This was his territory. Here he skipped over the cobblestone byways of the city's oldest region. Here, he frequented shops and rest houses, made friends of the street regulars, romped with the boys from a nearby orphanage and begged from the young gallants of Edinburgh's Castle Military Guard.

This bronze likeness is across the street from the inn he frequented with his master. Bobby sits atop a water fountain positioned well above most people's heads. Like all Skye Terriers, he is small. His hair is curly thick, his chest is full and round, his tail, bushy, and his ears turned down. His head is erect, his eyes dark, his nose cold. He has a canny, mischievous look. He's pensive, poised and obviously "his own dog."

History has it that John Gray was a retired policeman. How he came by Bobby is not known. Perhaps Bobby was a gift from a Pentland farmer north of Edinburgh or a runaway. What we do know is that Bobby was a pup when they met, that he and John were together for about a year and a half, and that they quickly developed a bond of friendship which for Bobby did not end in death.

Every day at one o'clock when "old Meg," a huge cannon on top of Edinburgh's Castle Hill terrified the whole city with a single blast, Bobby interrupted his antics to run to the tavern where he knew John was waiting. There, at the back, by a great stove, Bobby stripped the bone scraps provided by the owner, the same person who would feed him for the 13 years after John died. There he would fall asleep at the feet of his master, the lonely, poor, sickly John Gray.

Greyfriar's Cemetery where John Gray was buried in 1858 was named after the Franciscan Friars who had a monastery there from 1447 to 1860. In 1562 it became a kirkyard. The Church of Scotland owns it now. The monks were still there when John Gray died. Bobby, who lived from 1858 to January 14, 1872, would have known them.

Although dogs were not permitted in the cemetery, Bobby somehow managed to sneak his way through the gates to sleep on his master's grave. On cold nights, he slept under the tombstone that had fallen over the grave. On severe nights, the cemetery custodian who had a cottage outside the gates took Bobby into his home. Thus, in addition to receiving victuals from the tavern owner, Bobby was cared for by many friends enamoured by his loyalty to Gray.

Bobby spent his spare time patrolling old haunts. He chased squirrels and cats. He played catch. Sometimes he went into the country with young people. Other times he visited the Heriot Orphanage or chatted with country shoppers in the city for the day. But at dusk, everyone knew where to find him.

When Bobby died they gave him his own grave at the entrance to the cemetery, some 15 yards from his master. When one considers the number of people buried in that cemetery over 600 years, around a million they say, the placement of a master and his dog's remains in such honourable spots has to be one of mankind's finest gestures.

Today the graves, under softly broken brown earth and wild roses, give evidence of loving care. It's a tranquil place. All around a green carpet covers slightly rolling ground. Broad-spreading trees cast shadow and light on the tombs.

Certain authors and even Hollywood, have tried to dress up Bobby's story. But the truth does not need adornment. It is not a legend. It is a fact. Simply put, 145 years ago in the hovels of poverty-stricken Edinburgh, a man and a dog became friends. Soon after, one died in the comfort of the other. The survivor spent his life mourning that death. In the night, he lay on or near his master's grave and he did so until he himself died.

This story has been known to much of Scotland for 140 years. Even Queen Victoria, living at Balmoral, not far from Edinburgh, expressed her desire to see Bobby, but Bobby was not well enough to travel.

The Scottish see themselves in Bobby. They admire tenacity, spunk, sacrifice and loyalty. But mostly loyalty. For loyalty is the expression of love. Loyalty is going to war over beliefs and tenets and righteousness. Loyalty is love in practice. Loyalty is the proof of love.

Bobby, ye were some dog.

Thank God for Overtime

Marty received a phone call from his daughter, Judy, from the Island of Crete. In the middle of her holiday, nerves and loneliness had put her at her wit's end. She wanted to come home immediately and expected Marty to make the arrangements.

Marty did not know where to begin. It had taken three airlines and a great deal of planning to get her from Canada to Crete. Setting up a schedule from his end to return her home was almost impossible. And even if he *could* do it, the price would be astronomical.

Marty bit the bullet. He told her to find a drugstore and ask the pharmacist for a "calming down" prescription. She said she wouldn't and couldn't because all the drugstores were closed.

Marty then said, "Judy, in two hours you will be fine. Meanwhile, look for a drugstore. I shall call you back in two hours exactly."

Marty then got in his car and drove to the evening service at his church. There, he prayed intensely for one hour.

Later, at exactly the agreed upon time, his daughter came on the line. "I'm okay now, Dad. I'm staying. I found a drugstore. It was closed, but I knocked anyway. The pharmacist came to the door. I explained my situation. He said it was only on rare occasions he ever stayed late. He gave me some medication. I feel great. See you later."

Judy was calm. Marty was a wreck.

The Whistling Deer

Sylvester had been tracking "Big Daddy" for years. Their hunting ground was a chunk of Leeds County, Ontario, which many years before had been closed to the public because someone had been shot there. Only owners could hunt on such land and Sylvester was its owner. His adversary was a 300 pound deer with antlers wider than a barn door.

"Big Daddy" had a remarkable ability that kept him alive: he could whistle. As soon as the hunter whistled back, giving away his presence, "Big Daddy" took off. Eventually, Sylvester got wise to the whistle trick. The battle was on.

One evening, Sylvester came upon "Big Daddy" whistling safely behind a bush. Sylvester, overcome with buck fever, fired wildly. It was a lucky shot. The bullet hit an antler and ricocheted forcibly off the head of "Big Daddy." "Big Daddy" was down.

Now, the only way to be sure if a deer is dead (and for that matter, any animal), is to check the eyes: open, dead; closed, alive. Sylvester didn't know that. "Big Daddy's" eyes were shut. Nor did he know that wounded deer are unaware of where they are; so they remain perfectly quiet until the foe approaches.

"Big Daddy" waited until the last moment and then whipped his hooves into Sylvester's face, hitting him flush in the forehead. Both antagonists staggered around until Sylvester finished him off.

Somewhere in Leed's County, a stuffed "Big Daddy" hangs over a fireplace, a fitting reminder of his struggle with one Sylvester McNamee. It's called "the Whistler's Hunt," part of a tale from long ago. Sylvester died in the spring of 2002.

David's Rose

Before she died in 1897, Thérèse Martin of Lisieux, promised she would spend her heaven doing good on earth. She also promised to send roses when possible to those who prayed to her. The roses were proof she was doing what she could to help.

Once, in Lisieux, in 1981, I saw why Thérèse loved roses. All around her childhood home, bushes of wild roses scented the air. There was pink and white and her favourite colour, red.

It wasn't too long into the twentieth century that Thérèse became God's flower girl. In fact, God sent so many flowers through St. Thérèse that people nicknamed her the Little Flower.

Over the last 100 years, this petite Carmelite nun has become a Saint and a Doctor of the Catholic Church. At present she has admirers all over the world.

One such devotee was Lucy from a small town in the Ottawa Valley. In fact, Lucy's friendship with Thérèse was so well known in the district that when Lucy died at age 95, her admirers sent dozens of red roses to the wake. Among those present at the wake were Lucy's dear friend, Nancy, and Lucy's great-grandchild, David, who had both loved Lucy.

The funeral was particularly difficult for David. He sobbed at Nancy's side during the service. He had lost his best friend. Nancy did what she could to comfort him.

In the graveyard on a dreary January afternoon, Lucy's friends followed the coffin up a knoll. Nancy's husband and two sons were pallbearers. Nancy and David brought up the rear. The site was not without some cheer: dark red roses carried by the funeral staff glowed amid the trees, patches of snow and shades of green. Then it happened.

Halfway along the path, Nancy suddenly spotted a single red rose resting on the muddy turf. A hundred footsteps had missed it. When Nancy, also a friend of the Little Flower, saw the rose, she immediately heard Thérèse say, "This rose has fallen unblemished to show you and David that Lucy is happy and that I am with you both on this sad day."

Nancy picked up the rose and said to David, "St. Thérèse has sent you this rose. It is a remembrance. Keep it in memory of your grandmother and St. Thérèse."

Postscript

This writer is also a friend of St. Thérèse. A few seconds after he had finished the above article, his wife came in the front door. She was carrying ten red roses given to her at the nursing home where she volunteers.

And the Clouds Got Wide

My elder son's wedding was threatened by torrential rain. At 2:30 p.m., a half-hour before its start, the chances of a let-up appeared slim.

Now an old Irish belief contends that placing a rosary on a clothes-line will chase away the rain. I thought I'd give it a try.

By 2:45, the situation remained bleak and everyone got out umbrellas and raincoats for the five-minute drive to the church. But they weren't needed. At 2:53, the skies suddenly cleared and the wedding party left under blue skies. During the service, the rain returned with a vengeance, only to stop again for the photos and social gathering on the grounds.

During the reception and dance that followed in the church basement, the rain returned. Later in the evening it dissipated and everyone went home under a canopy of stars.

Carmel

I was talking recently with a close friend whom I have loved since childhood. She is now 88. She and her husband raised ten children during the 1940s and 1950s on love, sweat, and faith. They had few worldly goods. Home-made cooking, a huge garden, some steers, cows, hens, geese, pigs, adequate pasture, and a few fields in crops helped them get by.

She never regretted one moment as a farmer's wife. She sowed good seeds. Her children are now so solicitous of her welfare that she can barely keep her independence. She claims she is the luckiest person in the world.

The privilege of old age, however, has its price. Bad hips have slowed her down. She uses a walker. A weak heart regulates her energy.

During our discussion of physical handicaps, she startled me with a statement that showed the depth of her spunk and the height of her faith. She said, "Until lately, I've always said my prayers kneeling down. One day I came to realize that I had to accept the cross of not being able to kneel. I became so upset by my inability to praise God on my knees that I would often cry like a baby. It was the least I could do for Him, and now I can't even do that. I hope He doesn't mind."

Not likely! There was a day when He couldn't get down either.

The Short Circuit

The slant of her crimson tam said it all. Here was a character. She had just entered the aisle of a large downtown church in Vancouver for the late afternoon workers' Mass. She was agile, petite, and not unattractive. She had purpose and focus.

She carried a large paper shopping bag. A purse dangled from her shoulder. A simple coat, grey gloves and matching scarf filled out her ensemble. She looked like a well-to-do bag lady.

At the end of the service I spoke with her and I offered her a small gift of money. She refused, "Thanks just the same, but I'm fine. I have plenty to get by on. I have a pension from my teaching, and St. Joseph looks after all my needs."

And off she went.

At that moment, a priest of the parish walked by.

As I pointed her out, I said, "Who is that lady in the red tam?"

"Ah," said the curate, "her name is Lillian. Everybody knows her. She's our resident saint. By the way, it's her birthday next Friday — close to 80, I think."

"Father, she wouldn't take any money from me. So would you mind saying Mass for her birthday this Friday." And I gave him a donation.

"Sure, I will. And I'll tell her about it."

The following Friday morning, while I was attending the morning service at the Star of the Sea church in nearby White Rock, some 40 miles from downtown, an odd event took place.

Just before the end of the Mass, the old priest sat down on a bench at the side of the altar for a minute of contemplation. At that moment, for some reason, I wondered if Lillian had appreciated her birthday gift.

Suddenly, the microphone around the priest's neck exploded in sound. He jumped from his seat. The amplifying system was loudly broadcasting a conversation in a foreign tongue between an in-city taxi depot and an irate customer.

The wired-for-sound priest laughed. He then asked the people to spread a different kind of word, "Don't call the taxi company while Mass is being said. It's too unnerving."

And I said, "You're welcome, Lillian."

Sweethearts Forever

By far, Canada's most beautiful island is Prince Edward Island. The mercurial Atlantic laps its sandy shores. Green pastures, fishing villages and rolling knolls tease the eye. Stands of spruce, blue lakes and silver streams make it a tourist's paradise.

Naturally, the Island's people reflect its ambience. They make fast friends; have droll humour, unsophisticated pride and steadfast determination.

Two such Islanders were Lorraine and Arnold. Theirs was a sweetheart marriage. In spite of hardships they raised a fine family. Marvellous heights of joy made everything worthwhile. Married for 46 years, Arnold died the day after their last anniversary.

I recently met Lorraine at the anniversary luncheon of mutual friends. That particular day, Arnold would have been 75; so Lorraine became rather melancholy during the family reminiscences.

As we ate side by side I asked her how she and Arnold met. She traced their relationship up to the time Arnold asked for her hand in marriage. She said, (I paraphrase), "For years, I had thought of becoming a Sister of the Precious Blood. Finally it came down to the Sisterhood or marriage. I prayed and prayed and prayed.

"One day my answer came in a flash. I was praying in chapel when suddenly a firm voice told me, 'Arnold needs you.' I got up and went to him. We soon married.

"I never regretted my decision for a second. It happened that Arnold soon developed heart problems that lasted 46 years. I was there for him every single day. He was my sweetheart."

Love has no room for selfishness. Love satisfies each other's needs no matter how demanding. Arnold thanked God every day for Lorraine and Lorraine did the same for Arnold. God had brought them together.

God does speak to us if we listen.

AN ADAGE

Yesterday is history.
Tomorrow is a mystery.
Today is called the present,
And that's why it's a gift.
— A Friend in Souris, P.E.I

The Execution

Oakley was once a common name among the Irish pioneers of Huntley Township. Many Oakleys in the 1830s were carpenters. As itinerant workers, they rode into the many farmyards of my mother's ancestors in search of employment. If hired, they roomed and boarded in the clients' homes until their work was finished.

One story concerning an Oakley has survived the years. It shows how the lack of police and medical services affected the pioneers' lives. The pioneers were truly left to their own devices.

This happening took place one summer afternoon. An Oakley carpenter drove his wagon and team into a prospective customer's yard. Finding no movement about the place, he walked behind the house. There he came face to face with terror.

On a knoll under a maple tree, two men held another man standing on a bench. A fourth was trying to place a noose about his neck. The victim's hand and feet were tied; a cloth plugged his mouth.

"Hey, what're ye doin' thar?" shouted Oakley.

"What does it look like?" came the answer.

"Ye can't to that there sort of thing. Thar are laws, ye know. Let him go."

"Go way, Mister. Clear out unless ye want the same. We're desperate. So back off, and mind yer business."

Oakley softened his approach. He had stumbled on a moment of fierce passion. A man was being executed. The die was cast. Nothing could be done.

"Can ye at least tell me what led up to this? I won't interfere." The oldest of the three, his body shaking and voice trembling, moaned, "This here's my son. He has lost his mind. He is a mad man. He bites, hits, sets fires, and beats the animals. We have no life as long as he is alive. We're in danger."

He added, "Call the doctor, ye might say! Who? Where? We have no medicines, no cures. Call the constables! Take him to an asylum! There aren't any 'round here. May God have mercy on my boy and on us!"

With that said, the father pulled the bench away. The lad sank like a stone. The men sobbed. Somewhere women wailed.

Before Oakley left, he put together a make-shift coffin. He helped the men dig the grave. The boy's father could be seen walking back and forth in the distance.

That evening, Oakley said some prayers for the dead and levelled the grave's ground to preserve its secret. Fortified with sandwiches and tea made by the women folk, he then headed out the lane.

Thought Oakley, "When no law exists and no help is available, man must take the law into his own hands."

The general location of the murder has been guessed at, but never found.

The Unnecessary

We can do without: prima donnas ... political promises ... eggheads ... sex consultants ... bluebloods ... academics ... whiners ... the intelligentsia ... crocodile tears...patronage ... bullies ... scoffers ... cynics ... debunkers ... immoral leaders ... windbags ... soap operas ... the rich and famous ... parent bashers ... crepe hangers ... boors ... canned music ... braggarts ... the privileged ... pornography ... liars ... meanness ... legal bankruptcies ... practical jokers ... dirty humour ... guns ...a nosey media ... casinos ... blabbermouths ... experts ... hypocrites ... tailgaters ... telephone soliciting ... *unreal* reality shows ... nudity ... cursing and swearing ... advertising ... and skinflints.

The Dolphin

One day, somewhere in the seven seas, a legendary event took place.

A fisherman crazed by the playful teasing of a baby dolphin, speared it to death. Its blood lapped the golden shore.

The witnesses by the sea that day were shaken. Their superstitious natures ran wild. A dolphin treated in such a manner could bring hardships on them all. So they went home chanting mantras and fingering their beads. They didn't have long to wait for their fears to materialize.

Within a year, word spread that the dolphin's spirit had had its retribution. The guilty man's wife had given birth to a baby with a dolphin's face.

Old Friends

Several miles away, air traffic controllers are seeing the geese as dangerous blips. Flying at different levels directly across the take-off lanes to the west, they are a menace. The geese have their own flight plans, their own "promises to keep."

They fly as if their lives depend on it. Flock upon flock race dusk to the fading glow of a northern river. On this particular evening, by the light of a tippy-canoe moon, thousands flap effortlessly in the emptiness of one another's shadows.

Every fall for 40 years, after eating their fill in the cornfields beyond the city, they have honked across the heavens near my home. It's a sign that they are preparing to leave. On the river they make their plans. Anticipation of the journey is shared. They are restless.

One night soon they will steal away. No one will see them go. The steely purpose of every heartbeat drives them on.

Soon the late evenings will miss their presence. I know I will.

But not the air traffic controllers.

October

The quietness of the fall season is in our little community park. It's afternoon. No children, dogs or bicycles. Just animals preparing for winter and birds passing through. Empty swings sway slightly in a biting breeze.

I sense the neighbourhood has died. I miss the children on the slides and the tots in the sand and the colourful strollers parked near the benches where young mothers watch.

I find myself pensive in this change of season. November is bare and harsh, but October has some colour and warmth left.

One day last week I drove up an old country road by my grandmother's farm where I had lived for nine summers. A whitish green covered the acres where I once romped as a boy.

The fields were full of dreams. I could see myself on the wagons of hay, hear the horses neigh, watch Teddy fetch a stick and see my grandmother walking in the lane. I hadn't a care in the world back then. Each day gave me happiness beyond understanding.

Then I sadly counted the number of friends gone from a small stretch of farms, nineteen in all. I remembered each face.

It hit suddenly — a pang of loneliness I had seldom felt of late.

But, in my reverie, I did leave there with their smiles and laughter in my heart. Isn't it strange how the good thoughts rise to the top?

Ah, October! You are like my memories! A treasure! Especially for those of us in our winter.

Margaret

Before she died, 85-year-old Margaret requested that her ashes be scattered on a small bay near her home by the Pacific Ocean. In grey glare and soft blue, the little boat with its 12 mourners cast a shadow as it weighed anchor at a chosen spot in the bay. Soon the boat rocked in time to hymns and prayers. Then one of her four daughters spoke and a priest said a few words. Finally the scattering of ashes began.

As the motorboat turned in a circle, each daughter took her turn shaking her mother's remains over the ocean. Except one. The last daughter could not bring herself to do it. She sat frozen with grief. Everyone waited. Eventually, after much persuasion, she did sprinkle her portion.

It was later that this reluctant daughter explained to the others what had happened to change her mind, "I felt my mother sit beside me and put her arm around my shoulder. Slowly she helped me up and together we walked to the stern. As she held and watched me, I turned her urn down into the breeze. I felt great consolation. She was there with me. Then she left."

For two hours, the boat moved 'round Margaret's tomb. The celebration of toasts and tributes went on. They hoped Margaret was pleased. She must have been, they said, because she had been there on board.

A Not So Graceful Miracle

Cap de la Madeleine is a beautiful shrine some 90 miles west of Montreal on the north shore of the St. Lawrence River. It is dedicated to the Virgin Mary. The faithful have been going there for nearly two centuries.

The site is unique. All the buildings back on a sunken artificial lake in the middle of the grounds. Sprays of water shoot up beneath a statue of the Virgin positioned on an island in the centre of the lake. At night, the lights shine 'round this impressive sight.

Not many years ago, a lady with no feeling in her legs was brought to the shrine. As was the custom, a volunteer was assigned to look after her. The volunteer was my friend, Mary Brennan, from Ottawa.

In the afternoon, Mary took the lady for a ride in a wheelchair 'round the raised edge of the sunken lake. For some reason, Mary lost control of the wheelchair. It took off down the hill towards the lake. At the water, it hit a small cement rise and tossed the lady into the drink.

Mary got help and soon the lady was in a warm bed none the worse for her experience.

Next morning, Mary went to see her. Mary nearly fainted. The lady got up from her bed and walked across the room.

She had been cured.

A Summer Day

Maybe I had seen too many old movies or my imagination ran away on me that summer afternoon in a park by a river.

Before me, was a scene of long ago.

Hundreds promenaded around a kidney-shaped lake, small bridges crossed over silver creeks and geese sun-bathed. Children romped among birch and spruce, dogs splashed in the river, ducks quacked and chipmunks tumbled for admirers.

Seagulls swept inland over children's toy boats. Fishermen cast from the big rocks along the shore. Park benches were filled with mothers and children. Families frolicked on knolls.

Occasionally, the breeze carried the strains of a Sousa march from the bandstand at the park's end. But, for the most part, all was silent in that summer's haze — ethereal and timeless.

In my time warp, these grounds could have been Phoenix Park in Ireland, the Bois de Boulogne in Paris, or St. James on the Strand. It was anywhere, anytime — a scene of shifting colour and shadow — a soundless serenity in one of God's gardens.

I was elated on that day to be part of a bygone era and I was equally pleased to know that today's families, like yesterdays, are still spending time together in the idyllic joy of summer.

True Art

Much of today's literature, theatre, dance, and celluloid productions has little to do with good art. True art does not treat the themes of death, evil, revenge, violence, and despair for its own glorification. True art, for its own sake, does not promote carnival behaviour and erotic dance. True art does not malign, mock or ridicule as a means to an end. True art is not gross, vulgar, abrasive or indecent. True art is not mundane, childish, amateurish and vitriolic. Shocking scenes do not make art.

True art is beauty, truth and light. It is simple and subtle and pure. It touches souls with grace. It stirs our beings. Beauty, truth and light are not in the eye of the beholder. They are in the art itself.

True art defies time. Its quality always shines. It remains young and pristine.

Taking Stock

Since his childhood, my 75-year-old first cousin has loved the farm animals. He has always felt a close bond with them. He has mothered them from birth through sickness, storm, feed shortage and death.

Even today as he looks out on his herd of cows from his front window, he feels their comfort. They're his family. They're not stupid. They listen for him, watch for him and go to meet him. He shouts and whistles; they gambol and call out. If he's a bit tardy in sending down water or throwing out bales of hay, they get rambunctious.

In the spring the mothers hide their new calves in the bush and deliberately lead my cousin away from them. Later in the night they go to their hiding places. Sometimes it's a game they don't mind losing. Some calves need help. They cannot feed properly or have birth defects. Some mothers have complicated births. They reach out to him for assistance.

The cattle are his care. He worries about them. He comforts them, looks after their needs, their diet and well-being. They give much in return: patience, appreciation, companionship, even beef.

On those raw winter nights when the north wind crushes everything with a paralyzing cold, he'll throw down a few bales of straw by the side of the barn and watch the cattle spread it. Soon they'll snuggle together as a family and even take turns being on the outside. Then my cousin will head home, content that he has done his best for them.

Putting in a Good Word

Many people have their agents in heaven that intercede with God. These agents have God's ear because they are His saints. People pray to them, they pray to God, and God, if He desires, answers as He knows best.

Interestingly enough, God often sends irrefutable proof that He *has* been swayed by one of His Saints. The following powerful story illustrates my meaning.

Since childhood, my favorite saint has always been Thérèse Martin of Lisieux, France. Before she died at age 24 in 1897, she promised to continue to pray for souls after her death. I take her at her word and over the years she has never failed to help me.

Recently, I had wondered if I would see my wife after our deaths. Christ promised His apostles they would see Him again in Heaven. Why shouldn't I meet my wife? So I prayed to God for a sign that my wife and I would one day be together in heaven. I didn't ask St. Thérèse. I thought this request was very personal, something God Himself should answer. God did reply, and in the bargain, used St. Thérèse as the go-between.

It happened like this. My wife, her sister, and I were driving to Toronto. It was a Thursday, September 30. I was in the front seat and her sister in the back. I had forgotten about my request.

I certainly hadn't received an answer.

Suddenly, the back left door was hit a resounding crash. My sister-in-law had seen a big bird, probably a seagull, sweep by the car. With my wife driving 75 m.p.h. and the bird swooping in on 40 m.p.h. winds (tracker trailers were being blown off the road), the collision was forceful.

A half-hour later as we were driving along, the significance of this happening came to me.

When the bird hit, I noticed the time on the clock was 12 minutes after noon. I had taken note of the time because I am superstitious about birds.

I had driven that route to Toronto some 50 times in 50 years and had never once seen a seagull near my car. Now, that one *hit*, I was disturbed.

Suddenly I realized that the bird had smacked into the car at exactly the same time little Thérèse Martin died in 1897: the same day, Thursday, the same date, Sept. 30, and at the same minute as in France, 7:12 p.m. which in our time in Canada was 12:12 p.m.

I took it all as a sign from God through St. Thérèse that I *will* see my wife again in heaven. And no one can convince me otherwise!

But there's more.

An hour after the bird hit, we checked the left side of the car during a stop for lunch.

St. Thérèse had left her calling card. Stuck in the top slit of the left back door were three small feathers in the perfect shape of the fleur-de-lis. They were exactly the same size, colour and shape. They had defied the high winds.

Oaty

Meeting old buddies from my sports' days gives me an emotional lift. Somehow these friendships never die. The death of any one of them saddens me deeply.

Recently, Ralph, a popular hockey player from the early days, passed away. Although I had seen him only occasionally, I remembered him as a good-hearted lad.

In those times, most hockey teams carried four defencemen. Ralph and I were on defence together along with two other players named Oaty and Lyle. The team was the Brockville Magedomas, a fine collection of players. Oaty, Ralph and Lyle, since they lived in the same area, had been in close contact for 50 years.

One morning, after Ralph's funeral, I phoned his out-of-town residence to offer my sympathy to his wife, Iris.

Iris told me that Oaty, in spite of his crippling arthritis, had come to
Ralph's wake. He walked in on his crutches, made his way to Iris's side, looked
up at her and said, "Iris, I guess we're dressing only three defencemen tonight."

And that said it all.

Oaty died a year later.

Now, we're down to two.

Edna

My late good friend, Edna, a lady of extraordinary graciousness, loved walking
along ocean beaches. She would spend her summer holidays strolling the
shores of such holiday centres as Ocean City and Atlantic City. She claimed the
ocean eased her cares and put everything in perspective.

The beautiful Dalvay Beach on Prince Edward Island would have been to
her liking. At Dalvay one summer I thought of her as I walked near sea and sky
with a breeze running on the dunes and the sands swirling out to sea. I had
the ocean to myself that afternoon. As far as I knew, she had never come to
Dalvay. Yet, I felt her presence.

And just in case she was there, I shouted her name towards the ocean.
Once or twice I prayed aloud for her into the winds.

Two months later, I was talking to Edna's son and I told him of my trip to
Dalvay and my awareness there of his mother. And he said, "That's spooky! My
mother often spoke of Dalvay by the Sea. She walked there many times. She
loved it!"

Crawford

Crawford and Marjorie had an idyllic marriage. Crawford was a gentleman's
gentleman and Marjorie a lady of grace. Crawford was a retired Naval Com-
mander who served in the Second World War as an Intelligence Officer. Mar-
jorie followed him around Canada, waited for his return from assignments,
and supported him in every way she could. They had two children. They were
married 60 years.

When Crawford died, the family's love of privacy deterred them from mak-
ing any public announcement. I heard about his death several months later.

I called Marjorie and she told me something that warmed the heart.
Crawford had died at home surrounded by his Marjorie, two children, two
grandchildren, and the minister. Later, an intimate service was held in their
living room. Each had something to say about Crawford. His granddaughter
wrote a poem and read it, and that gathering was Crawford's memorial: neat,
sweet and meaningful!

On the phone Marjorie added, "You know, Gary, I was crazy over Craw-
ford. Everyday before we married, I was crazy over him. Every single day of my

marriage, I was crazy for him. And even now, not a day goes by that I don't say, "Crawford, I'm crazy over you."

Omagh

On August 15, 1998, a popular Catholic feast day throughout Southern Ireland, a small red car full of explosives blew up on a busy street in the peaceful town of Omagh, Northern Ireland. Some 30 people were killed and over 100 injured.

At the very moment of the killings, 3:10 p.m., a High Mass with hundreds in attendance was being celebrated at Knock Shrine in County Mayo in honour of the Assumption of the Virgin Mary. It began at 3:00 p.m.

Advertised for weeks as a prayer service for the success of the recently promulgated National Peace Accord in Northern Ireland, fanatics chose this day to set back the progress already achieved. They made a mockery of the people's prayerful attempts to seek God's help.

Not surprisingly, the media, in order not to disturb the delicate balance of religious tolerance, said little about the significance of the Holy Day. Instead, they rallied to the defence of the Accord. Such a sacrifice of innocent people, they said, demanded that all Irish people pull together to eradicate those sinister forces that would prolong the years of distrust and revenge.

Now it happened that my wife and I were seated in a tavern in Limerick, Ireland, on the evening of August 15. We had driven through Omagh just three days before. We watched the scenes on television: the injured wandering around, the dead, the many souls in shock, the shattered cars and wrecked buildings, the police, the ambulances, the ministers, the children — confusion, noise and fear.

Why would anyone do such a thing in that lovely town of Omagh where religious discord had not existed for decades? Could such madness ever be explained?

My wife and I decided it was the work of Satan. Only he could put these people to death; only he would punish the people of Omagh for their record of peaceful existence; only he would use his evil powers to destroy good; only he would bring religion into the fray. What a perfect opportunity it was on that feast day to embarrass God and fly in the face of the Virgin whom the Bible says will one day crush the devil's head with her heel. The terrorists did what they did at the very time a popular celebration was being held in her honour.

A small coincidence is associated with this tragedy. Before I left home, a priest told me he would say a Mass for our safety on August 15, a favourite feast of mine. When I got back, he told me he had indeed said that Mass on August 15. I asked him what time of day it was when he said it. He answered that the time of the Mass was between 10 a.m. and lo:20 a.m., Ottawa time — the exact time in Ireland when the bombs went off.

Elizabeth

In Georgetown, Washington, in the year 2000 the Mother Superior of a clois-
tered convent leaned over the frail form of Sister Mary Elizabeth in the infir-
mary. "Sister," she said, "is there any wisdom you would like to leave the order
before you die — something about the religious life, perhaps, that you have
followed so faithfully?"

Sister Mary answered, "Let me think for a while. Perhaps, in the morning
I shall have something — if I'm still here."

Next morning, Sister Mary of the Visitation Order was ready. Her eyes
moistened as she spoke, "Tell the Sisters — they must live like warm wax to
be moulded by God, having no desire, wish or hope other than the will of God
... they are the breath of God ... God is breathing in them."

— Sister Mary Agnes, Georgetown, Washington

A Roguish Heart May be the Sweetest

Kathleen Kennedy, younger sister to the President, lived with her family in
London in the late 1930s. As the daughter of American Ambassador, Joe
Kennedy, she hobnobbed with the caviar society of a not-so-merry England.

Her brash innocence and offhand Irish ways made her popular with the
eligible bachelors of the Ascot world. After several flings, she became
betrothed to Billy Cavendish, heir to the Dukedom of Devonshire.

Unfortunately, marriages between persons of different station and reli-
gion, especially at that time in upper-echelon England, could be anathema.
But there was more to it than that.

The Cavendishes had hated Irish Catholics (like the Kennedys) ever
since they helped their benefactor, William of Orange, stifle the late-seven-
teenth-century Irish. Over the decades, the seven Cavendish dukes in the
British and Irish parliaments continued to thwart all hopes of Ireland win-
ning Home Rule and any measure of Irish political and economic inde-
pendence. The IRA meanwhile drew Cavendish venom when they put a bul-
let in the brain of the ninth Duke as he took the air in Phoenix Park, Dublin,
in 1882.

Meanwhile, the Irish Kennedys, being old-sod and Boston-cod, had
detested the likes of the Cavendishes. They also felt that their money made
in stocks, bonds and booze was every bit as good as the wealth of the
Cavendishes, which largely came from patronage, grants, and tenants' rents.

Naturally both families put pressure on Billy and Kathleen to stand pat.
Billy would have to wait to take his "Kathleen ... home" which at that time
could have been any one of five mansions on 180,000 acres of Cavendish land.

Unfortunately, the circumstances of war didn't allow any lengthy mari-
tal jousting. The Allies were preparing for the invasion of Europe, and Billy,

as an officer in the Coldstream Guards, was destined for the front in a matter of weeks.

As time ran down, the stalemate prevailed. The very idea of Kathleen marrying outside her faith was enough to put Rose Kennedy in bed for several months, while the prospect of the next Duke of Devonshire becoming a Roman Catholic was tantamount to a sheik buying Big Ben.

In the long run, Billy wouldn't relent and Kathleen had to give way. She chucked her family honour, Irish loyalty and religious fidelity for the love of Billy. She put Billy above everything and everyone. At the risk of hurting her loved ones, and supported by no one but her brother, Joe, who gave her away, Kathleen, dressed in blushing pink, wed the uniformed Billy in the Chelsea Registry office in 1944. She did it her way.

After a five-week honeymoon, Billy went to Normandy. Kathleen continued work at the American Red Cross. Rose rose from her sickbed and Joe preoccupied himself working off disfavour with Roosevelt, who had fired him as American Ambassador. The Devonshires continued to run their estate, helped with the war effort, and spent more time at Lismore Castle in Waterford, Ireland, where for once they felt safer than in England.

But all's only well that ends well. In June, 1944, Kathleen's brother Joe volunteered to test-fly a TNT-loaded suicide bomber. The idea was to fly these planes to England's southern coast and then bail out and let the remote controls take over. Near the sea, Joe was blown to bits.

A few weeks later, a sniper in Belgium shot Billy through the heart.

Suddenly, religious bias and social status didn't mean much.

Kathleen carried on as the Marchioness of Hartington. With her head in a bit of a twist, she wandered around in the upper-crust milieu until she finally took up with an older already-married wealthy earl. In 1948, on a junket to the Riviera with her new love, she died when their plane crashed on the same soil where her Billy had died.

Within five years, four members of the Chelsea wedding party were gone: the bride and groom, Joe Kennedy, and the groom's father, who died in 1950.

Kathleen's story is but one of thousands of war stories. Better families than the Cavendishes and the Kennedys felt the pain of world conflict. Heartbreak touched every castle and bothie.

Yet, somehow Kathleen's story has a special pathos, the tale of a spunky kid on her own trying to make a mark. Everybody liked her. She had that *something* that opened doors and hearts. Was it her honesty and love that went beyond bigotry, law and propriety?

Who among us would judge her? We leave that to heaven, where reasons of the heart are kept and love covers a multitude of sins.

"Kick" Kennedy, the loving, loveable rascal that she was, may well have been the finest of the lot.

> ## FAITH
>
> We do not know the future,
> But we do know the One who controls it.
> — Cloistered Carmelite Nun, Dunbarton, Scotland, 1998

Ballantrae

The Northern Highlands above Toronto are 900 feet higher than Toronto itself. There, wild streams feed ponds and lakes. Cottages hide in the trees. Highways run into sky. It's a walker's delight.

One evening, near the town of Ballantrae, just as I walked out of a canopy of walnut trees, a flock of blackbirds swirled up from corn fields. As they swooped into the sun, a thousand shadows raced to the hills.

Just then a golf ball from an errant swing bounced under a tree. I waited and pointed to the spot. The golfer threw it out and drove it down the links. I was alone again. The wind had a bite. I turned up my collar and ambled on in that tranquility where nature and mankind play — in the beauty of the Canadian Highlands.

Father Ockwood Remembers

Can guardian angels punch? Father Art Ockwood claims they can. The following event happened shortly after he was ordained.

While driving home alone one evening, Father says he must have fallen asleep. All he remembers is waking up to a sharp blow to his right shoulder and finding his car heading for the rhubarb. He pulled up safely. His bruised shoulder hurt for days after.

He explained, "I know I was punched by an angel."

Another time, Father Ockwood was sitting on a bench near the altar waiting to begin a service. Suddenly, he looked up and saw Christ in flowing robes walk across the alter front, up the stairs, and into the tabernacle.

All the Way

Over the centuries the animals had blazed a trail through the great forest. It straddled streams and brooks, passed by pools and springs, went over pastures and meadows. It even allowed for rest stations and escape routes. The trail was the only safe way to move in the forest.

One afternoon a fawn wandered off the path and soon was lost. Darkness came eventually and the fawn curled up in a pile of leaves to wait the morn.

Next day, after a breakfast of berries and leaves, the fawn began to look for a way home. A bear came along and the fawn asked him if he knew how to find the great road that ran through the forest.

"Sure I do," said the bear. "See that dead tree over there — on the other side, you'll find a creek that winds to the great road. Just follow it home."

Well, the fawn couldn't find the creek — it must have been farther down from the tree. After looking around for the longest time, she finally lay down.

"Where's your mother?" asked a voice and the fawn looked up to see a smiling raccoon.

"I'm lost. I am trying to find the great road to my home."

"Well, I'm just the one to help you. You see that dead tree lying over there. Well just beyond it, and not too far away, is a creek that runs downhill to the great road. Look. I'll draw you a map on this bark with my paw, and you'll be home in no time at all."

The fawn carried the bark in her mouth and even though she checked it carefully, could not find the way. The raccoon must have been guessing.

Next morning, after a cold night among decaying trunks, the fawn awoke in a dismal mood. By now, the poor thing was desperate. Even a fresh apple sapling did little to calm her nerves. Suddenly, a rabbit chanced by. She said, "My friend, you don't look happy." After the fawn's story, the rabbit said, "I shall help you to find the great trail."

"Yeah, I have heard that before," the fawn said to herself.

Before she knew it, the rabbit was riding the fawn's back. "Now, head for that dead tree over there, the one lying down and we'll take it from there."

As the afternoon light dimmed, the fawn and the rabbit found the creek and followed it. The fawn said, "You're a long way from home, rabbit. Won't you get lost?"

"No," the rabbit answered, "my fellow rabbits are all around us and they'll help."

Soon, the main path to everywhere appeared and the fawn arrived home. The rabbit scampered away in delight. He had shown what real brotherhood was, something the fawn's other so-called good Samaritans knew nothing about. He had truly gone out of his way to help someone.

He had become involved.

The Man on the Corner

A 90-year-old lady friend was talking about angels. "Once, many, many moons ago, as a young driver, when I stopped my car for a red light at a busy intersection, I had a panic attack. I froze at the wheel — perspiration mixed with tears — my knuckles were white — my heart raced.

"Suddenly, amid the turmoil, I saw a dark-suited man standing in the crowd on the far corner. His hand was raised with the palm facing me. He had somehow spotted the mess I was in.

"Soon he began giving me directions — his hand gracefully orchestrating me out of my dilemma. When I crossed the intersection, I turned to look. He was gone. I felt he was an angel and I still feel the same way 60 years later."

Blessings at Lourdes

The following invocations quoted from the Gospels have been used at the healing shrine of Lourdes, France, since 1888. They have been compared to the power of an electric storm on a hot summer's day. Traditionally, a priest calls out each request in a litany during the candlelight procession. The pilgrims en masse (sometimes thousands) repeat each one:

* Jesus, our Master, have mercy on us.
* Lord, he whom Thou lovest is sick.
* Lord, grant that I may see.
* Lord, help me.
* Lord, if Thou wilt, Thou canst make me whole.
* Lord, save us, we perish.
* Son of David, have mercy on us.
* Lord, I am not worthy that Thou shouldst come under my roof, but speak the word only and I shall be healed.
* Master, we perish.
* Lord, save us.
* Lord, my daughter is dying, lay hands on her that she may be saved and live.
* Jesus, Son of David, have mercy on us.
* Hosanna, to the Son of David, blessed be He that cometh in the name of the Lord.

Clare

At a social gathering, a friend, recently bereaved of her husband, took me aside and softly said, "This is my first social event since my Clare's passing three month's ago. I miss him so much. We had been married 53 years. Cancer claimed him slowly. At the end he was totally blind.

"But I must tell you how God prepared me for this loss. He used my sister's death as a trial run.

"She died shortly before Clare. I was with her. What a great privilege it was! So beautiful and natural! As I held her hand, she slipped away. Within seconds it happened. A sensation, not of this world, flushed my spirit. I felt the warmth of joy and the coolness of peace. I was drifting on another plane. There was no anxiety, fear, or sense of loss. My sister's spirit was leaving her body and I was part of it. I was caught up in a moment of holiness — the going of a good soul to God.

"I wondered if Clare's death would be the same. And, do you know, it was. As soon as he gave up his last breath, that same feeling of deep serenity swept through me, that same comfort, that same breeze, that same happiness. It was as if I was handing Clare's soul to the Divine Master. Clare was at peace and so was I."

When she finished, her eyes swam with joy.

Last year she joined Clare.

A SCOTTISH TOAST

May the best you've ever seen
  Be the worst you'll ever see;
May the mouse ne'er leave your pantry
  Wi a tear drap in its e'e;
May your lum keep blithely reekin'
  Till you're auld enough to dee;
May you aye be just as happy
  As I wish you now to be!

— Anonymous

(lum – fireplace) (reekin' – smoking) (dee – die)

Is It Worth It?

The attainment of a goal requires sacrifice.

An old Gaelic story tells us of a Scottish hunter who had an on-going battle with a fox. Every time the hunter left his tent, the fox raided his catches.

One night the Scot devised a plan that cornered the fox. The fox ended up behind the fire inside the tent with the entrance blocked by the hunter.

As the Scot raised his pistol, the fox dashed to the very back of the tent, picked up the hunter's jacket and tossed it on the fire. The Scot reached in to retrieve his coat and the fox *hightailed* it.

A Good Start

Christ's forgiveness of His enemies as He hung on the cross is a lesson for people of all faiths. He said, "Forgive them, Father, for they know not what they do." (Luke 23:34)

Likewise, when it comes to our forgiving enemies, isn't Christ's admonition a good way to start? Confronted by hurt from others, can we not say, "Father, I forgive them, not only because You told us to do so, but also because they *may* not know what they're doing?"

Michael

One day at a special weekday morning service for two classes of school children, the old pastor taught the young people a beautiful form of prayer.

He said, "This very morning in Halifax General Hospital, a little boy of eight named Michael will be operated on. He is very, very sick! Now what I want all of you to do is imagine that we are all in his room in the hospital kneeling around his bed. And I want you to pray there, each in your own way that God will make him better." And then the priest paused. It was a solemn moment.

That was the day the children visited little Michael.

A Mother's Tears

The community Italian church as part of a drive for money planned an auction. They asked parishioners for the donation of articles.

Among the people asked was one Mario. A gifted oil painter well-known at home and abroad, Mario agreed to do an oil painting by a certain date.

About two months later, Mario received a phone call. The church officials wanted to know what had happened to the painting. The auction was the next day and nothing had been received. Mario said not to worry. He'd have it there in the morning.

Mario didn't tell them he'd forgotten and that he didn't have one ready. So he worked long into the night and came up with a beautiful oil of Virgin and Child. The organizers were delighted.

The evening of the show, Mario dropped in to see how much his painting would fetch. He arrived to see a great crowd surrounding his work. Then he noticed some were kneeling and praying and blessing themselves. Some were crying.

Mario thought, "I knew it was good but not that good." He moved closer. Then he saw the reason for the sanctity of the crowd. The Virgin's left eye appeared to be crying. That's what people thought. But Mario knew different.

The eyes were running because the oil hadn't time to set. So Mario told the parish priest who told the parishioners the truth.

Yet, all considered, the whole matter left an eerie suspicion among the people in the parish.

Some asked why another part of the painting hadn't dripped? Why that spot under the eye of the mother? Why not a finger? Or a nose?

Swing and Sway

Peggy had definite purpose in going to church that Sunday. She had been in a depressed state of mind for some time and was determined to ask God for a sign that her despondency would lift.

She arrived at church early. After some petitioning, she thought it best to tell God the kind of sign she would like. On the wall behind the altar was a large wooden statue of Mary holding Jesus. Over the lady's arm dangled a long rosary placed there by some devout soul. Peggy told God that if He would make the rosary swing back and forward, she would accept that as a sign that she would get well soon.

Some 15 minutes later, nothing had happened. Peggy was disappointed, but not deterred. Suddenly, just before the beginning of the service, the rosary started to swing. Peggy was delighted until she realized that the front doors had been opened and that the draught was causing the rosary to move.

But, then, Peggy concluded, and rightly so, that she hadn't told God how to arrange the sign. The swaying may not have been a miracle, Peggy thought, but it certainly was a good coincidence. And she took that for what it was worth.

NEVER QUIT

When things go wrong as they sometimes will,
When the road you're trudging seems all uphill,
When funds are low and debts are high
And you want to smile, but you have to sigh,
When care is pressing down a bit,
Rest if you must, but don't you quit.
Success is failure turned inside out —
The silver tint of the clouds of doubt,
And you never can tell how close you are,
It may be near when it seems so far,
So, stick to the fight when you're hardest hit —
It's when things seem worst that
You must not quit.

— Anonymous

Will You Be a Friend?

An old black and white Hollywood movie has for its theme that one's thirst for friendship begins early in life.

It's the story of a four-year-old girl so deprived of playing companions that she creates in her imagination a lady friend whom she meets regularly in the family garden for conversation and games.

The movie patron sees the lady friend as a ghost, the parents see her as a hallucination, and the child views her as a real person.

Not surprisingly, the girl needs her garden friend particularly in times of social stress. The playmate gives her the answers she wants to hear and the love that she desires. Without this friend, the child may not have kept her sanity.

It was only when a real *human* friend came into her life that the child closed the book on fantasy. One replaced the other. The child never knew the difference, because for her none existed.

The longing for friendship must be recognized for what it is — an intense desire to be wanted by others. A contact may be with someone outside a family or even from another world.

For a short time, dolls, toys, pets, even imagination, answer such a need, but one day little minds must reach out for recognition and love from contemporaries.

We must look around, tread softly and listen — we could well be the lady in the garden for some lonely child.

So Near — So Far

Inside the convent wall, two religious Sisters walked in the garden at dusk.

Suddenly, one Sister remarked, "Look at the beautiful castle beyond the valley. How majestic — the winding road up to its door — the sun on the ramparts — the fountains on its lawns."

"Yes, it is beautiful," answered the other. "Notice the great hall, the cars pulling up in front, the scurry of the footmen, the lights in all the rooms. It must be a special occasion — perhaps a celebration of marriage. There, you can see the special car."

"What comforts they must have," said the first. "Having all they wish for, must make for happy living."

The other Sister did not speak.

"What are you thinking?" asked the first.

"Nothing really. I'm imagining the dress and orchestra and food, the glitter, the laughter, the warmth and joy of it all. As for the happiness of the rich, it's an okay life for those cut out for it."

At the door, they parted.

For a while, the more pensive of the Sisters stood silently in her sparsely-furnished room. She looked at the single bed, the light, desk and chair, a small end table, the bare floor and the cupboard. She knelt down and prayed, "May God bless my younger sister married on this day. May she have as much happiness as I."

DON'T BLAME ME

I am the Light
And you do not see me …
I am the Way
And you do not follow me …
I am the Truth
And you do not believe me …
I am the Life
And you do not seek me …
I am the Master
And you do not listen to me …
I am your great Friend
And you do not love me …
I am your God
And you do not pray to me …
If you are unhappy
Don't blame me!

— Author Unknown

Reflections

The recently deceased parish priest had been treated poorly by his parishioners. Their stipends were small and their criticisms many. The parish had not prospered!

Before his death he left instructions that a letter from him to his parishioners be read at his funeral. His coffin was to be kept closed until that time.

In his letter, he said he was not entirely to blame for the parish's lack of success. If the members wanted to know the real cause, they need only file past his bier and look in at his worn-out remains.

They then opened the coffin. As one line moved along on either side, each person looking in saw his or her reflection. The sexton had put mirrors on each side of the body.

The pastor placed the major portion of the guilt squarely where it belonged: on every parish member's shoulders.

If Christ placed a mirror at the base of Calvary, how many images would we recognize?

Julian

I was setting out for Lourdes, to the Shrine of the Immaculate Conception and I asked a friend, a devout 84-year-old nun, Sister Mary Julian, if she wished to send any special request. I knew she had had some poor health of late and that her sister, also a nun, was in an advanced stage of Parkinson's.

The petite nun with deep amber eyes looked up at me and said, "Yes, I would like you to ask Our Lady of Lourdes to send me and the other Sisters in our monastery the grace to love God more deeply. You know," and she became very intense, "we can never love God too much!"

Sister Mary Julian died on September 25, 2004, never satisfied that she had loved as much as she should have.

The Bells

I was standing in the drizzle one cold Easter at the Grotto of Lourdes in southern France where 14-year-old Bernadette Soubirous saw God's mother in 1858. In front of me, under the overhang of a shallow cave, an Italian priest was preaching to Italian pilgrims. In behind and to his left was a small altar and to his right, along the wall, a single line of benches for shelter. The tempo of the ascetic priest increased as he neared the end.

The spirit of the occasion — Easter, Lourdes, Mary, his own people, the majestic Pyrenees — all moved him to eloquence. His eyes and gestures emphasized the melodic fusion of idea, word and feeling so characteristic of the Romantic tongues.

The air was full of "magnificoes" and "benedicites" when, suddenly, all the bells in the town of Lourdes began to peal. It was noon on Easter Sunday, time to celebrate the holiest feast in the Christian church.

No Easter bonnet or mitre for this day in the rain. Just a holy place in the misty foothills of a great mountain range, a song of praise from a good priest, and a tumultuous ringing joy in Lourdes.

Octavia

Some fellow Christians can be inspirational. Their faith runs so deep it flows into their thoughts and duties and words.

Not long ago, on my way out of morning service, I passed by a friend sitting in her pew. She looked up and said cheerfully, "And how are you this morning?" I said, rather unconvincingly, "Not too bad, Octavia, thank you. And how about yourself?"

"Oh, I'm fine." And then, picking up my malaise, she added, "When we have the Lord with us what else can we be, but on top of the world?"

The Spoiler

Her cane clicked as she shuffled down the cement ramp of the church. A stronger summer breeze would have turned her around.

Her determined spirit prompted me to say, "Good morning, Ma'am. You look like a lady with things to do and places to go."

Without so much as a look, she retorted, "I certainly have, Sir. I certainly have!"

As she left me in her dust, I blurted, "Whatever you do do, try to be a good girl!"

And quick as a twitch, she replied, "Ah, there you go, trying to spoil my day."

Alf

In matters of openness to other religions my Uncle Alf had tunnel vision. As a staunch Presbyterian, born and bred in Glasgow, Scotland, his tolerance for the Roman Church was zero. Naturally, intermarriage with Catholics was not acceptable. In fact, any participation in a Catholic service by a follower of the Church of Scotland was anathema.

When his parents came to Montreal in the early twentieth century, the whole family was wary of the strong Catholicity in that province.

Their first test came when Alf's sister became engaged to a Catholic. Her father refused to give her away. A second test saw Alf's brother become Catholic. His parents threw him out. That's the way it was in those times. They weren't bigots. History showed they had justification. Life went on.

It wasn't until many years later that Alf faced a test similar to the one that had beset his father. One of Alf's daughters announced her intention of marrying a Catholic. Naturally, Alf said he wouldn't give her away. That was final. His beliefs ran deep.

But a strange event changed his mind. Alf's father wanted to speak to him. His father told Alf not to make the same dreadful mistake that he had made years before. The old man had always regretted not taking his daughter to the altar.

Well the upshot was that Alf buried the hatchet and gave away his daughter to his new son-in-law. Alf seemed to have changed. But not really.

Within a year, the invitation to his first granddaughter's christening salted old wounds and Alf refused to attend.

A few years later, however, another situation pulled Alf off his perch. The same daughter developed life-threatening complications in a second pregnancy. She had a malignant tumour on the liver.

Everybody started praying, especially Alf. The outcome was a Caesarean birth during which the doctors removed half the liver to cut away the tumour. The doctors thought the whole process a miracle. The daughter recovered, the baby was healthy, and Alf was on top of the world.

So enthralled was Alf that he went into see his daughter in the hospital and said to her, "My dear, I want you to know that I shall be attending your new baby's christening. I am absolutely convinced that this miracle was not due to Presbyterian prayers alone, but to the prayers of people of all faiths, especially my friends, the Catholics."

Pauline

In a dream, my friend Pauline saw an ugly woman hovering over her bed. The woman smiled fiendishly. Arms draped in black reached down. Pauline was terrorized. Suddenly, behind the spectre, Pauline saw another woman. This woman was beautiful and her presence put the run on the evil one. Pauline awoke.

The next day, a nearby neighbour and her two children dropped by for an expected visit. While Pauline and the mother chatted over coffee and toast, Pauline's children took their playmates into a small bedroom.

When the visitor decided to go home, she went to the bedroom to get the children. Pauline became somewhat alarmed when the woman was gone a long time.

She went to the bedroom only to find the door locked. She called out. The lady said she'd be out in a few minutes.

A while later, she came out with the children in tow. She thanked Pauline and left. Pauline went about her work.

The lady's strange behaviour was forgotten until Pauline's children came running to say that smoke was coming from the bedroom where they had played. Pauline called the Fire Department.

The firemen discovered a table light inside a toy box. Various articles had been thrown in over the bare, burning bulb and the box half shut. The papers stuffed around the bulb had caught fire.

The fireman didn't think the visiting children were clever enough to contrive such a plan. So Pauline decided that it was the mother who had tried to burn her out. Pauline didn't call the police.

When Pauline recalled her dream, she was even more convinced of the visitor's guilt. She knew also that it was the beautiful lady in the dream who had helped her children discover the fire. The evil image had been a precursor of the evil-bent visitor.

Later that week, Pauline and her husband invited the lady's husband over to discuss the situation. Apparently his wife had done such strange things before. Eventually the sick woman received badly needed psychiatric care and as far as is known regained her health.

Why So Early?

I realize as I grow older that for many people rejection of God takes place early in their lives. It is as if they have prematurely studied their faith, found it wanting and thrown it away. Living life without religion becomes a habit and as such becomes as difficult to break as drinking, smoking or sleeping in Sunday mornings.

The Power of Song

A Father Fagan from Prince Edward Island, in true Irish fashion, loves to sing. I first met him in White Rock, Surrey, British Columbia, where he was a veteran pastor. Besides singing, he had two other loves: the Church and golf.

On Sunday it was the Church, and during the week, golf. In his chatty sermons he kept the parishioners informed of his progress on the course as zealously as he urged them to love God, especially in song. About the latter he would say over and over: "Prayer in song is twice as strong." Another version of that maxim is: "He who sings his prayers, prays twice."

In the Jewish faith, prayer in song has always been uppermost. Christ sang hymns with his apostles at the Last Supper and on other occasions. The Jews would have known from childhood all the songs of the synagogue, especially the psalms.

The psalms are Judaic poems set to music, written centuries before Christianity as prayers of supplication, thanksgiving and praise. The Book of Psalter, a collection of some 150 hymns written by kings, prophets and temple singers was sung individually or collectively, in and outside synagogues.

Today the Psalms are integral, not just to the Jewish faith, but also to the 300 or more branches of Christianity. They are, as ever, concise, meaningful, beautiful and powerful.

Once, years ago, a strange happening in regard to these song-prayers occurred while I was reading Bible verses as part of the Sunday service. The psalm spoke of God as our shepherd and of the repose and delights to be found in His kingdom of verdant meadows, laughing streams and cool shades.

I had only read one verse when a powerful presence seemed to surround the words. It was as if the One about whom we spoke was there listening to the praise of that simple poem. Each thought I read jumped off the page in stark realism. It was saying, "This is true about me. Listen, my children. I am your Good Shepherd. I am among you. Come, follow me."

After the service, I asked my wife if she felt anything about the reading. She said no. So, just to check my sanity, I went to the sacristy and spoke to the visiting priest whom I knew.

"Father," I said, "were you aware of anything special during my reading?"

"Yes," he answered, "it was very noticeable. I sensed there was a special force in the Church, something holy and powerful."

"That's right," I said. "I even felt once that I wasn't speaking the words and that someone was speaking them through me."

After that experience in the little church of St. Monica's so many days ago, I heartily support Father Fagan's theory: "Prayer in song *is* twice as strong."

No wonder we set our most meaningful thoughts and feelings to music.

Trust

A male teacher suffered 18 months of emotional stress before being cleared of false charges of child molestation.

One day after, a reporter asked him what his ordeal taught him. He answered, "I learned I must get to know people, *before* I trust them."

Those who trust too readily are prone to being taken in. They must devise methods of checking "character authenticity."

In doing so, they'll make errors; with luck, small ones; by being patient and wise, they'll learn to recognize people of true value.

Taking a Chance

Any person in his or her right mind is free up to the last breath, to choose heaven or hell. It's never too late to make peace with God. Even obstinate sinners have a chance.

Joseph Stalin's housekeeper swears she saw a priest leave Stalin's room the night he died. Whether Stalin's confession was contrite enough to warrant absolution is another matter. We must presume it was.

Jesus made it very clear that any sinner's conversion causes rejoicing in heaven. His parables on the vineyard-workers' pay, the recoveries of the lost pearl and lamb, and the return of the prodigal son, emphasize how repentant sinners are welcomed with open arms by God.

The questions remain, however: how many last-minute deathbed confessions *do* take place and how many people *actually* find God after years of rebuking Him?

After listening to sermons, reading biographies and autobiographies, visiting the elderly and following the lives of my friends and relatives, I believe that returning to God in one's latter days is the exception rather than the rule.

Most atheists and agnostics hold *steadfast* to their beliefs. Many lukewarm Christians *remain* just that, lukewarm. Most avaricious men continue to hoard.

Most selfish women continue to think only of their own welfare. Some proud men are *always* right, and so on. Such habits are so deeply rooted that any changes in inclinations are very difficult. Like rowing against a tide or running into a stiff wind. The old fox in us does not die easily.

The difficulty of deathbed conversion is illustrated by a story told by the Curé of Ars, France, St. John Vianney (1786-1859). Writing about avarice, he said, "Misers generally die ... in despair and pay eternally to the devil for their insatiable thirst for riches."

He then related a sad but amusing tale about a miser receiving the last sacraments. The Curé lit a candle set in a beautiful, heavy, silver candlestick. When the man saw the silver, he couldn't help but say, "That must be worth a fortune."

Naturally, countless souls near death do receive God's grace and ask for forgiveness. Such miracles are the business of the Holy Spirit who goes where She or He wishes. Often, God is swayed to use this saving grace by the prayers and sacrifices of someone, somewhere in our world. But can we take a chance?

If we are at odds with God, maybe we shouldn't wait for sudden reconciliation. Death comes like "a thief in the night" and "we know not the hour." Sickness may rob us of opportunity. But so can dalliance and procrastination.

Friendship

Friendships must be nurtured. They cannot be taken for granted. Left unattended, they die.

A saying like "Love means never having to say you're sorry" is poppycock. Apologies *are* necessary if we hurt a friend. *Patching up* friendships makes sense. Acts of affection keep friendships fresh. Forgiveness takes the cake; acts of kindness are the icing

The Power of Innocence

Many theologians agree that every person has the natural law written by God into his or her psyche. This psyche's externalization is called the conscience. This natural law enables man to determine good from evil without the guidance of commandments, laws and customs. Every sane person intuitively knows that killing another or coveting another's spouse and property is against the natural order.

The proof of this genetic moral code's existence is illustrated by the Biblical story of the cities of Sodom and Gomorrah. *The Book of Genesis* tells of their destruction by God around 1850 BC somewhere on the Palestinian plains below the Dead Sea. These were well-established Semitic cities known and visited by Abraham. Whether they were Hebrew and followers of Abraham cannot be verified. However, we do know they were morally corrupt and paid dearly for it.

According to *Genesis*, written to show the genealogy of Abraham from Adam by way of Noah to David, three men, one of whom was God, came one morning to Abraham's tent near Sodom. God said to Abraham, "The outcry against Sodom and Gomorrah is so great and their sins so grave, that I must go down and see whether or not their actions correspond to the cry against them that comes to me. I mean to find out."

So He sent his two accompanying angels into Sodom to the house of Abraham's nephew, Lot. Shortly after entry, the townsmen of Sodom, both "young and old" surrounded Lot's house and demanded the two strangers come outside "so we may have intimacies with them." Lot refused their request. When the crowds tried to batter down the front door, the two angels blinded them with light and escaped.

The next day, according to the Bible, God reduced "the plain," "the cities," "the produce," and "all the inhabitants" to just a "dense smoke rising like fumes from a furnace."

The kind of sins of these people that brought down the wrath of God has been open to conjecture. Some historians say homosexuality was the main cause, but the prophets suggest it may also have been social injustice to the poor, or an insidious immorality.

That it was the violation of the natural law which sealed their fate becomes evident when one considers these people had no written laws, commandments, or wandering prophets to teach them. At best, they had a few traditional laws set down by the leaders of tribes. It *had* to have been their consciences that made them guilty in God's eyes. Their own guilt condemned them and they knew they had done wrong.

There's a lesson here. The presence of conscience makes us all vulnerable. The pagan, the atheist, and the agnostic as well, must beware. Conscience is the silent judge of *all* behaviour.

When it comes to sin, the buck stops with ourselves. The laws of God regarding life and death are written where we can all read them. No public edicts or political ethics promulgated by courts, press, government and even some churches can "rub out" the "damned spots" of sin. Society may set aside the moral codes put forth in the Good Book. But it cannot so readily dispatch the natural law. "Conscience doth make cowards of us all."

Another lesson, on a more positive note, comes from this same tale of the two damned cities. It tells us about the power of good people. Abraham, obviously upset by the possible destruction of Sodom, asks God, "Will you sweep away the innocent with the guilty? Suppose there are 50 innocent people in the city, would you wipe out the place rather than spare it for the sake of the 50 innocent people within it?" God replied, "If I find 50 innocent people in the city of Sodom, I will spare the whole place for their sakes."

Abraham went further and asked: What about 45? Then 40? 30? 20? And finally 10? And each time God said he would not destroy Sodom for their sakes. Abraham pressed God no further. He may well have guessed God would have deterred His judgement for even *one* innocent person. Or perhaps Abraham knew in his heart that Sodom hadn't one person to offer except Lot and his family.

Imagine these scales of justice: in one pan, ten God-fearing loving persons, and in the other, two cities of reprobates. Yet, in spite of the imbalance, God still would have tipped the scales in favour of the innocents.

The writers of *Genesis* then, had four lessons to convey and Abraham was there for all four: God dislikes sin and will punish the unrepentant; man carries *within* himself God's natural laws; God attaches great importance and power to goodness; and goodness will overcome evil. The last two lessons are inspirational.

The whole idea of innocence being so pleasing to God gives confidence to anyone trying his or her best to become better. Not only can such a person move mountains, but he or she can also save cities, families and individuals. The presence of evil pales in the light of goodness.

So when we pray, even though we are only a few, we should pray with faith, knowing that if God chooses, He may allow any number of souls, otherwise doomed, to be given another chance to *live* again in His name.

He can sprinkle stardust wherever He chooses.

GREED

A cousin remembers a story from one of his early school readers: A dog with a large bone in his mouth comes upon a pool. In the pool, he sees another bone bigger than his own. He dives in to get it. For all his trouble, he loses the first bone and almost drowns.

One Day in '31

A certain good man was not happy about his third daughter leaving home. His first two had gone to the convent. Now his youngest was off to nursing school.

The family were all there that final Sunday night for a farewell dinner. The father gave a toast and his wife cried. Their princess stood for a moment to say goodbye.

Next morning, in the September mists, the man and his daughter set out for the college some 70 miles away. Their hearts were heavy, but reconciled.

Then it happened. They never did see the train.

A few days later the bell of St. Michael's, Corkery, Ontario, tolled across the country fields as father and daughter were laid to rest side by side on a knoll by the road where the wind forever sighs.

Francis and Jane

With or without physical gratification between people who love one another, the spiritual attachment of love is of paramount importance.

This tenet is as true for those in the religious life as for those outside it. In fact, spiritual *affairs* prudently developed in the religious life may well be the most enriching of all.

The story of such a "marriage of minds" between François de Sales and Jeanne de Chantal in the seventeenth century illustrates how two souls dedicated to God in the religious life can strengthen and complement the other. Both lived in those decades when Champlain discovered Québec, the pilgrims came to Virginia and Massachusetts, and Willie "the Bard" wrote his works. They were both Burgundian from France — intelligent, refined, rich, upper class, and destined to become saints.

François de Boisy, known as "de Sales," was born near Annecy, France, in 1567. Studies in Paris and Padua led to a Doctorate of Laws in 1591, the priesthood in 1593, and at age 35, a bishopric. His Episcopal see was in Geneva-Annecy, part of the Duchy of Savoie between France and Italy. It consisted of 450 parishes scattered through the mountains.

A man of gentle, almost reticent persuasion, he felt honey drew more flies than vinegar and that the pen was mightier than the sword. He stood for conviction, perseverance, and common sense in religious practice. His writings were standard reading in European castles, courts, and ecclesiastical institutions.

De Sales was a first class essayist long before the essay came into vogue. His style was straightforward with little pretence or superficiality.

He urged readers and listeners to worry less and pray more. Abandonment to God's will was crucial to spiritual advancement. He encouraged aid to the poor, lonely and destitute.

He reached out constantly to be with his parishioners. He counselled people from all walks of life by letter or in person. So well-grounded was he in his vocational fervour, that friendships with Henry III and IV, Louis XIII, Catherine de Medici, dukes, countesses, archbishops and Popes, never turned his head.

One morning while praying in Annecy, it became known to him that he would one day found a women's religious order. He saw in his mind the image of a lady dressed as a widow accompanied by two similarly garbed women. Later, while preaching at Dijon, he noticed a widow, whom he recognized as the person in his vision. And so it was that he came to meet Jeanne Fremyot, a chestnut-haired beauty with a brilliant mind and dynamic energy.

Together they would set up the Order of the Visitation, which 400 years later has a membership of 4,800 sisters in 180 monasteries throughout the world.

Jeanne Fremyot's family, unlike that of de Sales, was of noble blood. She was well-educated, energetic, cheerful, impulsive and the perfect catch for her husband, Christophe Rabutin de Chantal, whose blood happened to be richer than his purse. Of their six children, four lived.

Nine years after their marriage, Christophe was shot while hunting. At age 29, in the year 1602, Jeanne was a widow. She then spent seven unhappy years with her mercurial father-in-law. As no home can suffer two mistresses, Jeanne gave way to a dominating, scheming, well-entrenched housekeeper whose fealty to her master probably included upstairs responsibilities.

Although the Freymot and de Sales families knew each other through business, the bishop and Jeanne did not meet until 1604. Their friendship was to last until his death. Although separated by 200 miles between Annecy and Dijon, they often met in their parents' homes.

Jeanne had once asked the Bishop for spiritual direction because she, too, had been the recipient of a vision from God that had encouraged her to seek *his* assistance. One day, her prayer had been interrupted by the image of an unknown bishop who said, "Here is the guide, beloved of men and God, in whose hands you must put your conscience." Sometime later, she recognized her "unknown bishop" as he was preaching in Dijon abbey. He was François.

From 1602, until Jeanne and François established the first House of the Visitation of Annecy in 1610, they had their share of troubles. Jeanne struggled with her calling to the religious life as well as her domestic plight. As a new bishop, François faced the power of Calvinism complicated by the intrigue of royalty and parliaments.

Death also tested their faith. Jeanne lost a daughter in 1610, and François, his favourite sister in 1607 and his mother in 1610. Jeanne also had the painful duty of leaving her son at Dijon in the care of her father. Another daughter married and one came with her to the Annecy convent.

The establishment in France of some 30 Visitation Convents took place over the next 20 years. François did his best to help find accommodation, money and Roman approval for each new monastery. He also worked on the Order's constitution and rule. It was he who directed Jeanne in her vocation and never abandoned her. Jeanne did most of the organizational work but depended greatly on his advice and influence. Their heroic example drew many novices to the order and many converts to the Church. Their work with the poor and broken was legendary.

Over the years, they met to discuss strategy at Lyon, Paris, Moulins, Thorens, Annecy and Dijon. All the while, their spiritual admiration for each other grew deeper. They were soul mates.

François died at Lyon in December, 1622. At his final meeting with Jeanne (their first visit in three and a half years), they talked for four hours, after which he sent her on a road tour of monasteries in order to spare her being present when he died.

To the end, he emphasized simplicity in religious practice. Analyzing a problem ad infinitum was not his way; better to put it in God's hands along with any anxiety. Implored by his friends for some exhortation on how to become a saint, he asked for paper (since his illness prevented his speaking), and wrote in large letters "humility, humility, humility."

At heart, he was always the *peasants' bishop*. Two of his favourite people were a deaf mute girl from the hills of Savoie to whom he gave life employment in his father's house and a servant girl who became the fourth member of the first convent in Annecy and the last person he said goodbye to before he died.

It was Jeanne who arranged for the bishop's open coffin to be placed just outside the black grille in Annecy's Visitation Convent's chapel. The first time the Sisters came as a group to pay their respects, Jeanne knelt alone on a prie-dieu inside the cloister's grille side to offer prayers.

She felt devastated. How could she manage the Order without his guidance especially at a time when constitutional changes were imminent? The story has it that she asked François for a sign of direction.

Suddenly, she felt a gentle hand, from behind, grasp the top and side of her head. It was François. And what's even more astounding: all the Sisters in the choir gasped as they saw her cowl collapse under the weight of the hand.

The King and I

Advice couched in a good story or anecdote is far more readily accepted by listeners — it's like "a spoonful of honey" helping "the medicine go down!"

Saint François de Sales, already mentioned, had the knack of using pleasant interplay of either real or imaginary characters to make a moral point.

In real life, Saint Louis, King of France, once went to the Orient with his wife, Marguerite, a very saintly woman. In order to emphasize the best way of surrendering to God's will, de Sales imagined this interview before the trip between himself and the king's wife whom he knew.

"Where are you going, Madame?" asked de Sales.

"Where the king goes."

"But do you know exactly where the king is going?"

"He told me in a general way. I am not concerned to know where he is going. I care only about going with him."

"You have no information then about this voyage, Madame?"

"None, save the idea of being with my dear lord and husband."

"Your husband will go to Egypt. He will stop at Damietta, at Acre, and in several other places. Do you wish to go to all these places?"

"I think only of being near my king; the places where he goes have no importance at all for me except for the fact that he will be there. I am not so much travelling with him as following him. I do not care about the voyage, but am content to be in the presence of the king."

Tinus

St. Monica's is a small close-knit parish. So when the parish priest came out with a personal message as part of his Father's Day sermon, no one was surprised.

He said, "This morning I received a phone call from a former parishioner now living in Calgary. Her name is Marilyn. She's married with her own family.

"She asked me to forward a message to her father on this special day. She intends to phone him later, but for her own reasons wanted me to convey her feelings ahead of time.

"I see him from here. At the back. Tinus, would you mind standing for a moment?

"Thank you. It was your daughter who called. She wanted me to tell you what a good father you are, how you taught her the value of prayer, and how by your sacrifice and devotion to family, you left her with values that will never fade."

The burly, handsome Tinus humbly smiled and sat down to the applause of the entire church. That episode was the sermon that morning.

DOUG

Marriage and wit have helped my 96-year-old friend Doug. At age 93, he married his third wife. His first two wives had been wonderful ladies. So was his third.

Another bride, another wedding, another reception — Doug was an old hand.

So casual was he that when the priest asked him at the third marriage if he would take Estelle for his bride, he quipped, "I have! I did! And I do!"

A Matter of Sharing

"God moves in mysterious ways, His wonders to perform."

Many years ago, an unwed mother-to-be went far away to live with relatives. She gave birth to a girl.

Due to her young age, she decided to give up the child for adoption with the proviso that she could have a say in the choice of parents. She did so and went back home to begin again.

Years later, she married. But not for long. She and her husband died in an auto crash. The girl's parents were devastated. She had been their only child.

One day, in their loneliness, her parents had the idea to search for their granddaughter's adoptive parents. After all, their daughter had chosen them; so it wasn't as if they were strangers. Wouldn't it be something if the child's parents would be willing to allow the natural grandparents to see the girl?

Not long after, they *did* find the child's parents who *did* open their hearts.

The joy of that first embrace with the grandchild was immeasurable. Their deceased daughter's love flowed through the child's arms.

Recently, the grandparents attended the wedding of their grandchild.

MEDITATIVE POEM

I sought my soul, but my soul I could not see
I sought my God, but my God eluded me
I sought my brother, and I found all three!

— Author Unknown

Payne

Many professional athletes have such strong religious convictions that they wish to share these feelings with the public.

Some give testimony by crossing themselves. Others kneel down after scoring a touchdown or jumping a bar. Some wear medals. In such ways, they are publicly praising God for helping them.

They have come to realize that they can't survive in their highly pressured lifestyle without divine help.

Payne Stewart, a great golf talent who recently died, often shared God's role in his life with his fans. It showed in Payne's personal example on the course and off. It showed in his charity and love. It came out in little things.

After his death, his buddies found four letters of the alphabet sewn on the outside of one of his golf bags, four letters that showed the mettle of the man, four letters that said it all: "WWJD."

"What Would Jesus Do?"

The Circle

A friend holds the theory that some people have an evil power that enables them to extract goodness from others. When he is in a room of strangers, he protects himself by drawing an imaginary circle of goodness around his body.

The idea of an evil presence being present in certain people, places and things is not new. Nor are the items used to ward them off. Medals, incantations, blessings, feathers, jewellery, bits of clothing, holy water and incense are just a few things used by different cultures.

A circle drawn around our psyche is really not that far out.

There's merit in avoiding certain people and places. The world is full of leeches that drain our power. It follows that we best arm ourselves with inner strength and goodness.

Following Your Heart

Years ago, as part of a two-day retreat in a Cistercian Trappist monastery, I happened to be out walking with a middle-aged monk of whom I asked the following question, "If the Abbot told you tomorrow to leave this monastery and return to the world, how would you react?" He answered immediately, "I would lie outside the gate until I was dead."

Thirty years later this very scenario happened to a friend named Céline. After six and a half years of intense preparation for her final vows, the Mother Superior asked her to leave the convent before taking them. She had been rejected by a secret ballot among the House's 16 members. The Sisters had voted by dropping black or white balls into a wooden box. The vote had to be unanimous. One black ball was enough to send her on her way.

Céline was disappointed, even bitter. The Superior had suggested she come back and try again in a few years. But that advice did not placate her. She was a fish out of water. On the day she left, she sat on the convent steps with her suitcase beside her. It was a sad, sad moment and she hurt all over.

In truth, she understood the Order's position. A person not suited to the religious life can cause problems, particularly in a small group. Obviously some Sisters, perhaps just one, thought she was unacceptable. Was it because she was too outgoing? Did her hearty laugh unnerve them? Possibly her tendency to frolic unsettled a few. Was her guitar playing and singing of French melodies too much for the measured constraint of the silent life? Or was her religious development not yet good enough for final vows? She liked to think that it was the last reason. More of God's moulding was needed.

Now Céline was no quitter. She still felt that God really *did* want her in religious life. After all, she had spent six and a half years in it already! Those years proved she had a reservoir of physical and emotional strength. All she needed was another try. And not years away either — the sooner, the better!

Not long after, she received permission from the Mother Superior to visit the public part of the convent chapel. There she sat on the floor with her back up against the grill-wall of the cloister. There, she continued to sing the Hours (the Psalms) with the Sisters. Like the monk mentioned earlier, she was slowly dying outside the cloister.

After months of floundering, her former Mother Superior, impressed by her perseverance, arranged for her to try again at a different branch of the same Order. It was a smaller, younger group more in keeping with Céline's personality.

There, after another four years, the new group voted her in. No more black balls. At her ceremony of Final Vows, 11 family members and my wife and I joined the celebration. Céline was ecstatic with joy. It had taken ten and a half years — almost a lifetime.

One day on a visit with Céline, she reviewed her long voyage this way: "I wasn't ready the first time. My Sisters could see that. I needed more development. As to how I finally made it through those final years, I offer two factors: God wanted me and helped me, and secondly, a few precious friends believed in me and encouraged me to go on. My friends kept me above water and God did the rest. In fact, I truly believe that even one earthly friend beseeching God in another's behalf can save even the most destitute."

Near Is Not So Far

The late Scottish tenor host, Sir Harry Secombe, was unusually sombre on one segment of his travelling television show "Highway." In Letterkenny, Ireland, his director had arranged an interview between Harry and a lady who had recently lost four children in a house fire.

Sitting in her humble home, Sir Harry carefully began, "My dear, how did you ever manage to bear your loss?"

Without a pause, as if she were talking to a neighbour, she answered, "Sir Harry, they're gone and the shock will never go away. But my husband and I comfort each other knowing they have not gone very far. They are as near as God, and God is always close. They are only as far away as God."

Leslie

Can you imagine anyone insinuating to roly-poly Pope John 23rd that he himself cooked spaghetti in a cauldron? One Leslie Costello did just that and somehow escaped excommunication.

Leslie was never much for protocol. The product of a mining town in Northern Ontario, where men are men and the taverns are there to prove it, he needed both brawn and smarts to find a way. His Irish wit got him out of hot water as easily as it got him in. His physique suggested raw onions for breakfast and slightly cooked beefsteak for supper.

His general appearance had a black Irish beauty about it. His devil-may-care attitude included blarney, badgering, quips and zero respect for pomp and circumstance. In short, this unpredictable Irishman's behaviour antagonized every disciplinarian in his path.

His first career was as a professional hockey player with the Toronto Maple Leafs. It was his speed that was the talk of Maple Leaf Gardens. He could fly. Young people imitated his piston-like strides that drove him like the wind. Hockey scouts admired his talent and ferocity. He gave his best. He hated to lose.

Naturally, sport pundits were surprised when he gave up hockey for the priesthood. In the seminary, where I played against him, he showed why he made the big league. He had talent, flair, and grit.

After his ordination he went back to the communities of the North where the parishioners soon became attracted to his easy, border-line-sacrilegious manners. They realized that his nonchalant approach was just a front and that underneath he always gave his full attention to the purpose of his calling. Colourful, yes; entertaining, yes; but always on the job.

Not surprisingly, Father never quit hockey. Along with several Irish priests, like McGee, Coughlin, Smith and Fenlon, all of whom I knew, he formed a travelling hockey circus called the Flying Fathers. They made thousands of dollars for worthy causes with their all-star games against celebrity squads from radio, television, police, and fire departments. The Fathers even travelled in Europe.

On the ice they were incorrigible, full of tricks and shenanigans. Referees, mainly retirees from the National Hockey League, were willing dupes. Every game had its pies, pile-ups and disregard for rules. The biggest laugh for the crowd came when Leslie escorted the referee to the penalty box and slammed the door.

But, back to the Holy Father. In the early 1960s, the Flying Fathers once played a few games in Rome and before coming home met with the Pope. As the Pope moved down the line of young athletic priests, the solemnity of the moment suggested that any joviality be instigated by the Pope.

That is, until he got to Les. Les was ready for him. He had brought a gift for his boss, a new hockey stick signed by all the Flying Fathers. Naturally, the Pope had a few special words for the founder of the team. But wouldn't you

NATURE'S CHORUS

"The axe falls on the wood in thuds — 'God, God' ... the cry of the rook, 'God,' answers it ... the crack of the fire on the hearth, the voice of the brook, say the same name; all things, dog, cat, fiddle, baby, wind, breaker, sea, thunderclap repeat in a thousand languages — 'God.'"

— Chesterton

know, Les *had a few for him.* He said, "We've brought your holiness a hockey stick. You'll find it the greatest thing for stirring your spaghetti!"

Les died in 2003. You guessed it, while playing hockey. He was 75. His funeral filled the hockey arena in his home town, Schumacher, a suburb of Timmins. Already he is a legend in Northern Ontario. And in my heart.

The Repairman

Not long ago, as a result of a fever that affected his normality, a young man from Minnesota was mistakenly confined to a mental hospital. He was soon forgotten.

One day, by chance, a new doctor examined him and pronounced him sane. After his release, he led an ordinary life. He married and held down a job as an outdoor telephone repairman. He was back to normal — normal, that is, but for one small twist.

Somehow, somewhere, and no one knows when, he developed extrasensory powers. He could read men's hearts, predict the future and even catch glimpses of eternity. He could see spirits standing beside relatives and tell guests secret details about their lives.

His popularity spread to radio and television where he talked about God. He stressed that entrance to heaven depended on a person being at peace with God. He urged people to pray for souls being cleansed in purgatory. He depicted heaven, purgatory and hell. He saw the souls there: the saved souls were *in* the light; the suffering souls *in* a gloomy grey; and the damned souls *in* bottomless black.

The little repairman had come along way. His sixth sense was amazing. Just how great it was, is shown by the following incident: one night, he was on stage during a live television performance when a man in the back row shouted, "You're a phoney. You've no power. Nothing but a fake!"

The repairman answered his critic without mercy. The audience was astounded. He said, "Doctor, that's not your wife you're with tonight, is it?"

The man rose, stared blindly at the stage and ran into the night.

Dave

I don't know how we got around to the subject of dress code, but my friend, Dave, from Burlington, Ontario, said, "My mother set the standards for dress in our house. My brother and I couldn't get out the door without an inspection. And, you know, the training has stuck. I'd never think of going to a social event without a tie and, if not a suit, certainly a sweater."

We had agreed earlier that the men of our present society were dressing down for social occasions, especially those with the wherewithal to afford the best.

Dave surprised me with his next statement: "Suitable dress is a matter of respect. Sure the business world has its reasons: it opens doors, sets moods, makes a statement, and builds confidence.

"But even in everyday life, proper dress shows good manners. Special occasions like wakes, christenings, and anniversaries require appropriate dress. So do some dinners and parties. Showing regard for our guests and hosts; that's the ticket. Being well-groomed means a person has made an effort to look his or her best."

I agreed and added, "My mother had an expression for those who dressed sloppily. She said they looked like 'something the cat dragged in.'"

Wally

On the drive home that morning from his oldest brother's funeral, Wally felt an emptiness. It would be a long day.

Suddenly, he remembered he had a hockey game that afternoon. He said to his wife, "Mary, I have hockey with the fellows today, but I don't think I'll go. I don't feel up to it."

"Wally," said Mary, "your brother would want you to go. 'Whatever makes you happy,' he used to say. Remember."

"Yah, I know," countered Wally. "He always put my happiness first." Wally paused. Then he said, "Okay, I'll go."

Now, generally speaking, Wally was not a star hockey player. He worked hard and made enough good plays to keep his interest alive in the sport.

But, it was a new Wally on the ice that afternoon. Wally had the idea that his brother was watching him play; so he decided to dedicate the game to his memory. He turned his game up a notch.

In the first period, the puck popped on to Wally's stick and he drove it home. Wally felt great. His team-mates wondered what had happened to change him.

In the second period, Wally whistled a desperation shot from the blue line. The puck ricocheted off an opponent's leg into the net and Wally felt his brother's presence even more. As the teams retired for a rest before the third period, Wally entertained the dream of scoring a hat trick.

Wally said to his brother, "What do you say to a hat trick? Can we do it? If we do, I'll know you are truly alive and happy. How about it? Let's give it a try."

Wally hit the ice that period in overdrive. He skated and checked with abandon. He was a player with a mission.

Sure enough, in the last five minutes, from out of nowhere, the puck hit Wally's stick in front of the net. Wally whipped it in, and he had his hat trick. His team- mates joined in his celebration.

Later, at the front door of his home, Wally greeted Mary, "My brother is still watching over me."

"How do you know?"

"Well, he and I got a hat trick today. He set up the plays and I fired the goals. Just like that! Just like that! Wow! We're together again. Ain't that something?"

And for a long time, no one could say anything.

Meeting Places

One morning in Halifax, I came upon what was for me, a great find. Across from the railway station, beyond a park, was a cozy corner restaurant, the kind frequented by locals, truckers, retirees, and out-of-towners like me.

Every big city has got them, those spots of sanity where neighbours gather for the heck of it. As a bonus, these restaurants offer nourishing fare, quick service, the right price, and company as good as you give. Mind you, comfort is rare and space at a premium, but no one seems to notice.

Such establishments have been around for along time. Back in the midcentury, before the arrival of the fast-food outlets, they were popular with every walk of life. I remember they had a daily special — for example, sausages, whipped potatoes, peas, and bread — all for about 90 cents. Next day, the entré might be ham or chicken or hamburger. Only a single choice each day, but it didn't matter.

Other places for socializing in those days were the barbershop, the general store, the blacksmith's shop, the post office, the country store and the bread shop. Along with the corner restaurant, they remain for me wonderful places full of good people and good cheer.

Joseph

One evening Joseph slipped into a church for a visit. He knelt in front of a shrine. On either side at the top of the ornate marble altar, an angel was holding a candle with an electric bulb as a flame.

Joseph had had a tough month. He laid out his cards. He was just hanging on.

Suddenly, after a half-hour of praying, the two candle bulbs began to flicker. They did not stay on — they danced like a flame — licks of amber in the darkening church.

Joseph was sure they hadn't been on earlier. Maybe it was a sign. He left.

About a month later, he happened to meet the pastor with whom he was acquainted. He said, "Father, do those electric bulb candles that the angels hold ever come on?"

The pastor answered, "Not in years. In fact, the switch isn't properly connected. Why do you ask, Joseph?"

And Joseph said, "I was just wondering."

And his heart lightened.

Charles Gordon

In Old Aberdeen, Scotland, Father Charles Gordon was a legend. From 1795 to 1855, his figure was a familiar sight. Aberdeen's 5000 souls loved him — Protestant, Catholic, rich, poor, Gael, Saxon. Dressed in his long cape, wide-brimmed hat and brandishing a black walking stick, he greeted friends as he patrolled Aberdeen's cobblestone streets.

He carried in his *deep* pockets, candies, cookies, fruit, medical supplies and a good supply of coins. Four pence might go to a beggar, a half crown to an old man, fruit to a mother, and hard candy for a child. Some days he carried an old sack filled with clothing and blankets for the poor and sick. He also ran a daily soup kitchen where he himself regularly ate with his guests. He gave away sums of donated money to the needy.

Gradually, he wrote his name into the history books of Northern Scotland. For six decades, this indefatigable vagabond priest filled his small, poorly lit, draughty, damp house of worship with Scottish charity and a measure of incorrigible rascality.

The youngest of nine, he grew up on a farm in Banffshire, Scotland. Advanced education did little to take away his country ways. He spoke *broad* Scots on the street and in his sermons. His homespun turns of phrase were as pure and as natural as his personality. He had a colourful nature. He was an entertainer, a ham, and definitely, a character.

Like most Scotsmen, particularly the Gordons, he could be curt and satirical, especially in the pulpit. It was his *soapbox*. He hammered home his messages. He demanded attention and punctuality. He fingered the guilty: he'd point out a Robertson for checking his pocket watch too often; he'd tell an Anderson to put on her hat; he'd praise a Murray for his fine Sunday attendance, and shame an Ogilvie who came only once in a while.

His habit of questioning his audience from the pulpit kept everyone on edge. For example, he used his sermons to check the children's catechism, which he took pride teaching in the schools. Often a child's correct answer was embarrassing to the blank minds of some adults. Playing one group's answer off against another was a favourite ploy.

His popularity extended to the Protestant students of Aberdeen's University. Every Sunday night, they came to his evening service where they enjoyed his ecumenical sermons and his reintroduction of music into church worship.

Protestant acceptance also came from high officials in the Scottish church, government, and education. Donations from dignitaries and citizens of all faiths paid for gifts such as a beautiful oil painting of the Gordon, a stained glass window in his church of St. Peter's, and a large black granite statue of *himself* placed out front. The Press praised him as a humble servant of God and true friend of the Scot. He reached out to the people. Hands on. Gloves off. They reached back.

My wife and I found out for ourselves about his lasting popularity. We were having supper in a small fish and chips restaurant on the Aberdeen Strand in June, 2001. Two fellow diners at separate tables welcomed us to Aberdeen. I told them about reading of Charles Gordon in a 1967 *Scots Magazine* and asked if they had ever heard of him. Surprisingly, they had. They spoke of him with pride. They told us of his efforts to aid the victims of a cholera epidemic in the nineteenth century. They also gave us directions to the church outside of which stands the granite statue of Charles Gordon.

We *did* find the statue and his church of St. Peter's. And we found the cemetery of Our Lady of Snows where the people of Aberdeen buried him on November 28, 1855. It was an honour to touch parts of this man's life.

I imagined the mile-long funeral procession moving solemnly through the streets of East Aberdeen. Crowds lined the route. At first, no sounds but the horses and hearse on the cobblestone. Then the skill of the 79th Highlanders' Pipes and Drums released the tears of a loving people. Behind the Highlanders come the Provost, Bishop, Magistrates, adults, school children — and finally the tattered, ill and handicapped.

After his funeral, one professor said the priest was a dear gentleman respected by the Protestants of Aberdeen. Another Protestant Doctor of Laws said he translated "the Sermon on the Mount" into daily practice ... he had a single-hearted desire to serve his day and generation."

A final note about the statue of Charles Gordon we found that day. Darkness had almost set in when we got there. So we rushed to take a picture of me standing beside the black sculpture. My wife took it. Upon development of the film, the priest got the last laugh. My wife had decapitated him!

It's Time

The summer sun rose over Germany and quickly ran across France to Toulouse and the Pyrenees. On its way it lit up the hillside town of Lourdes, where pilgrims would soon fill the streets on their way to the Virgin's shrine.

Father Larry from Saskatchewan, was there that day. He had come to Lourdes two days earlier with a young teaching Sister who had asked him to bring her to the shrine. She was in a wheelchair because of multiple sclerosis.

The Sister was firmly convinced that God would cure her. She also thought that Father Larry would be instrumental in assisting God in that miracle.

Father Larry was an experienced priest. As a worker in the John Bosco Centre for wayward youth in Saskatchewan, he had faced challenging situations. He knew miracles were scarce and that eventually the victims of most handicaps have to face up to the realities of life. But the Sister's faith touched him and he decided to do whatever she asked.

On the first day, the priest said Mass in the Grotto where Bernadette saw her vision. At the finish, the Sister said simply, "It's not time yet."

The next day, another Mass by the priest at the Grotto was followed by the same comment, "Father, it is not time yet."

That night, Father Larry went to bed exhausted. He looked forward to a good night's sleep and a miracle. In the early morning of the third day, his phone rang. It was the Sister. She said, "Father, we must go to the Grotto. Now is the time."

Luckily, the single altar inside the grotto was not being used. The Sister sat beside him. A few other pilgrims surrounded the altar. In the middle of Mass after the consecration, it happened. Father Larry felt a strong jolt enter his body. He shuddered. He knew *something* had happened. The Spirit had passed through him.

At the end of the Mass, the Sister stood up on her own and walked. She went up the 70 steps to the Basilica's main entrance and waved to Father Larry standing below.

The Sister came home and returned to her teaching. According to Father Larry's friend and mine, Ed Kohlman, who told me this story, both Father Larry and the Sister are happy and well.

For Father Larry, it was an experience that totally strengthened his faith. For the Sister, it goes without saying.

BE STILL AND KNOW

When the cares of the day overwhelm us
And its tensions are hard to bear
There's a refuge that's sure and a shelter secure,
In the quiet communion of prayer.
For there in the hush of His presence
We lose all our sense of despair,
Our hope springs anew, and His peace comes through,
In the quiet communion of prayer.

— Anonymous

The Poster

A friend on a holiday bought a large coloured poster of a little girl and boy walking together down a country lane. They were holding hands and staring into each other's eyes. The caption at the bottom read, "I can't make it alone." At home, my friend rolled it up and put it in his bedroom cupboard and forgot about it.

About a year later he remembered the poster. He thought he would give it to one of his daughters as a present. But he couldn't find it in the cupboard.

He and his wife looked everywhere, to no avail. They gave up.

Months later, in the middle of the night, an object falling from their bedroom cupboard shelf, awakened them. My friend went over and found a shoe on the hardwood floor. He picked it up and went to replace it on the shelf, but something was in the way.

He reached in and found a rolled-up poster. He opened it up and read the words "I can't make it alone."

As he got back into bed, he suddenly remembered that that night was the first anniversary of his mother's death.

The happening was a message from her. She could not make it alone.

He then remembered that his mother had been with his family on that holiday when he had bought the poster.

The Magnifying Glass

Canadian Higgerty was determined to locate the original homestead of his kin in Ireland. He planned his trip carefully for he had neither time nor money to waste.

For two weeks in Ireland he visited graveyards, churches, archives and farms with nothing to show for his efforts. He and his wife resigned themselves to a lost cause. They made ready to go home.

Before they left, however, they had to attend to a small matter. During their romp across Ireland, they had borrowed a large magnifying glass from a local resident. This person had noticed the Higgerty's glass was inadequate for reading old maps; so she insisted they use hers. It had to be returned.

But the Higgertys lost the glass. They looked everywhere they'd been: hotel rooms, laneways, farmyards, even taverns. No luck.

Since the magnifying glass had probably been a family heirloom, the Higgerty's decided the least they could do was replace it. Since none could be had locally, they had to drive 30 miles to Cork City. In Cork, they found one to their liking. They were getting ready to leave the area when Mrs. Higgerty suggested that while there they should check the Cork city archives on the chance they might find something about the ancestors. They had nothing to lose!

Amazingly, at the archives, Mr. Higgerty found a clerk who directed him to the exact piece of land where the Higgertys had first settled in Cork. They had found the original homestead!

The day after returning the new magnifying glass to the lady, they drove to the Dublin airport. To their surprise, didn't they find the missing magnifying glass under a paper in the back seat? Its unexplainable disappearance had inadvertently led them to their ancestral discovery.

The next summer the Higgertys returned to Ireland, bought the family land, and began repairs to their *new* eighteenth-century farmhouse. Since then, Higgerty has contacted hundreds of Higgertys in the United States,

Ireland, and Canada. In 2002, they had a reunion on the old homestead. Three hundred attended. And it all happened because a magnifying glass that was apparently *lost*, *wasn't*.

A Tribute to My Uncle Eddie, a Man of God
(Read at his funeral)

Eddie was my mentally handicapped uncle who lived out his life working on the family farm. I lived with him for nine summers. He was an inspiration.

* Thank you, Eddie, for your life of innocence, your patience and endurance, your gentle ways, your infectious laugh and your good-natured acceptance of our badgering, and silly jokes.
* Thank you for never cursing, lying, stealing or gossiping.
* Thank you for not carrying a grudge, for never hurting anyone, and for never trying to get even.
* Thank you for your goodness to animals who saw in you a true friend, a person who understood their plights and loved them.
* Thank you for not being demanding about your needs or whining about your lot.
* Thank you for always being so friendly. Thank you for being such a good listener. You made a good companion.
* Thank you for being so kind to your mother. You respected each other. You were always her baby.
* Thank you for teaching us the appreciation of life's little blessings. Your needs were simple: a trinket, a tie, socks, new shoes, cake, tea, soft drinks, gum. Among the items you loved most were those that everyone said you should restrict: butter, salt, chocolate bars, sugar, honey, preserves. You continued to eat as much as you wanted of these treats and lived 83 years doing so.
* Such an ordinary kindness as a drink of cold water on a hot day in the field brought rapturous thanks from your parched lips.
* Any touch of pride you had was easily satisfied by good "slickum" for your curly hair, a pleasant after-shave lotion and a gentle talc for your rosy skin.
* Who among us can, as you did, Eddie, go through life without making enemies? Who among us can say we have never sinned? Who among us can live in the present? Who among us can love God with such a pure faith?
* Thanks for being around, Eddie.

* We may have failed a little in loving you, but we know you didn't mind.
* So long, Jack! And go easy on the butter, no matter where you are.

Alone in a Crowd

She sat alone on the garden bench taking no notice of the other hotel guests. She was leafing through a magazine. She appeared content. Yet in actuality I felt she was sorting out some problem. She had come to this hotel to think things through. She was absorbed in thought.

Suave in manner and dress, she was every bit a self-possessed lady. I could see her holding a position of authority in business or even running her own company.

She appeared on the whole vulnerable. Her docility was a front. I was tempted to speak to her. Perhaps just a few words about the weather, the garden, anything at all to show I noticed and understood. Instead, I chose only to admire her.

Even today, I regret not saying say hello, be it for a few seconds. Just to let our souls touch. I left her to her concerns and took away mine for her. A day later she had gone — a happier person I hoped.

Somewhere, she touches other hearts.

Mrs. Merton

Back in the 1920s, teenage girls from neighbouring farms often helped out when other farmers' wives needed help. A 90-year-old friend, Mrs. Merton, told me about the time her mother sent her to work on a nearby farm. She was nervous. It was the first time she had *worked out*. She was only sixteen.

Her employer put her in a bedroom on the ground floor. Not long after falling asleep on the first night, she woke to find her room full of a bright white light. At the end of her bed stood a big man. He wore farmer's clothes and a wide-brimmed hat. He carried a cattle driver's stick.

Mrs. Merton said she shook herself as she cowered under bedcovers. Was she awake?

The image spoke, "There is money in this room and it belongs to me." He repeated this message several times. Each time, my friend answered, "I would never touch your money."

The vision left.

Mrs. Merton said nothing to the owners, but, later she told her mother everything. Her mother explained it this way: the ghost was the father of the farm's present owner. He was a cattleman. A big person, shrewd, rich, and honest. The wide hat was the trademark of cattlemen.

"His coming tells us a lot," she said. "He liked money and he obviously attached much importance to it, even after death. He couldn't take it with him, but he didn't want anyone else to get it either.

"He hadn't trusted many people. He was the only one who knew where the money was. It was probably there in the room. He must be nervous about that money because you shouldn't have looked dangerous to him. He is not a very happy ghost. Too bad."

"How could you deduct all that from one appearance, Ma?" asked the daughter.

"Logic, my girl, logic. And a little knowledge of local history. I don't think we'll tell the present farmer about the money. Better to let 'sleeping ghosts lie.' Besides when you didn't take the money, he probably went away to his rest, completely at peace. Ghosts are funny that way."

SLOW DANCE

Have you ever watched kids on a merry-go-round,
    Or listened to rain slapping the ground?
Ever followed a butterfly's erratic flight,
    Or gazed at the sun fading into the night?
You better slow down, don't dance so fast,
    Time is short, the music won't last.

Do you run through each day on the fly?
    When you ask "How are you?" do you hear the reply?
When the day is done, do you lie in your bed, with the
    Next hundred chores running through your head?
You better slow down, don't dance so fast,
    Time is short, the music won't last.

    Ever told your child, we'll do it tomorrow,
And in your haste, not see his sorrow?
    Ever lost touch, let a good friendship die,
'Cause you never had time to call and say "hi"?
    You better slow down, don't dance so fast,
Time is short, the music won't last.
                — from a Restaurant Menu, Surrey, BC, 2000

Ownership

Ownership can be vital to our happiness. The prospect of being put out on the streets was the main reason why many bankrupt financiers jumped to their deaths during the Depression. They could not face poverty. They could not live without material possessions.

Oddly enough, some people *choose* to own nothing. Religious monks and sisters and missionaries don't own even the clothes on their backs. Even their energy and time are given for nothing.

The Russian writer, Trotsky, in his old age tried to give away his belongings because he felt having nothing would bring him closer to God. Many elderly widows and widowers live on next to nothing in order to build up their estates for offspring. Christ chose to own nothing.

Eddie Cantor, the round-eyed, big-hearted star of song and dance, said no one in this life owns anything — we just rent, and pay for the privilege of renting by doing service for others.

Suffice to say, then, whether people have nothing by design or fate, the going is tough. That's why those of us who *have* something must serve and share. That's why we must clothe the naked, feed the hungry, visit the sick, and comfort those who mourn. A coin, a hand, a caress, a smile, a letter, a candy, a joke, a song, a sandwich — all are rays of sunshine on a struggling humanity.

That way, everyone becomes better off.

Au Revoir, Bill
(On the Death of an Old School Friend)

On a lush green meadow of a place called Hope, in the patina of a summer sun, we came to bury Bill. As a soft breeze scattered the scent of flowers 'round his coffin, a great peace settled in our hearts and on the land.

True his family circle had been broken by his passing, but not for long. For here, at his graveside a new circle of love was formed by the joined hands of family and friends, adults and children, young and old.

It was a privileged moment … to help form this circle. On my left was Bill's beautiful grandchild, Christina, and on my right, her father, Bill's handsome son, Stephen. Who was I to separate them at this tender moment of farewell? But they had parted to let me in and I felt it an honour.

This family circle had taken nearly 50 years to develop. Today there are 7 children, 6 spouses and 15 grandchildren. But in 1954, Bill and Pat were only two.

Their romance started innocently enough. Bill was playing ping-pong in a church hall, when suddenly in the doorway stood a dark-haired beauty. Immediately Bill became a vagabond suitor and let a loose ball fly across the room in her direction and rushed gushingly to retrieve it.

The colleen coquettishly played along and soon set up her own web of romantic intrigue. In 1954, the very Irish, Pat Kelly married William the Conquered. Like Gary Cooper in Bill's favourite movie, *High Noon*, Bill got a Kelly girl. Their love grew.

So here we were together on that afternoon in June to bid farewell to Bill. I felt his presence in that circle. He wandered about in that nonchalant way of his, touching hearts. He was young and handsome, nay blissful. His pants were baggy, his favourite sweater a little worn, his Norway Bay Tournament cap of the Massel Clan slightly askew. He placed a kiss on his wife's cheek, patted his daughter Susie, steadied his old friend Tony, whispered in his daughter-in-law Moira's ear, put his arm 'round his missionary brother, John.

Bill gave us all gifts that day. I could feel the bonding in the group, the healing, the peace, the strength, and the joy. Clearly this gathering was a celebration of a good man's life. Clearly, love triumphs over death. Clearly, we shall all meet again in eternity.

The Magic Way

If God has a weakness, it is love of praise. In essence, all prayers whether of thanks, petition or reparation are forms of praise.

The good thief's immediate acceptance into paradise after he defended Christ on the cross is a perfect example. First the praise and then the miracle. It's like that all through the New Testament. All prayer is praise. Let's face it, and I beg forgiveness for this remark, "God's a sucker for praise."

One Sunday

At church on Sunday, I saw a young blind man led by his mother into a pew. Nearby sat a beautiful young lady with one crossed eye, and not far away a small boy with glasses over a black patch on one eye. Later on my way out, I saw a baby with the tell-tale eyes of retardation hugging his mother.

When I walked outside that morning, I thanked God for the gift of sight. Everything seemed so much more beautiful.

A Place of Comfort

And the old retired fisherman said, "You don't find many atheists on a small fishing boat in a storm off Newfoundland. You can feel pretty alone sliding down a 36-foot wave into a valley of darkness. Professional fishing is a terrifying business.

"Every man, you know, has his own way of dealing with fear. As for me, I took heart from the "jug, jug" of the diesel motor. I'd go down below and snuggle near the stack and listen to its power. It sounded like a great heart working. I knew as long as that engine never gave up, I'd be okay. It gave me confidence."

Even Angels Came To See

Last Sunday at church, I saw an example of love. Ahead in a front pew, a small woman held a sleeping baby in her arms.

The child had his fat legs wrapped around her sides and his arms around her shoulders. The mother weighed about 95 pounds.

Occasionally the child felt his mother's face and she in return would kiss him on the head. In spite of the dead weight, the mother never failed to stand as required by the service. The child was not a burden.

As I watched her carry the child up to communion, my admiration increased. The child was retarded. And I knew then that their love was special.

On my out, my wife said, "Did you notice the mother and her child ahead of us? Aren't they marvellous?"

KINDNESS

The kind heart is the garden.
The kind thought is the root.
The kind word is the flower.
The kind deed is the fruit.
— An an antique plaque in a store window

God's Blackbirds

About 4:30 p.m. on October 4, 1922, in the Northern Ontario town of Haileybury by the shore of Lake Temiskaming, the curate of Holy Cross Church, Father Dupuis, climbed up on a rock. Before him were 75 girls around 15 years of age, school boarders from the local Providence House Convent. They had been marched there two by two by their teaching Sisters about three o'clock that afternoon.

Straight south by west from the children, the heavens looked like the end of the world. A forest fire of the most dangerous kind called a crown, was leaping from treetop to roof to treetop towards the 5000 souls in Haileybury. The sun was copper red, the noise deafening, the air heavy, the wind horrific.

Haze circled the area. Waves capsized boats. Eyes stung and stomachs turned. The winds hit 60 miles per hour. Wagons, cars, bicycles, and walkers made for the lake. Soon as many as 500 people were huddled under blankets by the shore, watching live cinders go by.

The first warnings of danger had come at 11 a.m. on a gorgeous summerlike morning. Soot-covered fire-fighters had returned from the southwest side with cries to evacuate the area. The fire's tenacity had shrunk the survival time. The fire was in a frenzy. Miniature tornadoes swept out of oxygenstarved vacuums. By 4:30 p.m., a full western gale fed the fire.

The 75 students had already been sitting by the shore on logs and rocks, nibbling on pieces of bread and cheese. In their black tunics and white blouses, someone said they looked like white-winged blackbirds. Steadying himself in the wind, his black soutane flapping and white collar flashing, Father Dupuis shouted from the rock to his flock, "I wish you all to get in the water as far as your knees. The wind is so strong you must be careful. While you're in the water, hold hands. Stay in the water and don't be afraid; put your confidence in God. The Lord will look after us."

For the next hour and a half, until about 6:30 p.m., the students, Providence Sisters, and the other town people, were slowly driven farther backwards into the lake. As fiery debris fell around them, they ducked under the water. Habits and hair caught fire. Several children were burned.

The situation was reaching a crisis. Father Dupuis, a gentle God-fearing man, knew it. Something had to give. The combination of fumes, darkness, wind and waves was deadly. The children would suffocate, burn or drown. The young curate was frantic. He jumped back up on the rock and shouted to the children, "Let us pray together and ask the dear Lord to change the wind. At the same time be sorry for your sins and I will give you absolution."

As Father Dupuis prayed, the kerosene and gasoline barrels stored at the lake-front sheds began to explode. Red tracers followed the liquid into the lake. Orange rockets pierced the sky. Parts of the cathedral's spire and roof took off across the water.

Then, according to little Blanche Boivin, a convent border from Timmins, who has already been quoted above, Father Dupuis "put his hands like that and then the wind changed and everybody in the lake was screaming, 'We're saved.' You could see that was on account of the faith he had. We knew that there was something to that."

Another student, Velma Labranche, standing in the water near Father Dupuis, said, "Suddenly, the prayers were answered. The wind changed directions completely, shifting to the north." Just before this happening, Velma said, "A crazy jangling noise was carried on the wind. The cathedral bells had crashed to the ground."

A Gladys Anderson, five years old, was with her mother that night. In the water, the mother remembers "people … screaming and praying and children … crying … and the wind veering around. Up went shouts of joy and hope. Prayers of thanks were audible and many sang hymns."

Countless other witnesses whose stories appear in the fine book *The Great Fire of 1922* by the Haileybury Heritage Museum Society, experienced the wind's turn for the better. It blew all the dirt and embers back to the southwest. Within minutes, the children were out of the water and warming themselves before bonfires. Cows, horses, goats, dogs, cats, birds in cages, even a lone lamb milled among the hapless populace. That day Haileybury lost 90% of its homes, all its churches and manses, two schools, the Providence Sisters' Convent and their Providence 100-bed Hospital. Five thousand were homeless. Father Dupuis's uncle, Bishop Latulipe, who lived at the cathedral, already a sick man, died three months later. But the 75 convent girls and hundreds of others in the lake were saved, as were many homes and people in areas south of Haileybury.

At this point, the reader deserves to know what enticed me to do some research about this fire, officially recognized as one of Canada's top ten natural disasters. I was having breakfast with a friend who asked me, "Have you ever heard of the Miracle of Haileybury? My grandmother, now dead 40 years, once told me how a priest assigned to this small but enterprising town, saved a group of convent girls from a great fire. He prayed before it and it turned away.

"My grandmother who lived near Haileybury got the story from Blanche Boivin, her niece, who was present when the priest performed his miracle. She was my first cousin. She came to visit my home many times. She was a pleasant, personable person who loved everybody. My grandmother was a Boivin."

Unfortunately, the only existing written confirmation of a possible miracle was confined to what I have reported in Blanche Boivin's quotes and one or two others, all taken from the book *The Great Fire of 1922*. Further attempts to find a miracle were fruitless. I called newspaper editors, archive directors, and church historians around the 18 townships hit by the fire, but none knew about any miracle. My friend's story was my only present-day proof. A conversation with a Sister Tremblay in Haileybury offered no supporting evidence of a miracle. But she had known both Father Dupuis and Sister Blanche. She said Father Dupuis was a devoted curate and Sister Blanche a very popular principal of several schools in the North. In the northern town of Cochrane she is a legend. Both the priest and sister died in the early seventies. A sister Irene Morrisette, also from Haileybury, told me on the phone she knew Father Dupuis to be a very holy priest.

Can one imagine a more convenient time for a miracle? The fire had reached its worst — barrels of fuel were igniting — rockets flew in the night — the church bells gave a last gasp — children's lives were in jeopardy — the priest gave them absolution — he shouted to the heavens — they all prayed for a miracle. If God were going to save His children, He didn't have a better opportunity.

Of *course*, He acted. He turned the wind around that night as easily as He calmed the waters at Galilee. How could He refuse?

A PLACE TO HIDE

The squall swept in along the river's edge and I ran underneath the nervous branches of a poplar bush to watch the sheets of rain slanting the sailboats home ... soon, a setting sun brightened the gloom and the scent of mists came down ... the air was fresh ... and I stepped out into a nature glistening in repose.

A Love Story

One of the rank and file died the other day. The victim of a stroke, he had been confined to a hospital bed for six years.

He had been a success. He was handsome, witty, and a first-class salesman. He loved his family, a drink and a fling at the horses, but not necessarily in that order. He had intelligence, charm, and a beguiling free spirit.

Unfortunately, his downfall was beyond his control. All his life he fought manic depression. It led to alcoholism and the breakdown of his marriage. He lost his business and declared bankruptcy.

To his everlasting credit, however, he always showed courage in his adversity. He rode out failure and depression. He never complained about his blisters; he sat on them. Friends say it was his determination and independence that helped him to survive. Poor as he was, *he* controlled his situation. He never blamed anyone or anything for his troubles. He called the shots whenever he got a chance.

For some 17 years a son returned to live with him. The father found respectable work and altogether, life wasn't too bad. But after the son left to return to his mother, the bottom slowly gave way. The fall came when his health failed: diabetes, blindness, high blood pressure and always the curse of manic depression.

Gradually, his daily sojourns around the city grew less frequent. In the long nights he listened to radio and phoned into talk shows. He read the newspaper with the help of a large magnifying glass. Friends came to visit or phoned. He was a good listener. He impressed them with his richness of spirit.

Then came a crippling stroke. While in hospital, the number of his friends dwindled. The absence of his family (his wife had died) left him at the mercy of the social and medical systems. A few friends fought for his rights and needs. Eventually, caring administrators placed him in a local hospital for the chronically ill where he received the care that he richly deserved. If he had been sent to an out-of-town nursing home, the isolation would have finished him.

Those who got to know him best over the last six years learned that of all his crosses, the separation from his only daughter was the heaviest. He had always loved her and she him. He would tell people, "I am afraid she may be on the streets of the big city. I can do nothing. I shall never see her again. It's been 20 years. She was a great success, you know, a top model, beautiful and talented. But, like me, she has suffered from manic depression. It stole her life. She struggles. I miss her most of all."

As it turned out, amazingly, in the last two months of his life, a miracle occurred. This gentle man must have been praying. Certainly several friends were.

The chain of marvellous events started when the daughter, after spending five recuperative months in a hospital ward, was well enough to return to her own apartment. She was coping again on her own.

Then one day her brother told her that her father's sickness was getting more serious. So she asked for his address and sent him a letter and pictures. She wasn't sure if he ever got them, but he did, and he was delighted.

Soon, a friend of the father took it upon himself to get her address. He wrote a letter urging her to come to see her father. He also arranged for them to exchange phone calls.

In those special moments on the phone, two suffering souls said all the things that should have been said long, long ago.

When she finally did manage to see him a few weeks before he was to die, their conversations must have reached the stars. She promised to return.

A few days before his passing, she and her brothers came to see him. Together they talked to their father. From his pillow, he raised his head and with almost-blind eyes looked directly at the face of each child. He knew they were there.

The effects of the stroke quickly worsened. He could say nothing, but nothing needed saying that wasn't already felt. The family was together. The father was at peace.

The funeral was attended by a few friends who mattered. They all knew that the father's illness was his ticket to heaven. How proud he must have been to look down upon them from that beach in heaven where the priest at the service said he was probably basking.

Before the daughter returned home, just before she went to the plane, she hugged the father's friend who had written to her and whom she had come to like. As she did so, he whispered in her ear, "I don't have a daughter. Would you be my daughter from now on?"

And she whispered back, "Oh, yes, yes. I would like that very much."

This part of the story is over, but somewhere the daughter carries on. Surely, everything will be better just as her new-found father promised. Her heavenly Father will make sure.

Willard

God does help us when we need him.

At lunch one day my friend Willard told me he had recently buried his wife. He spoke proudly about how his seven children and their families helped him cope.

He said, "You know, my wife and I had eight children, but we lost one, a son. His death was so different from my wife's. She lingered in pain for two years and in a way death was a blessing. But my son died suddenly and tragically.

"He was sixteen. The sight of him in his room that morning was beyond belief. My wife found him. My grief was so great that the top of my head from forehead to neck felt it was going to crack wide open. Our sorrow knew no bounds. About two o'clock in the afternoon, I fell asleep, emotionally spent.

"But later that day a strange thing happened. I awoke, totally calm. The tears were gone. I was in total control of myself. During the funeral, I remained at peace."

"Willard," I asked, "how do you account for the sudden change?"

"The answer is simple: God. He gave me the grace of understanding and repose. He held me together as sure as He holds up the universe."

My Father's House

There's something to be said for small homes on small properties — the ones with cozy rooms on one floor, and picket fences and shutters on the outside.

During the Depression, my Glaswegian father built such a home, really a cottage. He used second-hand lumber for the framing, ten-test for insulation, and green spruce for the siding. The basement, dug out by dynamite and pick and shovel, was just deep enough to hold wood, coal and a furnace. Its uneven floor was damp earth. The ceiling was low.

To my Dad, who spent his first 12 years in a tenement apartment in Glasgow, his home here in Canada was a step above. Small though it was, he had a dining room, living room, kitchen, bathroom and two bedrooms. Off the kitchen, he added an enclosed veranda, and to one side of the house, a garage. Every area was *just big* enough. In Glasgow, his parents had adequate space in a living room, a small kitchen and a bedroom. In his new home, he had a little more.

Modern people today want space. It's a sign of having arrived. Many homes have three stories, three garages and three bathrooms. Manicured lawns sprawl inside tall fences. Front entrances open to high ceilings and winding staircases. Living quarters expand to vast interiors.

Surely the owners of these mini-mansions rightly deserve acclaim for their ingenuity and beauty. But, for some of us, size means little. You can only sit in one chair at a time.

A country cottage is my idea of reasonable size — big enough to be comfortable, small enough to chat, share a dream or play a card. The togetherness in such homes unequivocally suits the unpretentious folk who live there.

By the side of the road on an under-sized lot, my father built his own home with nickels and dimes. I wouldn't have traded it for all the castles on the Rhine.

THE BETTER WAY

I'd rather see a sermon than hear one
  any day;
I'd rather one should walk with me than
  merely show the way.
The eye's a better pupil and more
  willing than the ear;
Fine counsel is confusing,
  but example's always clear;
And the best of all the preachers are
  the men who live their creeds,
For to see the good in action is what
  everybody needs.
I can soon learn how to do it if you'll
  let me see it done.
I can watch your hands in action, but
  your tongue too fast may run;
And the lectures you deliver may be
  very wise and true,
But I'd rather get my lesson by observing
  what you do.
For I may misunderstand you and the high
  advice you give,
But there's no misunderstanding how you
  act and how you live.

— Author Unknown

Rosie

A year after her husband contracted a crippling nervous disease, Rosie had a stroke. The prognosis was she would never be her old self again. Doctors recommended a nursing home.

The husband, himself a doctor, decided he would use his retirement to look after her at home. For ten years, friends and professionals helped him care for her.

Contrary to the medical predictions, the wife eventually walked, fed herself, and did some painting. She also overcame her inability to talk by using voice inflection, facial expressions and gestures. However, the only words she could say were, "Okay, nothing good." And she repeated them over and over.

Everyone admired the doctor's love for Rosie. Every day he bathed her, read to her, and talked to her. The tightening grip of his own disease took a long time getting the better of his dedication.

As often happens in these cases, the one doing the caring died first. For three years, the doctor suffered dementia. One night near the end, Rosie sat beside him in a hospital for incurables. The family was there.

Neither Rosie nor her sweetheart could speak. They were both broken. Their journey together in Ireland and Canada with all its joyful memories was about to end.

At the bedside, a daughter broke the silence, "He loves you, Mom. He loves you!" It was then that Rosie, that beautiful, loyal, tongue-tied Irish beauty, leaned over her 76-year-old husband and from the depths of her soul said, "Love you. Love you. Love you!"

And somewhere a lightning bolt split a mountain.

The Test

His parents had chosen a perfect day.

The baby swallow rocked inside the round hole of its nest. Father and mother took turns hovering around, twittering encouragement.

Below the nest on the veranda rail, feathered friends looked up at the baby. Their cheery chirps also urged it on. Word had spread. Agitation grew.

Suddenly all the birds flew away. The fledgling was alone. I turned away for a second. When I looked again, the flight was over. The bird had gone.

He just had to leave. He couldn't bear to be left behind. He had followed *on his own* to be with his family and friends.

The True Light

At this moment, a poor mother in Washington, D.C., fully depends on the charity of her neighbours. She has three children, a sick husband and her own blindness. Fortunately, they never do without.

Recently, a Visitation nun, a social worker, who had come to Washington from the same Caribbean island as the mother, became acquainted with the family's situation.

After many weeks of working with the family, the Sister came to the conclusion that the mother has an extraordinary relationship with God. Since her blindness, she had become intimate with Him. He speaks to her. He assures. He consoles. He sends shelter, food, and money whenever the need.

At certain times, when the mother prays with her children in their Washington flat, God portends His coming with a strong wind and then speaks as Moses did on Sinai. In her darkness, she sees God and hears him.

One day, the Visitation Sister asked the mother a question to test her. She said, "If God returned your eyesight in full measure, would you be willing to give up the deep relationship you have found with Him in your blindness?"

The mother said, "No, I would not. What I see now is not found in the power of the human eye. God has given me the true light. Better for me that my eyes are dead."

The Violinist

At a Friday late-afternoon service in Vancouver's Holy Rosary Cathedral, a gentleman came forward in the sanctuary to read the Epistle.

His reading was precise and clear in keeping with his obvious refinement. He had the stealth of a valet seasoned in being inconspicuous by his presence. When finished, he slipped behind a great column of pink-plaster-on-pine. The service went on.

The parishioners and visitors in the cathedral were of many cultures: Mexican, Korean, Chinese, Asian, West Indian and Polish, to name a few. Being in a downtown parish, they were mostly blue-collar workers dropping in on their way home. Their dress and countenances told of hard lives. Their dependence on God showed in the way they prayed.

As the service went on, a heavy silence came over the church. Was it due to everybody being bone-tired? Or was it caused by the sincere prayers being offered? It seemed the Holy Spirit was moving through the church, helping, healing, strengthening, and working little miracles.

Suddenly the soft strains of a violin eased the silence. Behind the pink column, the earlier reader was playing a sweet melody. He was professionally trained. His body slightly swayed with each bar of delicate sound.

It was all done with such grace and ease that a stranger like me will never forget that humble Italian violinist who filled a cathedral one evening in Vancouver with music worthy of God.

Sometimes It Pays To Be Ignorant

Christ's attitude to his enemies as he hung on the cross is a lesson for people of all faiths. He said, "Forgive them, Father, for they know not what they do."

In *our* society when it comes to justice and law, ignorance is no excuse for breaking rules. But in the courts of heaven, where mercy abounds, it *can* be.

It sounds boorish to acclaim that our enemies don't know any better. But when it comes to forgiveness, it's as good a place to start as any. In truth, the soldiers were following orders. They had no education about a one God.

Christ's execution was just another example to them of the punishment needed to free society of degenerates.

Of course, Jesus's admonition about forgiveness that Good Friday also extended to many of those responsible for his sentence of death. If they really believed that Jesus was God, they would have never laid a hand upon Him.

As pilgrims, let's follow Christ's prayer when personal injuries come our way, "Father, forgive them for they know not what they do!"

Good Taste

Believe it or not, there's a line beyond which good taste ceases to exist. It can happen in dress, dance, song, dialogue, writing, design, and indeed all art.

At first, the intrusions into bad taste may be subtle. But given time, poor taste can grow to be so rampant that one doesn't recognize it anymore. Poor taste can become pseudo-good taste and soon no one can tell the difference.

People with no taste can do little to control taste. It is up to those who *do* recognize good taste to stand up against those who would vilify the world with trash.

Suggestive dialogue, movements and gestures in a Broadway play can never be in good taste. An erotic dance in a movie, no matter how well choreographed, is not in good taste.

Vulgarity is tasteless.

Kathleen

Present-day "native Irish" writers often present a warped, one-sided view of their childhood in Ireland. They speak of poverty, hardship, and social chaos. They picture shoeless waifs loitering in dark lanes. They see the Irish as railing against the Church and governments. They make us believe that society then was joyless, with no good times, laughter or cheer; just scar upon scar, never to heal.

Fortunately, not all of Ireland's deprived children were unhappy. Poverty is no guarantee of being a miserable sod. Beautiful flowers can grow in unfavourable conditions.

History records *poor* Irish minstrels of song and dance. Stories of the humourous ways of the wary, quick-witted, downtrodden Irish are countless. Impoverished Irish homes have always produced their share of good people.

Among the reasons for Irish home life maintaining a joie de vivre was Irish motherhood. The Irish mothers were the spark. Faith in God, love for others, a courageous spirit, and just discipline, turned out hard-working, happy sons and daughters.

I saw this nose-to-the-grindstone, unflappable devil-may-care attitude in my Irish grandmother, my Irish aunts, my Irish mother, Irish neighbours, my

Irish wife and our own girls. They set the standards. They sharpen the wits. They work the miracles.

A perfect example of a true Irish mother, herself the product of a poor home, was my friend Kathleen. This is her story.

I first met her in 1938. She was 23. I was seven. Even *then* I felt her spirit and goodness. Now, 66 years later, I think of her as an Annie Oakley and Annie Rooney rolled up in one, and I easily imagine her as a young girl standing barefoot on limestone belting out the lyrics "Tomorrow, tomorrow."

Around 1934, and married just a year, Kathleen moved to a small log house in an Irish community directly across from my grandmother's farm. By 1938, she had two children.

That was the year I started visiting my grandmother for my summer holidays. In time, I wandered up Kathleen's way looking for playmates and cookies. It was there I fell under her spell and was all the better for it.

I remember her as being a pleasure to be around. She was fun-loving. I cannot forget the kindness she showered on a snotty-nosed city kid back when dusty, country roads were his wonderland.

Don't think for a second that Kathleen was a sweet Mother McCree. She could shake up the neighbourhood. She didn't put up with shenanigans. She barked commands and didn't abide excuses. She could flay away with an open hand. She called them as she saw them. She rattled the dishes. She ruled the roost. She called the shots.

Even her husband, Paddy, jumped through her hoops. Kathleen at first gave him plenty of leash. After all, he was a fun-loving and free-wheeling Irishman with a taste for the malt. But she soon had to rope him in.

One time Paddy and his buddy, Boer-war veteran, Howard, failed to come home from a day trip to a nearby town. She sat up all night worrying.

The next afternoon, a taxi pulled into the yard and out stepped the two culprits. Kathleen's relief turned into anger the like of which bachelor Howard had never heard on the tundra of South Africa. Apparently, the afternoon before, Howard's Rio car had made jam out of a loaded berry truck. To the police, the smell of alcohol made it all the worse. The police put them behind bars for a night, confiscated Howard's licence, impounded the car, and fined them ten dollars each, big money in the Depression.

Paddy had brought Howard home that day to buffer Kathleen's reaction. But Howard never knew what hit him. They say he almost re-enlisted. Nor did Paddy escape. He was roasted like a chestnut. Howard lurched home and Paddy fell asleep with Kathleen still going around and around her campfire. But Kathleen was never mean and never held a grudge. Next day she'd be fine.

———

Allowing for her background, what else could we expect but fine characteristics? She was also the product of an Irish mother. One time her mother went to confront her relative, a priest at the rectory of the parish church. In those days, discipline often came with a stick or strap. On a Sunday afternoon at summer catechism, the priest, while punishing a nearby student, accidentally nipped Kathleen's fingertip with the strap. Although such an accident was usually given leeway by Irish parents, this breach, imagined or not, was viewed by Kathleen's protective mother as just one more incident in a series of unfair treatments of her children by the priest. It became known locally as "the battle of the bleeding finger." The hard-nosed, dedicated veteran-chaplain of the First World War never got a word in.

Kathleen was the third child of eight and the second girl. Her father had chronic asthma all his life. It was Kathleen's job as a young girl to bring him his camphor-filled tin can when his breathing became difficult. One morning in 1924, her mother told the nine-year-old Kathleen that she had found her father dead beside her.

From then on, Kathleen's older sister and brother ran the farm. Kathleen pitched in. She was used to a strong work ethic. In earlier years she would stand on a kitchen chair to wash dishes. She would collect eggs, fetch water, nurse piglets and calves, feed the poultry, pick berries and vegetables, turn the separator, and help rotate the butter barrel. She would chase down cattle and geese, hoe the garden, run errands, make beds, and knock down butter-nuts.

In the bush detail, Kathleen and her brother were second-in-command to their older sister. The sister marked off the territory, supervised the piling of the cut logs, pulled them from the bush with horses, split open the blocks left by the mobile saw machines, and carried and stacked the wood with demanding exactitude.

Kathleen says about those days: "To be seen and not heard was the rule. Responsibilities outweighed rights. No whining, whimpering or talking back, thank you. Putting down authority, including the neighbours, was not acceptable. Our parents and grandparents brought us up the same way they were brought up. No one bothered us as long as we did what we were told.

"Take privacy: non-existent. Sheer lack of space demanded compromise. Ten people sleeping in a *one-bedroom downstairs and two up*; think of it, imagine the proximity. I know some families where as many as 17 slept in a small log house and never complained.

"We didn't have much time for feeling sorry for ourselves. Many's the time I cried myself to sleep. But, I'd soon get over it.

"Our Momma never let us get down too low. We played ball at home and school. We made up card games; we played tug-of-war and swung in spare tires; we helped make cookies, buns, raisin bread and pies; we peeled turnips, cleaned green and yellow beans, and pulled tall green onions. We climbed in the orchards, especially for red crab apples. We knocked potato bugs for the burning into honey-pails, played with our cats and dogs, and waited for the men folk to bring home fish, deer, and rabbit.

"Every morning we had porridge and milk and thick crusty slices of toast. My favourite preserves were wild strawberries. After supper we said the Rosary. We took turns leading. We had a picture of Mary in the kitchen beside one of the Sacred Heart of Jesus.

"We went to school during the week and to catechism on Sunday afternoon. We ran over the fields in summer and along the main roads in winter. We knew the Baltimore Catechism by heart. Our religion put meaning into our lives. Doing a good turn for someone was engrained into us.

"Not surprising then that I grew up ready and eager to take on life! We survived rains and drought. We lived with diphtheria, typhoid, tuberculosis, polio, German and red measles, pneumonia, scarlet fever, appendectomies and Spanish flu. Deaths during childbirth were common. Old people had nothing for pain. Accidents lacked medical attention.

"Talk about calamities. I remember the day my brother cut off his big toe with an axe. My mother drenched three sanitized flour bags with his blood before she stopped the bleeding. The doctor arrived at 9 p.m. from eight miles away.

"My brother had just had the axe sharpened. It cut through three heavy socks and his gumboot. Took the toe off like nothing. Did it bleed!

"He was terrified and crazy with pain. He refused chloroform. They gave him dandelion wine.

"That day, no one could stand the sight of the blood and the missing toe. My brothers and sisters and I were passing out. About 11 p.m., the doctor finished the stitching.

"Next day they sent me to fetch the toe from the bush. I was the roadrunner then, over to the church to phone, back home, back to the church again — down to my uncle's — across to the bush. Well, when I saw the white toe lying there in the stained snow, I started getting nauseous again and couldn't bring myself to touch it. An uncle came over and finished the job.

"The next day, we put the toe in a matchbox, packed it in cotton balls and took it to the graveyard to plant at my father's grave. As expected, the sight of digging up a bit of earth for the toe, made us queasy again and yet another neighbour had to come over and save the day. We were a fainthearted lot.

―――――※―――――

"Accidents in the bush were frequent. My grandfather John and his wife Sarah lost their first son, Michael, when a tree decapitated him. He was only five. The year was 1878. At the time they had been married six years. Apparently,

Sarah went to the bush and carried the severed head home in her extended kitchen apron. She placed his head on a nearby wagon at the house and collapsed.

"Michael may well have been killed by a falling branch, dead as a result of the great fire that had ripped across that concession in 1870. John's brother James who had his farm beside John lost everything. In fact, according to the records, someone died on *that* farm in *that* fire.

"Imagine the sorrow on that winter morning when Michael's funeral procession left from the homestead for the two-mile ride to St. Michael's — the great Clydesdales pulling Michael's sleigh — the single horse-drawn cutters of John and Sarah, John's brothers, James and Michael with their wives, and bachelor brother, Timothy.

"And waiting at the church, the old priest Father O'Malley, himself from Ireland. Think of that damp stone church — the mourners huddled at the front — the black vestments of death — the old pump organ — and at the back, the Irish neighbours from all around, the Carrolls, Manions, Finners, Corbetts, Sullivans, O'Keefes, McGraths, Egans and Carters, to name a few.

"Next day they planted a tree in Michael's memory at the homestead — they called it Michael's tree. That was common practice then. When Tim, John's brother, lost a son, Michael James, a beautiful child, 15, in 1910, they planted a maple. It is still there on the property — a tender tribute.

"By the way, a special mourner that day for Michael was his grandmother, Hanna. She must have been heartbroken — her first grandchild gone. Hanna lived for 94 years, until 1914. Can we imagine her on that occasion surrounded by her grieving children and grandchildren?

"Alas, Michael's tree also met with tragedy. In 1955, I was a widow living on that homestead with my seven children. One day a wild summer storm ripped across the land. As I looked out a window, a lightning bolt split Michael's tree wide open. I took this as a sign to move my family again. No one from our clan has ever lived on that farm again. It had a good run — about 1845 to 1955.

"In spite of everything, we had our fun and giggles — the usual outside childhood games: softball, swimming in the quarries, one-scene skits, skating parties, and lawn socials at neighbouring churches. Sunday picnics in summer put on by St. Michael's parish were common. The older we got, the later we were allowed to stay up. I remember the fiddlers and step-dancers. I remember songs like 'Turkey in the Straw,' 'Old Dan Tucker,' and 'Camptown Races.' The men told stories, recited poetry and sang old favourites like 'The Black Velvet Band,' 'Colonial Boy,' and 'Mother McCree.' Kathleen paused in thought."

Kathleen grew up fast. She went to work at 15 and used her money to take an office-training course. Everyone around, remembers the adolescent Kathleen being a good looker. In those days, by 16, the girls wore rouge, perfume and fluffy dresses. Gone were the catechism classes and the curfews. The sweet girls of the Christmas pageants slowly evolved into provocative maidens. First kisses and some imbibing came much sooner for these flappers than they did for city girls. Kathleen's friends like Anna Mary, Carmel and Margaret bounced up and down the country lanes in Model A's, Durants, Whippets, and Maxwells. Social events in nearby villages and towns became more accessible.

———————

Kathleen was the bee's knees. Her wedding picture shows a pretty, self-possessed, sassy young lady. She wore the latest in fashion — a cloth coat with removable fur collar and sleeves, a smart kerchief and a chic cloche hat over her shiny, raven hair.

Paddy too was dapper. Irish men know how to dress. Standing beside Kathleen in their wedding photo, he was distinguished looking. Dark eyes peeked out from under a brown Chicago-style fedora. He wore a camel-coloured, double-breasted winter coat, an Ivy-League scarf, a new suit, a white shirt with cuff links, and a vest with a watch.

The reception was held at Paddy's red-brick homestead. According to Kathleen, the celebration went on and on. It never really ended — sort of faded away like smog. The next week many in the West-Huntley valley had a hangover. The consumption of booze was high. Very few remembered the party.

Paddy and Kathleen lived beside my grandmother's place for six years. They rented the farmhouse from my dear friend, Basil, for $10 per month plus the task of watching over Basil's sheep. More than once Basil forgot to collect the fee.

To supplement Paddy's small wages during the Depression, the neighbours helped the family. My grandmother sent over fresh milk, bread, and eggs. Hand-me-down clothes came from neighbours like the Williams and Mantils. One neighbour sent over a hind quarter, (already packed in brine), of every pig he butchered.

Their first house, some 80 years old in 1933, was sturdy enough. I spent some cosy winter evenings there with Basil, who took it over in 1940. Flour bags and horse hair and newspaper were used for insulation. Just about every summer night after the milking, Basil and I played a seven-inning softball game. Using the house as a backdrop, we pitched in turn inning after inning. The catcher was the umpire and his word was final, most times! Basil, you were the greatest!

———————

The house was only some ten feet from the "forced" road to town. It stood under the brow of a small hill that cut the west wind. Nearby on the property was the finest spring water in the country. On four hills of this road, rising like stairs to the rock ridge behind the house, choke cherry bushes, haw trees, wild crab apple trees, and strawberry and raspberry plants grew abundantly.

My grandmother often walked over to Kathleen's home. Granny was about 55 then and a big woman. Kathleen still laughs about the day Granny put her foot through a kitchen floorboard to a considerable depth.

Outside the house's back door was a limestone walk. One winter weekend, Kathleen had a younger sister, Martha, visiting. They were in the kitchen just inside the door when they heard heavy footsteps on the walk. Someone knocked. When Kathleen went to answer, no one was there. The step, a big flat stone, was covered with a light snow. There were no footprints. The episode happened again with the same results.

Kathleen, only 22, knew it was a sign. A few weeks later, Martha, just 17, got pneumonia. She had fallen into the creek early one morning on her way to light the school stoves. Not long after, Martha died in Kathleen's arms. The *little* mother was there again for her family.

Paddy's popularity and Kathleen's hospitality drew many visitors. The Kennedys came, the Mantils, O'Keefes, and Williams, the Newtons, Lynchs, and Carrolls — all pioneer families to that region.

Kathleen had a unique way then of making pin-money. Twice a winter she would run a "rooster euchre." Twelve invited men sat down to play a set number of games for three roosters. The winner of each rooster had to pay Kathleen six dollars for the bird. Eighteen dollars was real money in those days, but the roosters raised by Kathleen were apparently worth it.

One night at one of these euchres, a long-remembered practical joke took place. Some of the boys filled up the bottom of a player's pipe with live match-ends and fresh tobacco on top. When the man lit his beloved pipe, the anticipation in the room was almost too much to bear. When "she did blow" everyone fell down laughing. No one is sure if he ever smoked the pipe again.

To find out more about Kathleen I asked my friends who knew her. Herman never could forget her sense of duty. Clarence saw her as a good woman. Mary recalled her kindness to everyone. Carmel admired her fierce dedication. Angus remembered her quick wit.

Her children say she never complained. She just did her best. She never blamed God or fate or herself. She faced the music and even sang along when she could. A daughter of her second marriage, who saw her most often in the later years, says she is the strongest, most determined woman she has ever met.

Kathleen and Paddy moved to a nearby city in 1940. Until Paddy's death in 1948, they lived in a well-equipped house at a government building complex where Paddy worked. However, the 45-year-old Paddy died and the family had to move back to the Irish community where she had been born. Kathleen was 33. They had seven children.

For the next four years, Kathleen lived in an old log home that she eventually purchased and tastefully upgraded. She rented part of it to her brother and his family.

Kathleen continued with small jobs on the side to make money. When a construction crew came one summer to resurface the highway outside her door, she provided supper and lunch-boxes for three workers. Forty-five years later a member of that crew who remembered Kathleen's cooking and kindness sent her a present to show his gratitude. In those days Kathleen received $119 per month mother's allowance.

In 1952, on a cold winter night in that same log house, tragedy again struck. Gas in the stove-pipe of the newly refurbished home exploded across the four upstairs bedrooms and instantly killed two of her brother Will's boys. Kathleen's oldest, Mark and Milton, were burned. Milton rushed outside, his hair aflame and his flesh seared. He ran over fences to a neighbour where he knew there was a car, but the neighbour had sold it that day. He finally got a ride to the town hospital where he spent several months recuperating.

Neighbours helped those two families that winter. A local priest collected money in the nearby city while the priest at St. Michael's spearheaded collections from the local people. Someone gave the families a rent-free home for ten weeks.

Kathleen's brother and his wife never fully recovered from their loss. Yet, they carried on and raised a fine family.

Eventually, with nowhere to live, Kathleen and her brood were forced back to the homestead where her grandfather Michael and his wife, Julia, had settled around 1843. They stayed there until the day Michael's tree exploded in the storm. They then moved to a nearby town.

In 1959, Kathleen's mother died. In the mid-1950s, Kathleen remarried and had one child. She also raised the three young children of her new husband.

Kathleen is now 90 and lives in a nursing home. She talks about the good old days and never says they weren't. From the time she scampered as a child up the loft ladder, she has never ceased to fight for everything decent. In the Terry Fox drives, she collected thousands of dollars for cancer research.

I salute her and all Irish mothers. She took her problems by the throat and worked unceremoniously for family, friends and God.

She was an able dealer, but never wore the trousers. She was the sergeant-major who never pulled rank. She fought daily for survival, threw a few punches, but never hit below the belt. She was a free-wheeling, outspoken scrapper, but always a lady.

She and Irish mothers like her, lived in an environment totally unknown among the Irish mothers in Ireland. In one season of the year they would experience a cold that froze their faces in seconds and in another, a humidity that drained their energy. The rains came down in barrels. The winds flattened fields. Drought carried away crops and animals. Contagious diseases emptied their cradles. When the men folk worked "away" at the lumber shanties, these women carried all the responsibility of the farms.

These pioneers also experienced a vacuum of silence which ate into their sanity. The closing of roads in winter and spring added to their loneliness. Nothing but the howl of a wolf, a neighing horse, the cry of a loon, a barking dog, a whippoorwill's lament, the drone of a distant train-engine. The land they walked on was uneven, full of gullies, hills, rotting timber and snake-infested swamps. In summer, the mosquitoes, black flies, and horse flies, (all unknown in Ireland), drove them indoors. They retired at night with either bites or blisters.

Who among my Irish friends in that country setting has not felt Kathleen's warmth? Who has not benefited from her example or counsel? Kathleen, I think of you as the epitome of everything good about Irish mothers.

In heaven, you will join all Irish mothers whom I have known and loved and sadly lost.

All told, Kathleen has been a mother to 8 children, grandmother to 29, and great-grandmother to 37. During her life she has helped numerous in-laws, nephews, nieces, neighbours and strangers.

Let no one say that Irish homes, even the poorest, whether here or in Ireland, have not generated happiness, goodness, and fine people.

Let us be wary of native-born or Canadian Irish writers who emphasize only the wretched side of Irish life.

WHERE IS HAPPINESS

A youth approached the market-place and stopped a learned man … "There is a question I would ask. Pray tell me if you can … In which of these special shops can happiness be had … for I've a pocketful of gold … and my heart is still sad?"

The wise man looked at him and smiled. "No matter how you try, there are such things like happiness that money cannot buy … True happiness can only come from doing good to others … from treating all men everywhere as if they were your brothers … And all the gold in all the world could never buy a part of the great happiness you'll know … when love is in your heart."

— Anonymous

The Now

There are really no tomorrows and no yesterdays. The present is everything. God lives in the present. So do we. The present is now.

We are part of a spiritual family that transcends time. Time does not pass. It is at best only a series of nows. Our souls have no cycles or time frames or periods. They are in the *now* just as our friends and relatives who have gone before us are in the now.

This very second, moment, minute or hour are now.

His Door Was Always Open

Through the beautiful stained glass windows of St. John's Gothic church in Perth, Ontario, the noonday sun of a cold January day warmed the pastel walls.

In the sanctuary, the archbishop of the Kingston Diocese and many priests had come to bury their compatriot and my old friend, Father Tom Brady.

In the eulogy, his good companion in the priesthood, Father Frank O'Connor, gently wove without hyperbole or embellishment, the picture of an extraordinary man. So much so, that hushes of holiness periodically fell upon the crowd.

As Father Frank talked, we realized that Tom Brady had been a genuine people's priest. He had made himself available to anyone who needed him. He was always on call for Christ, day or night.

He loved to be with his people. He worked the trenches. He walked the line, paid his dues, and pounded the beat. He loved the mystical body of Christ. He visited the sick, gave the last rites, buried the dead, and comforted mourners.

As chaplain for nearly 20 years at the Kingston Federal Psychiatric Hospital and the Women's Maximum Security Penitentiary, Tom dealt with the abandoned and destitute. The hopeless clung to his coat. He brought Christ to these souls, no matter what their condition.

Tom Brady saw his priesthood as a great force. He was Christ's hands and feet — Christ's voice crying in the wilderness. As a follower of Jesus, he became a divine comforter. Just his presence brought grace to those in need.

At funerals when his services were not required for the liturgy, you'd find him sitting with the faithful — right in their midst. Just being there was his way of offering them his support. Father Frank said, "Being among his suffering flock gave him happiness. That's where he belonged."

During his 47 years as a priest, this tall, red-headed Gael became synonymous with service to the sick and lonely across the Kingston diocese. He didn't wait for them to come to him — he went to them in their homes, hospitals and prisons. The physically and mentally ill took his hand and looked into his tearing eyes for love.

When Tom visited healthy friends, he never stayed long. He had things to do, places to go, and people to see. His work was never done. He always heard the call of his people and answered.

Many years ago, in 1953, when I attended my first year of theology, Tom and I had adjacent rooms and every night at lights out, we would knock a couple of times on the adjoining wall to say goodnight. Even then, he was a comfort.

Tom, I shall remember you as a truly dedicated down-home priest always ready to serve God and your people.

At the end, your diabetic body was worn out.

You couldn't walk.
You were blind.
You had given your all.
Your work was done.

(Knock, Knock, Knock)

Goodnight, Tom.

YOUNG GIRL

The sight of the young girl seating on the cold pavement made the man angry.
  And he said to God, "Why don't you do something about this child's condition?"
  And God answered, "I have. I created you!"

A Heavenly Visitor

In a hospital waiting room, my wife met a patient who talked about his open-heart surgery. He told her he had had a bypass operation. He was 53.

He said that when he was first diagnosed with a heart problem, they told him he would probably need surgery and that further tests would show the full extent of his problem. He went back to his job, not too much concerned. He decided to catch up on work around his home.

One day, he began laying interlocking bricks in his front laneway. Such a job requires lifting, getting up and down, pushing, cutting, hammering — a real workout, even for a healthy man.

That evening his sister phoned from out-of-town. He knew something was up because she rarely called. She said, "What have you been doing? I had a heavenly visitor last night who told me you were doing work injurious to your health. The spirit told me, 'Your brother will get better but he must be careful!'"

When the brother told her about the driveway and about the pending heart examination, the sister became very upset. The brother wisely stopped laying the brick.

A few weeks later, heart tests showed that five arteries were blocked.

Sunsets

Where have all the sunsets gone? How quickly have they passed! Never to be seen again.

Recently, nature reminded me of this relentless fleeting of time. My wife and I had driven one summer's evening into the resort town of Malbaie in northeastern Québec. Here the St. Lawrence River laps a mile-long boardwalk. Pleasure craft play in the bay and couples take the invigorating air along its shore.

A brief history in a guidebook showed how the town was named. In 1610 (approx.), Samuel de Champlain cast anchor in the bay where Malbaie lies — just an overnight stop on one of his several exploratory sojourns into New France. He would wait there until morn so as to better navigate the St. Lawrence's treacherous waters.

What Samuel saw from the bridge next day was enough to curl his wig. His boat sat in the middle of a mud field. The water had been sucked back into the Atlantic. He was marooned.

Not without humour, Samuel told his men: "This is not a good bay, mes amis. In fact, it is a mal baie (a bad bay)." And from that day the name stuck as solidly as was Samuel's ship.

Next morning, I too saw those very mud flats. I was probably just as surprised as he. Nature had emptied that river in six hours, just as it had been doing for 400 years.

That noon as I stared into silver mist and dark cloud I thought how inconsequential are many of mankind's quests. Wherefore the Algonquins and Iroquois — the trading and immigration ships — the eagles' cries — the cannons' roar — the gunfires' crackle — the glory — the plagues — the loves and tragedies of our First Peoples — gone like smoke?

I saw in this mud the immutable will of God. Tide and time wait for no man. All is vanity. When the end comes, God and the good works of His people will remain and nothing much else of importance.

Some Allergy!

During his sermons, my friend Jim has little trouble in holding the attention of parishioners. The church takes on a hush as he speaks, a hush that lingers to the end of the service.

Jim is a layman in the Catholic Church; after his retirement from the military, he chose to become a deacon. Only three priestly duties are denied a deacon: saying Mass, hearing confessions, and giving the last rites. Other than these restrictions, he is allowed to baptize, marry, read the gospels, give sermons and practise corporal works of mercy, such as visiting the sick and caring for the poor.

Why do people listen when Jim talks? For starters, Jim's forte in preaching stems from a solid training in the spoken word back in Tipperary, Ireland. Since the Gaelic language is basically unwritten, emphasis in Eire has always been centred on oral communication. That's why the Irish race specializes in the art of storytelling so naturally.

In addition to this cultural inheritance, Jim has a velvet voice, fine logic, good coherence and unity. He is also blessed with intimacy, sincerity, and the "gift of the gab." He uses no elocutionary tricks like ranting or gesticulations. He comes straight at his listeners, right on the money, enveloping them in his charisma. That's it — charisma, a charisma refined by daily trials and God's love, a charisma that comes from within — an innate magic that enables him to charm and mesmerize and mould.

Deacon Jim is a man of God and always has been. God carried him through military postings, family crises, and serious illnesses. He has become a buster, barker, jester, ambassador — troubadour, roustabout, servant and brother of Jesus. So much so, that when he speaks of Jesus, Jesus speaks through him. That's why his talks are fresh and unrehearsed.

One morning after Mass, I congratulated him and added, "Jim, when you speak, even quietly, I make out every word." And then teasing, I said, "Except when you blow your nose several times during the sermon. You must have had those allergies for years."

He looked at me from under his Irish cap and said, "I have never had allergies. I am blowing my nose because I'm crying."

In Praise of Praise

Hal Holbrook has spent much of his successful stage and screen life portraying Mark Twain. So much so that Twain's philosophic musings have come to colour his way of looking at society. As a result, Holbrook can wax eloquent on many subjects.

In a recent interview, the forceful Holbrook evoked admiration with the following *Twain-Holbrook* advice. I paraphrase: "We don't praise enough in our society. Talent, especially, deserves recognition in a meaningful 'hands on' way.

"It is fallacy to assume that praise 'goes to a person's head.' On the contrary, praise inspires. When I was a young actor, I never knew if I was any good. Up until 15 years ago, I was always scared silly that my work didn't measure up to acceptable benchmarks. I needed an outside source to tell me. For some reason, no one ever did.

"Nowadays, after I have watched an impressive performance, I make my way to the dressing room to compliment the actor. Mark Twain said he could live for a year on a compliment. For young people, especially artists, any compliment at the right time will support them all their lives."

Standing Tall

At a recent gathering of old friends someone commented on Margaret's excellent posture. Since compliments don't come that frequently at our age, she was happy to hear one.

She then took the opportunity to tell us what had led up to such fine posture. She said, "Like many young girls of my day, I was more likely to respond to advice from a relative, friend or complete stranger than from my immediate family. One day when I was visiting a dear uncle, he remarked that my above-average height and slimness required good posture — otherwise, I could look like a sack of bones.

"Needless to say, I was impressed by his good-natured suggestion. And even more so when he continued with these wise words: 'Remember Margaret, proper carriage shows discipline of character. It is a habit easily imitated. Remember you are a *lady*, a member of our family and the temple of the Holy Ghost. You must stand tall, Margaret, and walk with pride.'

"I have tried to do so ever since."

A Poor Man's Holiday

Only the rich can afford the luxury of holidaying in those spots of the world conducive to good health. You won't find the low-income families in the resorts of the Caribbean, the Black Sea, the Mediterranean, the Swiss Alps, or Hawaii.

Fortunately though, nature does provide the less well-to-do with opportunities to enjoy the healthy benefits of the great outdoors. Campers and trailers rest in the woods and by lakes and rivers. Adventure seekers track trails and run rapids. Some barbecue in parks, climb mountains, and fish and hunt in the wild.

For example, what's to prevent a humble colleen from driving along a certain stretch of the Atlantic coast in Connemara, Ireland, in air so refreshing it's been compared to a shot of bracing whiskey.

In Scotland, too, the ordinary lads and lassies can gambol along the North Scotland shore from Inverness to Aberdeen where the freshness of the Arctic wind enlivens the spirit.

Recently, my wife and I found yet another area whose climate has such powers of rejuvenation — this time not far from home — in northeastern Québec some 200 miles from Québec City.

The St. Lawrence River widens there and the Laurentian mountains spread northward. In between, lies the district of Charlevoix, 100 square miles of beauty. There, the air whistles eastward up the St. Lawrence with such restorative powers that President Taft, who made Charlevoix his playground, called it "champagne without the hangover."

René Richard, a famous Canadian painter, born and raised in the Swiss Alps, proclaimed this scenery superior to that of his homeland. Clarence Gagnon, a Parisian-trained watercolourist, lived there too. His paintings capture the essence of this land in a bold clarity of earthy colours.

Go to this land. Drive through these Charlevoix dales and villages to where the Saguenay River meets the Atlantic Ocean. Here even the whales come to eat and play. Perhaps they too recognize the healthy atmosphere of the place.

A Father's Wisdom

Some people say they don't attend church because they get nothing out of it. In response, the clergy insists that they *can* get something out of it, but only when they *put* something in — bring nothing: get nothing. They maintain that active participation at church with faith and love can convince God to give worshippers peace, consolation and answers.

Last Sunday, after church services, I met a young man carrying his newly born infant. The baby was beautiful. I said jokingly, "Did everyone here this morning get one of those?"

The father smartly quipped, "No. You had to bring one to get one."

Touché. It's the same with church attendance. You have to bring something to get something.

Look In the Heart

Often when a friend dies, the enormity of the loss can only be measured by the depth of our mourning. How often these words are spoken: "I never realized how much I loved him, until he was taken."

That's because the heart has its own reasons and emotions which it keeps hidden from the conscious mind. Only a shock such as an unexpected passing releases them.

So next time your reaction to the death of a loved person is far keener than expected, blame it on the heart where the true worth of all our loves is stored.

Joe

Part of Joe's job as a roustabout with a petroleum company in Edmonton was safety inspection. He was very good at what he did, so good that the refinery's engineers relied greatly on his savvy.

When Joe's tenure came up after 30 years, a promised promotion was denied him. So Joe resigned and started up his own petroleum consulting firm. Realizing their loss, Joe's former bosses hired Joe on a contractual basis to help them with safety.

In addition to his *smarts* on the job, Joe was blessed with a sixth sense for trouble. A true story illustrates this power. As a young man, Joe used to take the family's threshing machine on the road. He'd leave Sunday night and return on Saturday. Once, while he was away, a horse on his father's farm kicked out a wooden slat that held a bin of fresh wheat. Three horses succumbed to overeating.

When Joe came home, his father approached him with the news that 3 of their 30 working horses and foals had died. Joe said, "I know!" and he told his father the names of the three dead horses.

On one occasion at the refinery before he quit his job there, Joe had warned an engineering companion about a danger spot in a certain valve. The engineer ignored the report claiming that any repair would have been expensive and in the end probably unnecessary.

A year after his resignation, in the middle of the night an explosion took place in Joe's old oil refinery plant near Edmonton. Instinctively Joe thought of that danger-spot. He hit the floor, dressed and drove to the exact building which contained the fire. He knew where and how the ignition had taken place. He knew that there had to be two men inside — he found them and dragged them out one at a time.

He was the first man there and he saved two lives — all on a hunch, courage and not a little savoir-faire.

The Touching Pond

Children are particularly susceptible to confusing reality with imagination. I was standing by a "touching pond" at the Marina in Maui when a girl of five or six said, "It's a touching pond, Mister. You can touch the fish if you wish. Go ahead."

In front of us, on the raised ledge of the pond, three coral backs invited us to touch them. One was yellow, one red, and one black.

As she watched, I reached out and put a finger on the back of the red one, withdrew it and said, "Look, my finger is all red. What shall I do?"

She watched intently, gazed at my clean finger but said nothing. She then touched the same red one and checked her finger for a mark. Then she touched the yellow one.

I followed by touching the black one. "Look," I said. "I've got marks on the end of my finger again!" This time she promptly added, "That's okay. If you touch the yellow one as I did, the blackness will disappear."

Through a Window

The Halifax fog soon enveloped Her Majesty's Corvette as it slipped into the submarine-infested waters of the North Atlantic. On board, military recruits who had just bid goodbye to loved ones tried to cope with their loneliness.

Among them was Floyd, a young man from Sydney, Nova Scotia. He wondered what his wife, Edith, and child, Matt, were doing that evening. Would they be all right? Would he ever see them again?

As the long months passed, Edith decided to enlist in the Red Cross with the hope she'd meet up with Floyd overseas. So her sister adopted Matt for an indefinite period, and Edith went to war.

Shortly after her arrival, however, Floyd was killed and Edith had a choice: return home or stay. She decided to remain in the service and take up where Floyd had left off.

Meanwhile, back at home, Matt, nearly six, was very much concerned about his parents. Where were they? When would they come back?

When Edith was interviewed in later years about this separation from her son, she said, "During one phone call I asked my sister if Matt was still inquiring about Floyd and me. She assured me he often did and that his favourite question was always, 'Where are they?'

"I asked her how she answered and she replied that she would wave her arm towards the sea and say, 'Over there.'

"I then asked what Matt said to that.

"And she said, 'Nothing. But a little later he would stand for a long time by the picture window and stare at the sea.'"

The King of Hearts

Doctor Wilbur Keon is slight, nay even delicate, like a young Edward VIII, and his features, refined, nay handsome, like Der Bingle.

In just 30 years, he had put his home town of Sheenboro in the Ottawa Valley on the map. In just 30 years he had built in Ottawa an Institute of Heart Surgery second-to-none in the world.

This graduate of Harvard astounded the medical world with new cardiac surgical techniques. Doctors have come from afar to be trained at his side. He helped bring about 10,000 surgical heart operations in those 30 years — and fine-tuned a total staff of 700 to perform them.

Now, in 2004, on an afternoon in April, he had stopped by at one of the many gatherings organized to bid him adieu. Among the people there was a

68-year-old man, the doctor's first bypass and transplant patient. He presented the doctor with a special gift, a two-and-a-half-foot tin man, reminiscent of the wizard of Oz. It was crafted by an artisan in Nova Scotia. Its silver head rattled, the waist folded, and the legs flapped.

As he thanked everyone, the doctor clutched his tin man. He spoke of standing over his father's grave when he was eleven, and the years spent helping his mother run the family store. He thanked his wife and family, re-created his early years of medicine, and praised the Institute's friendship with its many supportive charities. He teared when he spoke of the patients he had failed to save. For here was a sensitive, caring man who carried all his losses on his sleeve.

Doctor Wilbur Keon was indeed a *wizard*. The sick of heart sought him out. He turned no one away if there *was* a *way*. By his creativity, dexterity of hand, and love of mankind, he embraced and mended many defective hearts. I know because I was a tin man until one of Doctor Keon's protégés gave me back my life.

MAKING DO

In a Chicago airport, I met a friendly middle-aged woman from Idaho. In the course of conversation, I asked her how she would best describe the women of Idaho. She thought for a moment and said concisely, "I like to think that the women of Idaho have always had the ability to make do whatever the circumstances."

A Mother's Gift

Herman had decided not to attend the auction of his homestead's furnishings and farm equipment. Too many memories. Too much emotional stress for a man of 79. Instead, he consented to drop in one afternoon and watch his relatives preparing for the sale. It was the year 2004.

Fortunately, Herman's visit was a way of closure for him. His brother, the owner, had recently died and this brief re-acquaintance with the past seemed to ease Herman's difficulty coping with his loss. The day of the auction he wandered among the cutters and buggies of the 1920s and 1930s, sat up on farm machinery such as hand rakes, seeders, and discs. He caressed 125-year-old carpentry tools, bush saws, and axes. He checked out his old bedroom furniture, the summer-kitchen table, and looked into the old mirror in which he had watched himself grow into manhood.

At one point that day, Herman went for a walk with his brother's dog down into the valley behind the house. He had worked those fields, picked fruit in the nearby bush, and hunted beyond the limits of the farm.

As the youngest of eight and a strong, handsome Irish youth, he was an asset to his father and the pride of his mother. He grew up quickly. His father Michael died when Herman was 10 and two older brothers 15 and 16. For 15 years, the farm was run by these three boys. Nellie, their widowed 50-year-old mother, needed everyone's help to survive the Depression and war years. Nellie and Herman became very close. Herman denied her nothing.

I was a summer guest on that farm in the early 1940s. Herman's mother left me with pleasant memories. She had everything that a 12-year-old boy treasured: kindness, understanding, encouragement and love. Her cooking ability as you would expect had not a little to do with my happiness.

She taught me steadiness of disposition, gentleness of character, and the importance of being painstakingly dedicated to duty. She treated me much the same as she did Herman, then 15, and his brothers Alan and John — all good examples for me. I can see her now, over 65 years later, hanging out the laundry on a Monday morning in front of her pretty white house under a canopy of great oaks at the end of the lane.

Herman had but one request concerning the auction's items. He wanted the picture of his parents taken on their wedding day. He needed something to hold on to.

The heirs did arrange for Herman to receive the picture. But they had something else for him. When they were going through old cardboard storage barrels they came upon blankets, sweaters, and socks that Nellie had put away. Among the items found was a patchwork quilt that Nellie had made back in the 1920s. Tucked inside it was a calendar leaf for the month of April, 1961, and a small note pinned to the edging. It said simply, "For Herman."

They presented Herman with this 75-year-old gift and he felt once again the warmth of his mother's love. He remembered then the hours she spent in a draughty room cutting and stitching pieces of dresses and shirts. In his old age he could wrap this token of his mother's love 'round his lonely heart.

A Good Practice

A cardiac specialist once said to me, "I take as much time as the patient needs. Patients deserve to know the relevant factors about their conditions. Their concerns must be addressed. Of course, I must be satisfied, but so must they.

"That's why I never set rigid time periods for my consultations. Each case differs. Time and pressure do not dictate to me — I control *them*.

"The line-up in the waiting room does not disturb me. I have my own ways of catching up. Getting in the way of my patients' health is not one of them."

A Promise

In a preoperative interview a doctor offered this advice: "The result of any operation is by its nature unpredictable. That's because risk is always a factor. Therefore, for a patient to approach a serious operation with a carefree attitude is not recommended. Better to keep a reserved feeling.

"However, there are, in fact, many good reasons for having a healthy outlook. Especially here in this specialized hospital. Our staff can't promise that they won't make mistakes — everyone is human. But what they *can* promise, is that every person involved *here* with a patient will do the utmost to assure that *nothing* will go wrong."

Farewell

My friend, Stephen, had this to say about his father's death, (I paraphrase): "I needed finality. Although we knew his passing would eventually come after nine years of suffering, it still was a shock. Each family member had to find a way of handling the emptiness.

"As I pined, I realized that whatever form my closure took, it would have to be acceptable to my father. Its scenario would have to be something he himself could have easily orchestrated. It would have to be in accordance with his wishes, his style, manners and ways.

"The answer came one morning in a dream. Just like that. As if it were meant to be.

"I dreamed my father and I were standing on a golf tee. Where? I don't know. Somewhere, anywhere! The early morn was damp. Mists enveloped the course.

"We took our practice swings. Dressed in his usual nondescript cap, windbreaker and baggy trousers, Dad limbered up with his reliable callisthenics. He looked young and happy, and I caught once more his passion for the game.

"Three rounds a day were nothing for him. If he had company, all the better, but he didn't mind playing alone. He played golf the way he lived — not too much emotion — a controlled three-quarter swing — always within himself — a quiet intensity and focus — an explosive release of power when needed — and a deep respect for the game, its etiquette and rules. Whether as a guest or a host, his hospitality never wavered.

"Suddenly my Dad said, 'Son, would you mind if I took the honour this morning. It's a special day.'

"'Sure, Dad. But what's so special?' I asked. And he came over and looked me in the eye. He was crying a little. And I knew instinctively then the moment had come for him to leave.

"He raised his arm and pointed behind us. A crowd had assembled — family, relatives, friends, neighbours, school buddies, old golfing partners —

they were applauding, but I could hear nothing. My Dad smiled and waved graciously, like some king from a balcony.

"And he said to me, 'Son, I think I'll play alone today. Do you mind?'

"And I said, 'What can I say, Dad?'

"'Don't say anything,' he answered. 'Just be brave and remember, I love you, Son.'

"With that he took a final look at the crowd and drove the ball. It looked like the sweetest shot he had ever made. He smiled.

"I then handed him his bag to which he returned his club. He then put on the cover, placed the bag's loop on his shoulder and walked straight out. Some 230 yards down the meadow, he hit an iron to the green.

"It was then he turned and raised his cap with his head slightly cocked. His final farewell.

"The last we saw of him — he had reached the green. After he putted out, a group of people surrounded him. The flag was put in its hole and they all walked together into the folds of eternity."

— Based on Stephen's dream

Diana

Among the famous women of the twentieth century such as Roosevelt, Gandhi, Thatcher, Mother Teresa, and Garbo surely the name of the Irish-Anglo beauty, Diana Spencer, has a place. In a mere 16 years of public life she captured the hearts of millions. She became everybody's sweetheart.

In many ways Diana was an emotional misfit. Her confidence was easily scuttled. She trusted too many, talked too much, lacked stability, and lived in the fast lane. Her school marks suggest an inability to handle academic subjects.

These weaknesses, however, did not deter her rise to prominence. She had much going for her: position, money, beauty, personality, and connections. The mother in all of us empathized with her fairy-tale, soap-opera life. It appealed to romantics everywhere.

But Diana had something more. She had a tremendous capacity for love — natural, guileless, spontaneous, and fathomless. It swept up everyone in its path. It touched souls, especially those in need.

It showed in her playing on the floor with children, sitting on the beds of the sick, and kissing the shaking hands of the old. If anyone as much as opened his or her heart to Diana, she walked in. The forgotten side of humanity shared her royal spirit.

The trait of being so accessible to people came from the example of her maternal grandfather, Baron Roche, by way of her mother, Frances. Frances is quoted as saying, "Treat everyone the same whether they come from castle, cottage or caravan."

Sadly, Diana never did get enough love in her own life.

How could she? She kept giving it away?

She may well have been a lost child but she showed true charity to thousand.

In any century only a few women of her ilk ever come along.

The Pin

(A true story by Margaret Anderson, a great-granddaughter of Grandma MacCrae)

The occasion was special. Ten-year-old Martin wandered hopelessly through the Glasgow Protestant Cemetery. He thought he knew where his grandmother MacCrae was buried. After all, he had been there at her funeral. But now his memory failed him.

He was saying goodbye to his grandmother. He had brought along a posy. He was being sent to live with his aunt in Montreal. She badly needed company and support. He would go and do what he could. But he really had no choice.

His grandmother had been Martin's best friend. She ran fish and chip shops in the Gorbels of Glasgow where Martin worked cleaning tables and running errands. Her death in 1915 hit Martin hard. He just had to go to the cemetery and leave a token of love.

Needless to say, Martin was discouraged that late April afternoon in 1917. He was lost and cold. The flowers were withering. He was going to have to stop looking.

However, just as he turned for the iron-gate exit at the far end of the cemetery, he saw afar a girl about his own age standing among the gravestones. She beckoned him to follow her.

She took Martin to an older section of the burial ground and finally stopped before one gravestone. Martin caught up. He realized at once it was his grandmother's grave.

Quickly Martin placed the flowers at the head of the stone. He said a few silent prayers and then turned to thank the girl.

But she had gone.

At home, Martin told his mother he had purchased flowers with the money given him by a neighbour and taken them to the cemetery.

"But why were you gone so long, Martin?" she asked.

"Well, Ma, I couldn't find the grave. Finally a girl came along and showed me where it was."

"What did she look like?"

"My age, black hair, dark eyes, a grey dress with a white collar — pretty — a lovely smile. She acted as if she knew me."

"Do you believe in ghosts, Martin?"

"Don't know."

"Well it appears to me that the girl who guided you was your sister, Charlotte. She died as a baby. She was our first child. I've told you about her. She was named after my sister, your aunt in Montreal.

"She was Grandma MacCrae's first grandchild and she mourned her terribly. If Charlotte were alive today, she would be one year older than you. I remember we placed a small pin of Grandma's on her white dress when we buried her."

"What kind of a pin was it?"

"It was silver — shaped like a quarter moon."

"Ma, the girl had that same pin on her. Come to think of it — she wore no coat, just a white dress and the pin. She wasn't even cold. My dear sister, she wasn't even cold."

The Good Shepherd of the Snow

Across unmapped tundra of the North in weather seldom seen by man, a small band of Eskimo herds drove 3000 reindeer to the safety of distant valleys. The wind and cold were relentless, sweat froze, eyelids stuck, frostbite crippled. At night, no one wanted to go outside the shelters.

Finally, the herds became disoriented. They were lost. They sat down in their tracks and began railing at their leader. There was no point in going on, they said.

Legend has it that the leader stood among his men and said, "Look at me and believe. As sure as you see me, my words are true. *We* are not lost. I am *not* lost. *I* know the way. Follow *me*, I promise to bring you back home."

And they followed. And he did.

BEFORE I SLEEP

Underneath a Pacific Sky, out where the seabirds seldom fly ... where the full moon shines straight above my head and Lady Venus hangs as on a thread ... out where dark clouds tumble against the blue and storms from afar flash their hue ... I walk alone on promenade bare, by dangling life boats and empty chairs ... and hear the ship's prow pound the sea like some steel monster on a spree ... and watch it split the waves to ride the tide and lie spent on a foreign shore ... and later in the eve when the wind has bite, I look again into Neptune's deep and think of God before I sleep.

— the Author

An Invitation

An old 93-year-old friend from my childhood lives in a retirement home. She has a quaint room at the very end of her floor.

The other day as I was leaving she said strongly, "When I get to heaven, I hope I have a room just like this, a little out of the way but worth the walk. And when you get to heaven I want you to know that you're welcome to come and visit me there. Just like here. My door is always open to a dear friend."

She died four months after this last meeting.

Simple Ways of Praying

As we age, our prayers become more simple, more direct and personal, more from the heart. One elderly friend, unable to walk the Stations of the Cross in her church, used to follow the pictures in her prayer book. Each page brought to mind the fourteen commemorations of Christ's walk of death. She said these prayers several times a day whenever she could find the time and privacy.

Another old lady, crippled by a stroke, used the little eyesight she had left to meditate upon a flower. She would hold it up closely, study it, turn it and praise God for His beautiful works. She easily became lost in devotion.

Another friend, tired of repetitive prayers, said the only way for her to pray properly was to abandon herself to God. She described her method very simply, "I just let myself fall into God's embrace."

A Soccer Ball

I was standing in the asphalt playground beside Haghill Elementary School in Denistown, Glasgow. My father had attended this school in 1912, just a few years after it opened. He started at age five, and was graduated at age 12.

In 2002, I hadn't seen the school in 34 years. It was by then ragged looking, needed painting, fence repairs, etc. It was on its last legs. The School Board was slowly letting it slip into closure.

Now, it happened that this occasion of my second visit was the afternoon of the last day of classes for the year. The empty school grounds suited the general atmosphere of the place.

Near a wall in a corner under red brick, I spotted a small white soccer ball, a leftover from the games played in the yard that day.

As I walked up to it, I felt my father's presence. And my loneliness grew as I whispered, "Dad, I'm going to kick this ball across the schoolyard. When it settles, perhaps you would kick it back."

Well, nothing happened. I thought at least the wind or gravity would return it, but, alas, it was not to be. The ball stayed put. Yet, I knew he was there.

Then, I turned away. Dark clouds cast a gloom. The wind was cool. I'm sure my Dad watched me go.

Dr. Chummie

Dr. Archie Chummie had many children as friends in the small town where he practised. But none was so dear as a boy named Timmy whom he brought into the world and looked after, for ten years.

In addition to regular medical appointments, the two saw each other in other capacities since Timmy's father, as mayor of the town, was part of the same social whirl as the doctor.

Timmy often stopped by the doctor's side-door for cookies and milk and often helped out by delivering prescriptions, walking the dog, or picking up mail.

Over their years, their closeness was such that some people said the doctor later saved Timmy's life in a miraculous way.

This is what happened. On a snowy afternoon, ten-year-old Timmy was sledding down a hill near his home. His speed took him across a road and underneath an approaching automobile.

The woman driver saw the boy sliding beneath her car. She was sure she had hit him. Recognizing the lad as the son of the mayor, she raced to get the boy's father. She arrived at the father's door in a hysterical state.

Together, they rushed to the accident and there stood Timmy completely unscathed. The father and all the bystanders were amazed that Timmy had escaped the wheels, let alone the undercarriage. It was then that word came that Doctor Chummie had died an hour before the accident.

Timmy's family, whom I know, swear to this day that the just-deceased Doctor Chummie saved Timmy from an otherwise certain tragedy.

Four Walls

Just a cheap, iron bed with four chintzy gold knobs in the downstairs bedroom of an old 1854 country home. Yet it served four generations.

The inside of the house was gutted in 1990, but two sides of the bedroom walls are left.

Originally its four walls were covered by layers of flowery paper placed over thin slats stuffed with horse hair, rags and newspapers.

The two outside walls were of roughly hewn logs, their white wash never quite white and its limestone-chinking never quite intact.

The only window in the room faced the morning sun. A door joined the bedroom to the kitchen-dining-living room. The window could be raised for the summer breeze and the door left open in the winter for heat from the lion's-paw stove in the family room.

A picture of Saint Cecilia playing a musical instrument was just inside the door and a plaster cross rested above the bed. The Virgin Mary holding her Son was on a side wall.

The floor was grey maple boards with a thin rug at the side of the bed. On the left side of the entrance, shelves made of coarse spruce hid behind a curtain.

The furniture in the room consisted of a hope chest under the window and a three-drawer birch dresser up against the wall inside the entrance. The bed had flat springs, a straw mattress, bleached sheets, and a home-made patch-work blanket.

The first couple to share the bedroom were Tom and Margaret. Nine children were conceived and born there between 1850 and 1869. Tom died in 1890, his wife, in 1909. Tom's son, Tom, brought his 21-year-old bride, Genevieve, to the same house. They had seven children from 1900 to 1921. Both Tom and Genevieve died in that bedroom, Tom in 1934, and Genevieve in 1955.

That bedroom then had been a special place for some 120 years. It had witnessed pain, passion, joy. It had seen a thousand kisses, heard hundreds of endearing remarks, winced at the agonized cries of women in labour, shared the joy of 16 newborn babies, and watched death carry away loved ones.

It had played an integral part in the lives of two families. It wrapped them in comfort and privacy. A simple room. A powerful legacy. Where life began and ended!

Father and Son

At the sitter's house where he had spent the day, he ran down the lane into his father's arms. "Dah-dee, Dah-dee," he shouted as his father lifted him high above his head.

From his car seat in the back, he then directed his father to the nearest McDonald's. Along the way, they engaged in chatter about the little guy's day. They could see each other in the front mirror — both faces full of happiness. "I waf you, Dah-dee," he'd say. Then he'd run his toy car up and down the seat.

The little guy was moved around a great deal — his mother's home, his father's, his grandparents', not to mention his sitter's. You'd wonder how this constant change affected him — he was only three — being shifted from house to house — different friends, settings, food, rules. Yet he seemed resilient. Except for the odd burst of bad temper, he managed to charm his way through it all.

The bond between son and father was strong. The father attempted to love the child as much as he could in the time allotted. They read books, put together puzzles, arranged train tracks, raced cars, watched television and snacked on bachelor food. They had their arguments but made up and hugged and laughed.

The child had become somewhat used to their parting. He knew his father would come again. The days meant nothing; the hours counted.

But the father found the boy's departures difficult. He could never, never quite get used to it. The hugs were long — the goodbyes repetitive. The little guy would watch his father leave in his car, his wee hand waving, his face strained, his voice whining, "Bye Dah-dee, bye Dah-dee. I waf you, Dah-dee."

His father would call back as long as the boy could see him. Then he'd drive alone into the night, his heartache washed by tears. And he would pray, "Oh, God, keep my son in Your hands. He needs You. Will You do that for me?"

> **QUIET MOMENTS**
>
> The best of any day
>   Are those moments of repose
> When interludes of solitude
>   Refresh my restless soul.
> To close my eyes and nod my head
>   Wherever I may be
> And drift awhile in God's embrace
>   Is sweet serenity.
>
> — the Author

The Deacon's Duty

After his retirement from his career job, a friend decided he would like to become a deacon in his Church.

As it happened, one of his duties was the requirement to drink the left-over wine after the communion service. This caused him great anxiety since he was an alcoholic. Before beginning his studies, he told the archbishop about his problem. The archbishop said not to worry. They'd work out something.

But my friend was not sure. Any taste of alcohol could set him off for days. So he prayed and prayed as he went on with his plans.

Eventually, when the day came to drink the wine, he shuttered at the thought of what could happen. He put the tilted chalice to his lips and drank. Suddenly, his whole mouth began to burn — nothing serious, he said, but strong, uncomfortable and encompassing.

After his mouth returned to normal, he sat back and waited for the over-powering craving to kick in. But it never did. In the many years since, he has never once felt an urge for alcohol after consuming the wine. Naturally, he avoids all other alcoholic beverages, but not the wine. He claims it's a miracle and who should know better than he.

The Hooker

A certain group were in a tourist bus in a foreign country. Five of the passengers were from the same American city. Although strangers at first, after some days of travel they became close companions.

The five were made up of a young male student, a nurse, a teacher, a minister, and a young lady of the night.

One afternoon, the bus went down a cliff. Among the five friends, three died — the minister, teacher and nurse. But before the minister succumbed, he reached for his blood-splattered Bible and handed it to the woman of ill repute and said, "Take this and read it — it will change your life." All this was witnessed by the student.

Many years later, when the student was attending a religious service in a suburb of his own city, he was startled by the minister's sermon.

The minister was preaching about good works. In order to accentuate a point, he raised a Bible over his head. He said, "This Bible, my dear people, belonged to my mother. For many years, she led a wayward life, but that changed the day someone gave her this Bible. It happened while she was on a vacation. She and some fellow travellers were in an accident. One of the dying, a minister, handed her this Bible and with his last breath whispered in her ear, 'My daughter, it's not what we take with us out of this life that matters; it's what we leave behind.'"

THE HAWAIIAN HEART

At Culloden the gorse entwines.
At Waterloo, the flocks recline.
On Flanders' Fields, the poppies sway.
On Gettysburg's green, the chipmunks play.
On Hawaii's Isles, rocks ink the dales,
And on their mountains the greenery scales.
The plantations ripen in the sunny mists
And underneath the city's palms
The silver boulevards run on and on.
But such a beauty has a price
Nor was its peace won overnight.
It was the brave hearts of the silenced few
That have made all Hawaii's dreams come true.

— the Author

A Story of Forgiveness

The six daughters and wife of a certain gentleman did not mourn his passing. Now 20 years after, they still could not forgive him. He had sexually abused his children and beaten his wife. Their life had been a hell.

Of late the mother's health had been failing. Blindness took her eyesight and Alzheimer's took her mind. The daughters who lived nearby took turns sitting with her.

As the end drew closer, all the daughters became very concerned that the refusal of their mother to forgive her husband might well jeopardize her chances of getting into heaven. In fact, they themselves had reservations about their own spiritual disposition since they could not bring themselves to forgive him either.

So the daughters decided to meet at a Sunday service to pray over their problem. The presiding priest, unaware of their dilemma, gave a sermon on forgiveness which happened to be the theme for the Sunday reading. His words set all the sisters crying and two had to leave to gain control of themselves.

After the service, the priest having become aware of some difficulty in the congregation, met with them. A lively discussion followed. The result was the priest agreed to visit the mother in hospital on the following day.

Early next morning, the priest was surprised to find the mother had regained her sanity. The doctors and nurses were amazed to hear the woman talking intelligently. It was a miracle.

The priest took the opportunity to discuss the mother's attitude to the husband. Yes, she suffered from guilt, but felt no forgiveness. The priest was wasting his breath. So, he proceeded with his priestly duties: he gave her communion and the last rites.

But suddenly the lady began to speak kindly about her husband. Perhaps, as a military man, the war had twisted his mind, she thought. Perhaps he had no control over what he did. Maybe she didn't try her best, and so on.

By this time, the daughters had arrived in the room. The mother spoke to each one. And then she confronted the girls with the words, "You must forgive your father. I have. He will meet me in heaven. I must be able to tell him that all has been forgiven by his family."

In the presence of the mother and the priest, the girls individually announced their forgiveness. Everybody was crying, including the priest.

Later that evening, with a few of the girls present, another priest, the hospital's chaplain, dropped in on the woman. Not aware the last rites had already been given, he gave them to her again. When she went to sign herself at the blessing, her arm fell. She was dead.

The Café Owner

The flicker of Le Café Grand's neon light was a welcome sight that foggy evening. The wanderer had hardly settled into a chair by the fire when someone said, "Bonsoir, Monsieur. Bienvenue à mon café," and he looked up at a loveliness that took his breath away.

"I am at your service, Monsieur. Perhaps a brandy, some cheese and baguette." He agreed and she left him to his adoration.

That was the first time he saw her. The stranger, an oil painter by profession, couldn't get enough of her. He became a regular guest and every night she personally took his order seemingly oblivious to the spell she cast.

Some artists would search a lifetime to find such a prize. How fortunate he felt. It was as if he had been drawn to that little café by the waterfront in the French quarter of old Amsterdam.

Naturally, he wanted to capture her sweetness on canvas, but he had the idea she would not agree to an individual sitting. So he thought he might entice her to be included in a mural of the café's interior. And she agreed.

Before he began, however, the artist knew he had homework to do. He had to study his scene and players so as to have a definitive purpose for painting anything at all.

So he sat by the café fireplace night after night studying his objects over his brandy. He sketched and wrote. Gradually, the ambience of the place seeped into his creativity: the clinking, tittering, scents, songs, the chatter and always that refreshing spirit of the waitresses, their repartee, their saucy smiles, fluffy brown hair, roguish eyes shaded in blue, and the deep mauve richness of their uniforms.

His eyes would follow the proprietress especially as she moved exuding her charm from table to bar, to kitchen, to customer. Grasping her beauty and character was not easy. Yet he could not begin without first doing so. Every human being is so complex, with so much subtlety, so many shadows, masks and faces. He had first to see *behind* those dark eyes and faint smile. He had to work his way through all the sensual and emotional stimuli to find the essence of her beauty.

One night, he felt he had finally come to know her. Now his task was to capture her on canvas. So he went to work. Every brush stroke only strengthened his conviction that he had found what he wanted. Every scene he painted had her central to the viewer's eye. Every scene had her loveliness in it.

His paintings won her heart. She was ecstatic to see her café and friends on canvas.

The artist's paintings of that café have since made him famous in the Netherlands. Some compare his work to that of Degas with its mixture of the impressionist and realist, a style intimately at one with the passing parade of daily life.

Not long after, a friend asked this artist, "How did you know *when* you were ready to start your paintings?" And he replied (I paraphrase), "I saw suddenly an unpretentious woman of exceptional wisdom and courage who had reached a point in her life beyond which she did not need or wish to go. She had found herself. She had had her flings and known romance and joy. She had a peace no one could take from her.

"She had done her best with life as it had presented itself. No regrets, no guilt, no remorse — no more dreams or expectations. She was content to live her life out by that waterfront in a café with her friends.

"I saw in her what all of us should have — contentment, happiness and fulfillment."

WAYS OF SAYING GOODBYE

* Catch ya later
* Drop in anytime
* See you sooner
* We'll meet again
* Until next time
* Keep the faith
* Cheery bye
* May God go with you
* Hang in there
* The door is always open
* The pot is always boiling
* Don't be so long coming back

* The latch is always on
* Thinking of you
* Keep smiling
* Toodle-loo
* Keep in touch
* Call you later
* Au revoir
* Come again
* God love ya
* So long
* Now that you know where I live
* You don't need an invitation

Having Faith in Hope

Some theologians contend that mankind's universal quest for heaven is proof that a God does exist. They say some outside force ignites our being to desire eternal happiness.

Similarly, mankind carries an inner hope into other aspects of daily life. They look for satisfaction, retribution, solutions, and cures. They never lose hope for that treasure at the end of the rainbow. A *new* day is *another* day for dreams to come true. Tomorrow is a lovely day.

Mankind's hope is particularly strong in relations to the loss of precious people and things. A deep-sea-diving instructor recently told me about a famous family of underwater treasure hunters who lost a favourite son to the sea some ten years ago. They were determined to discover his body and every time they had a chance, they went down to look in that part of ocean where he had disappeared. They searched over ten years to no avail.

On the day of the 10th anniversary of his death, they decided on one final sweep of the area. On that hallowed day, they found him. Their longing was justified. Coincidence? Who knows?

Another story illustrates the feasibility of hoping. Some 20 years ago a friend and her two-year-old son were sitting on the sandy beach of her parents' cottage. Without thinking, the mother took off a favourite bracelet and placed it on a wooden walk beside her. She reached for it a minute later. It was gone. As she turned towards her son, she saw him throw it into the sand.

Twenty years later, the family was still looking for it. It was an heirloom, several generations old, and treasured by the different ladies who had worn it. Members of the family took turns raking the sand during the summer months. Not even 20 winters dulled their hopes of finding it.

What was it that spurred them on? Perhaps it was the original owner who wanted it found. Whatever the reason, they persisted. As it turned out, their yearnings were not in vain.

Twenty years to the day, in an area that had been searched countless times, the mother stepped on the bracelet. Their prayers and efforts and unaccountable faith that it would be found, were answered.

Footprints

It's difficult to walk in another's footsteps. But sometimes we must. A veteran military man was talking the other day about the times his army platoon had to walk through mine fields. The procedure was that a leader carefully went first followed by the others in single file. Naturally, each person had to place his feet exactly in the ones left by the leader.

Life's like that too. The world can be a minefield. Especially in matter of morals. One false move and figuratively speaking we can fall in a hole, go off a cliff, get stuck in a rut. To help us in this regard, one leader has left us the imprint of a path through these dangers. When the paths we make for ourselves become treacherous, look for His footprints and follow them.

Call Muldoon

As the visiting chaplain of his local general hospital, Father Muldoon had the responsibility of providing spiritual consolation to those Catholic patients who wished to see him.

Of particular importance was his giving the last rites to the dying. The nurses and doctors who knew from experience when death was imminent, would call Father Muldoon on his cell phone.

During the years that Father Muldoon visited this secular hospital, the nurses on duty, quite on their own, made a startling discovery. They noticed that not one patient given the last rites by Father Muldoon ever died on the same day as his visit. What's more, not one patient in the entire hospital died during the same time frame.

They concluded that Father Muldoon has the power of healing. Although those days of Father Muldoon's visits are long gone, the staff continues to bring these happenings back to memory.

The Greatest Magician of Them All

The Universe's existence, order, and beauty cannot help but increase our faith in God. Its magnitude, consistency, and precision are marvels. The energy, power and force that run it cannot be explained. The creation of the Universe is a mystery.

That the Universe is explainable by the "big bang" theory, as some scientists would have us believe, is about as plausible as a tornado in a junkyard producing a 747 aeroplane.

Scientists can take us so far. They can predict eclipses, comets, magnetic bursts; they can measure distances in space and the size of stars and galaxies; they can document the birth and death of heavenly objects; they can put man on the moon and robots on planets; they can photograph the transcending majesty of the heavens; but in the final analysis, when the crunch comes, they cannot explain how, when or why, the universe came into being.

The answer is a Supreme Being. It is He who created living cells from nothing. It is He who made the universe, all the gases and mass and light and energy and beauty.

Scientists attribute the maintenance of the universe to a power called gravity. Gravitation is an attraction of mass, which science thinks is a form of electro-magnetism. Gravity is the motor, fuel and glue of the universe. The slightest change in gravity's balance would paralyze the heavens. The shortest cessation of gravity and the universe would fall in, float away, and "crash."

Because of gravity, every mass attracts every other mass. The universe is engaged in a giant tug of war within itself. Unless the size of one of two masses or the distance between them changes, the power they have on each other is constant. The Supreme Being has programmed every dimension and distance to produce order extraordinaire.

A study of the universe brings faith and science together. They complement each other. Theologians and scientists must bow to a grandeur of such magnitude that it defies explanation or description. When our reason falls short, we can turn to faith. When faith weakens, look to science.

Science tells us that our galaxy, the Milky Way, rotates west to east just as the other millions of galaxies do. Gravity also moves the entire universe as a whole in the same direction. In addition, all the heavenly objects in each galaxy rotate the same way. Gravity also spins the earth on its axis, west to east, and swings the earth 'round the sun that way once a year. A few years ago, Greenwich, the time centre of the world, found a one-second discrepancy in one year between the earth's orbit and Greenwich's time machine. Naturally the clock was wrong.

No wonder human beings get headaches. We are on one great roller coaster ride. We are never in the same place in the universe.

Somewhere in or outside all this creation, God resides. He has contacted His creatures. He has told us what He expects from us. He has set up a code to follow.

To those who adhere to it, He has promised heaven forever in His company. He is not a machine or robot; He is a personal, loving, kind and understanding Being who holds the entire universe in one hand and all creatures in the other.

He who made the stars and roses also made souls.

A BLAZE OF GLORY

Parts of the Atlantic trade route from the Caribbean to the Mediterranean have always been a test of ship and seaman ... near the Azores, one May evening, where the deepest volcanic eruptions in the world are found, a bad-tempered sea rocked the great liner ... white caps snapped at shadows ... a cold wind cut the bow ... no one stirred outside....

But I — alone, on the stern's lower promenade, gazed westward in hope the sun would yet dot the horizon's edge ... and sure enough, a pin of orange lit the waves and expanded into the image of a fiery frigate ... it blazed long enough to show its glory of long ago ... and then as quickly as it formed, slipped beneath a cloud to wander in eternity.

A Child of Grace

Because Good Friday's date moves according to the full moon, occasionally it falls on March 25, the Catholic Church's celebration of the Annunciation.

It is a significant coincidence. While the Annunciation recalls the angel's announcement to Mary that a Saviour will be born to her, Good Friday celebrates the same Son's redemptive act on Calvary. On one day, Mary agreed to be the mother of God; on the other, Jesus fulfilled his Father's wish that he be the ransom for our salvation. Without one, there could not be the other.

Elsewhere in this book, a true story depicts the death of a saintly girl in Montreal. Her name was Annette. Her sister had told me about her. After a few short months, during which time Annette offered her illness and death as a prayer that her mother would live, Annette died on Good Friday, March 25 at 3 p.m. She was 16. The year, 1934.

Recently, another child of grace, whose paternal grandparents I have known since my teens, died on Good Friday, 2005, on March 25, at 3:30 p.m. She was 17. Her name was Colleen.

Now, it just happened that this child's grandmother was dying in the same hospital at the same time this girl was being born. Before the baby and mother went home, the grandmother, also named Colleen, asked to see her grandchild. The baby was placed in her grandmother's arms and at the grandmother's request both were left alone. The grandmother died in a few days.

Some three years later, the child Colleen developed leukemia. At age five, the cancer went into remission and remained so for ten years. In those ten years, Colleen lived life to the fullest. Small, vivacious and full of beans she was, so much like her grandmother. She played, danced and studied with gusto. But when she was 15 the cancer returned and claimed her two years later.

Colleen and her namesake had similar traits of courage under duress — neither indulged in self-pity, neither ever complained about their lot and both showed death-bed concerns about their families' welfare.

Since Colleen thought she wouldn't live for her seventeenth birthday, she held an early birthday party at home. Many friends came. From her wheelchair, she enjoyed all the activities. The tears of 70 people weren't enough to extinguish the birthday candles; so Colleen blew them out with the same spirit that filled her life.

Colleen died on Good Friday; her grandmother had died on Easter Monday. They were buried on the same date, March 28.

Obviously, the closeness of these two over 17 years was immeasurable. In her final hours Colleen never thought of herself. She approached death as her grandmother had. She asked a priest to ask everyone to pray for her mother and father.

Near death, she whispered to her mother a wish that shows the essence of this child of grace, "Mom, who's going to look after all the sick and poor children of the world?"

Of such is the kingdom of heaven!

Billy

Seven years ago I viewed the ruins of a flash fire that claimed two lives. The two under-age teens who had set a bonfire on the back steps of a two-storey apartment served five years in jail. They are now free. The victims, Billy and his wife, weren't so lucky.

Last week I met Joan, whose son was a good friend of Billy. She told me this story: Billy and her boy belonged to a fishing club comprised of old school chums. All the members mourned Billy and his wife. On every fishing trip since, they have held a moment of silence in remembrance. They can't forget.

Neither can Billy. Not long after the tragedy, the gang went ice fishing on an isolated lake. There, Joan's son, while separated from the others, went through the ice. He couldn't get out. He shouted. He struggled. He was drowning. Suddenly someone grabbed him by the back of his jacket's collar and pulled him out. Safe on the ice, her son realized he was still alone. How did it happen?

The group decided that it was Billy who had pulled his friend to safety.

A Gentleman Named Rod

Many believe that we tend to make friends with those in whom we see our own fine qualities. On the contrary, we are attracted to them because they have qualities superior to ours. Their example makes us all the better for being with them. Their goodness rubs off upon us. We improve. We learn.

I lost a friend last week named Rod Andrews. I liked him because he exemplified the characteristics of a true gentleman.

This is what he taught me about being a gentleman. A gentleman:

* is thoughtful and kind
* is a good listener
* is gentle in speech
* never condemns
* converses without rancour
* smiles easily
* forgives carefully
* rules compassionately
* never pouts
* gives in secret
* thinks things through
* never gloats
* never judges
* praises discreetly
* is content with his lot
* searches for truth
* treats equally
* never carries tales
* is loyal when required
* divides fairly
* forgives readily
* is slow to anger
* is never condescending
* speaks no evil
* never corrects unduly
* never brags
* is solicitous of family, friends and neighbours
* is never boorish or gauche
* never whines
* weeps alone
* prays often
* never flaunts
* never rails
* avoids foul language
* tries constantly to learn, to read, to search
* loves justice
* never flatters for gain
* shares happily
* has his priorities straight

All these qualities in varying degrees made up Rod's persona. What a friend he was!

A Long Nap

Father Steve was about to leave the Manor after the regular Thursday, 10 a.m. Mass when an elderly lady who had been at the service approached him. As she steadied herself on a walker, she said, "Father, I have something to ask you."

"Go ahead, Mrs. Emery, by all means," answered the priest.

"Father, the doctor told me this week that I have cancer. On top of my other ills, I'm not sure I can face more pain."

"Mrs. Emery, I am sorry to hear such news. I shall pray for you."

"Father," she continued, "I haven't asked you my question yet. Is it okay if I pray to God to take me to heaven? Do you think He'd mind?"

Father Steve thought carefully. He moved closed to her good ear, and said, "Mrs. Emery, how can God be upset about someone wanting to be with Him? He doesn't want you to suffer. He desires you to be with Him.

Father blessed her and she shuffled away. He never saw her again.

That afternoon, Mrs. Emery lay down for her afternoon nap and never woke up.

A Roman Holiday — "All is Vanity"

Rome never sleeps. Mopeds buzz, sub-compacts wait panting for the Indy green, ambulances, police cars and fire trucks wail. Jaywalkers defy death in clogged arteries. It's a people city — well-used — often abused — impatient, temperamental and indifferent — always on the go, pulsating to a thousand moods. It's a circus with a multitude of rings.

Twenty-eight hundred years in the making, her charisma still entices millions. First glimpses of landmarks like the infamous slaughter-house called the Colosseum and the marble statues of the Trevi fountain, stir the heart.

Just to walk where greats like Peter and Paul, Constantine, Charlemagne, Augustus and Pope John Paul II strode is a privilege. Michelangelo, Bernini and Raphael added to Rome's beauty and the English Romantic poets, Shelley, Keats and Byron brought their talents to Rome as did Shakespeare, Milton and Swinburne. To navigate the granite stone walks of the Roman forum where thousands and thousands clamoured to touch their kings and emperors brings a nostalgic rush.

Rome is at once for the romantic and the melancholic. On the upbeat side, beauty and truth, be they intellectual or not, are found there, even among the fallen arches and vaults, hollow ruins, and empty fields.

I heard Shelley's nightingale praising God behind a rosebush on Palatine Hill. I saw the leafy Tiber twisting along its shorelines of modern apartments. Atop majestic tombs and churches, sculptures of Aurelius and St. Michael look down on swirling piazzas, spouting fountains, lazy parks and me.

I stood near Janiculum Hill on the west side of the Tiber where Romulus and his shepherds in the eighth century first pitched their tents on the marshes. Beside this hill, Cleopatra walked in her gardens as she listened for Caesar's arrival. There she would have felt Shelley's "wild west wind," as I did, swooping up the Tiber from the Mediterranean Sea.

And while there, I felt the pain of this 24-year-old rather plain Macedonian maiden when word came that her sugar-daddy had been sucker-stabbed by Cassius and *friends*, not more than a few hundred yards from her embrace ... and I pictured Calpurnia sobbing at her altar of gods, the angry mob demanding her Caesar's body for burning, and Marc Antony getting up on a Senate rostrum to share their sorrow and at the same time co-incidentally eyeing Julius's mistress. The stuff of Shakespeare, Theocritus and Marlowe.

Occasionally we sat under umbrellas at corner cafés and watched the world go by. Here other weary tourists mingled with the locals as cheerful barmaids flitted among bright plastic-covered tables. Down a dark lane, in-your-face vendors waved the bright hues of silk ties and scarves, or blew soap bubbles from plastic pipes, or whirled satellite boomerangs out and back over the motley-dressed. Once, a well-dressed young man offered us each a free rose — provided we gave a donation.

Not far from where we were wandering in this older section known as Trastevere, Constantine built the first St. Peter's Basilica. He put it beside Vatican Hill where Nero had St. Peter crucified upside down in 67 AD. Just two miles from there, outside the ancient 11-mile-long wall with its 15 gates, soldiers beheaded the Roman citizen, Paul, on the Ostian road to Rome.

Testimonies to Rome's former greatness lie everywhere. In the third century, 2,000,000 within its 800-walled hectares swelled the byways — it had 1,000 baths, 1,000 public fountains, brothels, 300 reservoirs, outdoor theatres, zoos, the Parthenon, the Forum, gardens, libraries, triumphal arches and vaults and a four-horse-chariot racetrack that sat 300,000. And everywhere, splashes of gold, silver and marble.

On Rome's seven hills, the emperors and kings built their palaces and villas. Below in the streets and valleys, serfs, slaves, beggars, gypsies, gladiators and soldiers mingled with tribunes, patricians, senators, magistrates, and aristocrats.

All roads led to a pulsating Rome: soldiers marching to war, the triumphant returns of emperors, lavish dinners, gala entertainments, the crowning of kings and state funerals. So much pageantry. So much elegance. A monument to power, greed, terror, valour and courage.

The spirits of a zillion ghosts surrounded me: St. Dominic, St. Cecelia, Cicero, Attila, St. Francis, Tiberius, Pompey, Eisenhower, Pope John Paul II, the 40 Jesuit martyrs trained at Rome's English College for death in England. And what about our Canadian men and women who fought in two world wars — their field hospitals and playing fields, their mustering and carousing? Here my friend, Monsignor Leo Lesage, a chaplain in the Canadian Army, on behalf of all Canadian freedom fighters, read his speech to Pope Pius XII surrounded by our boys and girls.

On the other side of the Roman coin, Rome's melancholy nature is becoming more pronounced. Some say time has been a gentleman to the lady that is Rome. Maybe so. But in honesty the old girl's showing her age. Centuries of plagues, sackings, coups, military conquests, fires, droughts, not to mention civil wars, have helped pull it down.

The old has become old. Rome has almost had her day. She is becoming a scarlet lady, best seen in discriminating light. She lacks the order of London, the cleanliness of Lisbon and the grandeur of Paris. She needs a facelift. The damp cobblestones in narrow sunless lanes are treacherous; graffiti pollutes the eye; bare-armed tenants wave through their drying laundry on overhead verandas; vehicular emissions blacken the lady's face; a grey drabness hangs over a city that lives on its past.

As a guest of Rome, I hate to say anything too negative. She deserves respect and kindness. But the cold fact is: Rome is a perfect example of the maxim that "All is Vanity." The dust of its dead has blown away. Its monuments, mausoleums and catacombs tell us that "the paths of the glory lead but to the grave." Where has Charlemagne's might gone? Where are the Cardinals' red hats, the robes and jewels, the marble palaces, the shepherd staffs and the Popes that held them?

Shelley was not too much impressed with the Rome he saw 300 years ago. He put no store in pomp and heraldry.

In his poem *Ozymandias*, a traveller tells him the story of "two vast and trunkless legs of stone" standing in the desert. Beside them lies a "shattered visage" of a king whose disdain for his people is carefully captured by the sculptor. On its pedestal are the words: "My name is Ozymandias, King of Kings, look on my work, ye mighty and despair." Shelley closes with two haunting lines:

"'Round the decay of that colossal wreck,
    boundless and bare
The love and level sands stretch far away."

The six hundred miles of empty catacombs, the preponderance of impersonal sculptures in St. Peter's, and the morose tombs of Popes and Cardinals underneath, give one little religious comfort. As in Egypt, Asia Minor, Peru, and even Washington, such monuments are used partially for propaganda and the emulation of leaders.

The valour and courage and memory of the good is what counts. The rest is an exercise in futility paid for by the blood and sweat of the people of Rome and Europe. Life is for the living, not the dead. "Let the dead bury their own dead," Jesus said (Matt 8:22).

A final positive word. The populace of Rome are friendly — not pretentious — down-to-earth. I see them as kinder than the Parisians, more open than the Londoners, less serious than the Portuguese. They smile more. They go out of their way to assist you. Among themselves, they are also obliging and cordial.

In conclusion, a small story about a Roman beggar. She was in the portico of the Basilica of Santa Maria in Trastevere. It was our last few hours in Rome. She stood severely bent over. In her left hand, a thin cane; on her back, a purple pack; and over her left arm, a small white sack. As she wheeled about, she thrust a tin cup among the passers-by.

She was alone when I decided to walk over and give her a donation. When she saw me coming, she darted towards me. The sound of my few coins hitting the rather large cup prompted her to shower me with effusive prayers and praise. Before I knew it, she looked into my eyes, took my left hand, and kissed it. Then she was gone.

On our way out, she spotted me. There she was — black kerchief, black scarf, long black stockings, black sweater and skirt, and a pair of tan slippers. She stared at me. Suddenly her face lightened. She smiled radiantly. What a gift. I shall remember her smile that embodied for me the true Roman spirit and a million Roman sunrises.

She knew the secret of life. She was happy. And she had nothing!

Fred

My great-uncle, Fred Robertson, brought home to Glasgow many stories about his four years in a German concentration camp in France.

Since he was a teetotaller, he never drank his portion of rum given out each evening before bedtime in the camp. Instead, he gave his to a 13-year-old boy who was not allowed any. When the British sergeant in his section heard about it, in order to emphasize the importance of the rum to one's health, he forced Fred to drink cup after cup until Fred was drunk as a skunk.

In Fred's next letter home, he told his wife about the forced inebriation. When Margaret read it, she was amazed. The very night of Fred's encounter with the rum, she had had a wild nightmare about Fred coming home so plastered, she feared he would die. Such was her closeness to Fred.

Another story shows the inordinate height to which honour in battle can go. On one occasion in camp, someone stole Fred's boots. Without boots, survival was not possible.

An investigation proved that a Russian prisoner had taken them back to his section. Now the Russian people back home never sent anything to their prisoners of war, because the culture of the times dictated that the Russian military should die in battle rather than surrender. [Any packages for them came from other Allies.]

Because of his theft, the Russian was executed by his fellow prisoners.

The Tears

In 1904, or thereabouts, in Glasgow, Margaret, my great-aunt, had just given birth to twins. It was a calamitous moment. The twins died and Margaret went unconscious. Soon the doctor pronounced that she was dead. Another doctor confirmed this finding. Fred, her husband, called in to view the body, noticed tears on Margaret's eyelids. He called over the doctor who said such tearing often occurs in such cases and he wiped away the drops. But, soon more tears formed and the doctor decided to exam Margaret again. This time he heard a faint heartbeat.

Later, Margaret told everyone she could hear the doctor's diagnosis. But she couldn't speak. In fact she couldn't move any part of her body except one little finger. Unfortunately, the finger and hand were trapped under her body.

Was it the pain of her hand that made Margaret tear, or was her heart crying out through her eyes letting the world know that she was alive.

A Letter from Ma

Dear Son,

I hope this letter finds ye better than us. We've had atrocious weather of late. Our kitchen roof has so many leaks, it took your father an hour to finish his soup. If the creek gets any higher we'll be fishing off the veranda.

We enjoyed your last letter, but your Pa missed the President's pictures. Keep them for yourself, lad. We'll manage.

Your Pa has become crotchety of late. His cataracts don't help. He reached in to milk the bull last week. No one knows who was more surprised, him or the bull. He'll be going in for surgery as soon as he can stand up.

Grandma is no better. She still talks away to her dear dead Willy, but not as much. She says she gets tired listening to him whine about the ungodly heat. She keeps saying to him, "If you can't stand the kitchen, get out of the fire." Only Willy would understand that.

She's been depressed of late. Someone told her to count her blessings. She's tried several times, but couldn't think of any, and only got worse. Lately, she's put us in danger. When lightin' her pipe with rolled-up newspaper, she throws the pipe into the stove and sets fire to her hair. She needs wigs bad.

Cousin Alfred was held up on Moore Street last week. The thief demanded his money or his life. When Alfred starting spouting where he was born and went to school, the robber became confused and took off.

Father Costello and your Brother, Eamon, are at odds. Every Sunday Eamon takes up the collection to the front of the church after the sermon. One morning, a wiseacre slipped a foot under Eamon and the proceeds went flyin'. The sight of half the church on its knees for the wrong reason put the good priest in a flap. He told Eamon to make a quick retreat if he knew what was good for him. When Eamon asked him for the date of the next retreat, Father turned purple, the closest he'll ever get to the colours, said the Widow Sherman.

Your Uncle Dermot has been experimenting with fertility drugs. Not for himself, but for his hogs. He gave a trial dose to his prize sow and she became so big, they had to butcher her. All the pork was put in frozen storage except for one big roast. Your uncle took the occasion to have some neighbours over to enjoy it. And they all did. But since then a problem has developed which has all the women guests apprehensive. Two women who ate the pork are now expecting twins. One lady is 52. The vet says it's out of his league. If any kids have pug noses, there'll be hell to pay.

Old Dusty McKay had a big surprise. He's not over it yet. As ye know, he poaches fish. For years he has been raiding Hennessey's Trout Pond, and Hennessey never the wiser. Last month, the Kearney lads transported two large salmon from the River Suir (compliments of the Clomnel Fish and Game Club) to the Trout Pond. Sure enough, McKay came along before the rooster's crow and settled into a crevice known as Mrs. Hennessey's cleavage. He's been there about an hour when one of the salmon almost snapped him into the drink. McKay, to hear him tell it, thought he had a whale. He ran around the pool twice giving and taking line until he finally waded in and landed the weakened fish with his bare hands. That's the way the Kearneys found him — lying on his back with the five pound salmon across his chest. The shock alone almost killed him.

Father O'Malley is up in arms. The mayor gave him a mystery novel for his fortieth anniversary, the title of which offended the good father. As ye know, he hasn't seen his shoes on his feet for years, and to beat all, wasn't the name of the book, *The Death of a Glutton.*

To add to his troubles, at Mrs. Casey's burial last week, with the rain pelting down and himself with arthritis, didn't the coffin prove to be four inches too long for the grave. There was no "Singin in the Rain" that day. And nearly no prayers. By the time the hole was bigger, the priest's tootsies were a foot in the mire. Dinny Kennedy's suggestion to cut the end off the coffin brought an unnerving shriek from Sadie O'Farrell. Father O'Malley was steamed up like the Galway Local. His public chastisement of the dead Mrs. Casey as being the cause of the calamity many considered unkind. But they did hate each other. Maybe he thought she had put a curse on him. Even after they sank her, the coffin floated back up. It was then that Annie Mahaffy saw the priest unstick his boot and kick the coffin. Glory be to God, what's the world comin' to?

Some say Martha Gilagully, a trustee of the County Mental Hospital, may be on the wrong side of the wall when she recommended the fiddle tune, "Red MacCarthy's Breakdown," as an ideal choice for the Hospital's Lottery theme song.

Well, that's it for now, Son. My heart goes wid ye.
Ma

Reminders

My memory nowadays is easily jogged by a familiar word, sound, or smell, as if a chord is plucked and my mind runs on about a place or person ... the scent of approaching rain and I see the mists coming down through the bush across from my grandmother's farm ... the buzz of a bull fly and I'm sitting in a horse stable out of the summer sun ... the smell of liniment and there's the Watkins Man showing my mother his medicinal wares in our kitchen ... and so it is with the lonesome cry of a train or the sound of a horn or the sassy call of the crow ... a crackling fireplace log and I jump as I once did to the crash of falling embers in the country stove ... the odour of coal-burning gases and I hear my mother throwing fresh fuel into the furnace in our damp basement ... the searing sound of an igniting match and I remember my father jumping in pain as the burning phosphorus from a whole match package stuck to his hand, and my mother telling me that the incident was a warning and my father dying not long after ... a crack of thunder reminds me of my uncle talking about the furniture being moved in heaven, and the terror I felt as a child on the farm as the white light in the night lit up the fields before the rain swept down ... the sound of bagpipes, the lone report of a gun in the bush, the neigh of a horse, the sight of the frosty breath 'round a cow's whiskers take me down a familiar lane and 'round a bend and over a hill ... the sweet savour of maple syrup and I see my cousin Allan standing in his snow-packed bush over a steaming cauldron of boiling sap ... the sound of a hockey puck against the boards takes me back to early morning practices in the old hockey auditorium and the shouts of my buddies coming out on the ice ... who among us does not respond to the trumpet's last post ... the call of the geese ... the tang of onions and hamburgers at a country fair ... the howl of a wolf ... the whimpering of a child ... the clang of school bells ... the mournful toll from a church steeple? ... why, just a single whiff of your perfume and I am dancing once again with you, my arm around your slender waist and my heart beating against yours.

About the Author

GARFIELD THOMAS OGILVIE

Garfield Thomas Ogilvie is the author of three books, now collectively and affectionately referred to as the Garfield Ogilvie Trilogy. He was born in Ottawa and grew up in the boroughs of New Edinburgh and Westboro. A skilled hockey player in his youth, he was scouted by the New York Rangers, but decided to take a degree in English at St. Patrick's College instead. He then went on to study Theology at St. Augustine's Seminary in Scarborough. In 1956 he received a Specialist Teaching Certificate from the University of Toronto.

Garfield Ogilvie taught at Perth Collegiate for four years before going on to teach at Woodroffe High School in Nepean. Throughout his twenty-seven-year tenure at Woodroffe, he taught English at every level while holding office as the school's Director of Guidance.

Garfield Ogilvie is married to Marilyn O'Grady. They have four children (Catherine, John, Mary, Tom) and seven grandchildren (Colin, Heather, Kathleen, Laura, Rebecca, Sarah, and Shawn). Nepean is still home, as it has been for over thirty years.

Once Upon a Country Lane
A Tribute to a Gaelic Community

In the western section of Carleton County lies a region of hospitality once known as West or Upper Huntley Township. An Irish community has lived among its ridges and valleys for the past 170 years. *Once Upon a Country Lane* is the story of the land and of its people.

The author's fifty-five year friendship with this Celtic settlement began as a child. During summer, Christmas, and Easter vacations, from 1937 to 1946, he lived with his grandmother at O'Keefe's Corners, West Huntley. Here, oblivious to the hardships of the Depression and the turbulence of war, Garfield Ogilvie basked in West Huntley's pastoral splendour, a comfort he never again experienced in his lifetime.

In this book, the author reflects on those carefree days. Supporting personal memories with extensive research gathered here and in Ireland, the author presents an intimate picture of the Irish of West Huntley. With folklore, history, humour, pathos, and romance — all offered in a simple, chatty, down-home style — *Once Upon a Country Lane* gives pleasure to readers of all kinds.

THE GARFIELD OGILVIE TRILOGY
BOOK TWO

Silver Linings
Stories and Reflections for the Soul

This book is about everyday life. It speaks of simple folk trying to find happiness in a topsy-turvy world. It focuses on good thoughts, noble deeds, and deep feelings.

The stories and reflections come from the author's personal observations, experiences, and readings. As a student of life, he has never lost his sense of wonderment. His innate fascination with life's meaning shows in this intimate, childlike way of looking at and explaining people and events.

If the book has any purpose, it is to lift the spirits of readers. The author writes of courage and perseverance. He extols goodness. He urges us to rise above our difficulties. He writes of grace, God, blessings, and miracles, and encourages readers to look for the *silver linings,* which are constantly being tailor-made in another world for every person's needs.

THE GARFIELD OGILVIE TRILOGY
BOOK THREE

Tomorrow is a Lovely Day

Tomorrow is a Lovely Day illuminates the past with the insights of a gifted storyteller who possesses a keen eye for human interest.

In this book you will find prose and poetry, humour and pathos, warmth and understanding, woven throughout a series of concise vignettes. The author will take you across the Atlantic on journeys to find his roots. You will encounter religious devotion, past and present. Garfield Ogilivie offers personal historical insights, as well as snapshots of seasons, beloved pets, and the small creatures you find in city backyards.

This book draws you into a world that is passing away — a world that delivers, in its twilight, persistent, heart-warming messages of love and hope.